Scotland's Choices

The Referendum and What Happens Afterwards

SECOND EDITION

Iain McLean, Jim Gallagher and
Guy Lodge

EDINBURGH
University Press

© Iain McLean, Jim Gallagher and Guy Lodge, 2014

First edition published by Edinburgh University Press in 2013
Second edition 2014

Edinburgh University Press Ltd
The Tun – Holyrood Road
12 (2f) Jackson's Entry
Edinburgh EH8 8PJ
www.euppublishing.com

Typeset in 11.5/13.5 Minion Pro by
Servis Filmsetting Ltd, Stockport, Cheshire
and printed and bound in Great Britain by
CPI Group (UK) Ltd, Croydon CR0 4YY

A CIP record for this book is available from the British Library

ISBN 978 0 7486 9640 6 (paperback)
ISBN 978 0 7486 9639 0 (webready PDF)
ISBN 978 0 7486 9641 3 (epub)

Contents

Tables

Tables

Figures

Preface to the Second Edition

SCOTLAND FACES ITS biggest choice since 1707. The Scottish government will hold a referendum in 2014 on Scottish independence. As we go to press for this edition, the referendum debate is well under way. The referendum process has been negotiated between the Scottish and UK governments, and we know the wording of the question, the precise date and exactly who will be allowed to vote. The governments and the campaign are making their cases. It is an event of great importance, and it puts a heavy responsibility on the heads of the Scottish electorate.

Not only on their heads, but on those of everybody who wants to inform the electorate about the consequences of their choices. Politicians are already hard at work. Nationalists point to the sunlit uplands that will follow independence. Unionists point to the chasms of doubt and despair that will ensue. The Yes and No campaigns are in full flow as we write. But the substance of their messages is limited. We already know what they think. Arguments that seem to promote their causes will be marketed; those that do not will be ignored. The Scottish people will, in the end, have to make their own judgements. But it will help them to have the issues explained as clearly and neutrally as possible. Of course we have our own views – but that is what we try to do in this book.

The Scottish vote is of almost equal importance to people in the rest of the UK and to the UK's trading and treaty partners including the European Union (EU), the Council of Europe, and NATO. Whereas in Scotland there has been much heat but little light in the independence debate, furth of Scotland there has been little heat – although that is now changing as people suddenly wake up to the fact that Scotland could soon be an independent state.

The consequences of voting No are much clearer than the consequences of voting Yes. That is inherent in any independence referendum. Nevertheless, the consequences of voting No are also not well understood in current Scottish debate. That is because a No vote will lead, not to the status quo remaining, but to the full implementation of the Scotland Act 2012. That is in itself a significant change from the present situation, so we devote a chapter to explaining what it will do if it is brought into force. Moreover, the major unionist parties have also said that they would devolve additional powers – that go over and above those of the Scotland Act 2012 – *should* Scotland vote No to independence. For this reason we explore in detail options for further enhancing the powers of the Scottish Parliament.

We all live in an interconnected world. Therefore the consequences of voting Yes cannot be fully known because we do not know how the rest of the world will react. If Scotland votes Yes, it is clear that the rest of the UK (rUK) will respect this vote (which marks a huge step forward compared to British attitudes on Irish and Indian independence in past generations). But it will mark the beginning, not the end, of discussions. The current Scottish government has announced that if the people vote Yes, Scotland would wish to share embassies, the pound sterling, financial regulation, the monarchy, and maybe even some defence responsibilities with rUK. Some of these are easier than others to share. For instance, if it is wise, the government of rUK will keep out of any discussions between Scotland and Buckingham Palace about Scotland becoming one of the Realms (as they are technically known) of Queen Elizabeth II (I of Scotland) and her successors. Currency and financial regulation are another matter entirely. Though Scottish Ministers have occasionally given the impression that an independent Scotland could simply adopt the pound sterling without consulting anybody else, that is unrealistic. Montenegro has adopted the Euro without needing anybody else's agreement; but Montenegro does not have an enormous financial services industry that does most of its business with customers in rUK.

An independent Scotland will also have to negotiate terms with the numerous international bodies of which the UK is a member. Again, many of these are uncontroversial. For example: as a member of the Council of Europe, the UK has adopted the European Convention on Human Rights and observes the rulings of the Council's court, the European Court of Human Rights. As the present devolution settlement already binds the Scottish Parliament not to act in a way that contravenes the European Convention on Human Rights, it may be assumed that Scottish accession to the Council of Europe will raise no new or difficult issues.

The cases of the EU and NATO are much more challenging. Scottish

Ministers had argued that Scotland would automatically remain in the EU on the same terms as the existing UK, and implied that this was based on legal advice. The President of the European Commission, on the other hand, has reportedly stated that a new state: 'has to apply to become a member of the European Union and all the other member states have to give their consent' (J. M. Barroso, 11 September 2012, quoted in Carrell 2012). The UK government has published a legal opinion saying the same. It has now become clear that the Scottish government did not have legal advice from their Law Officers on this, and their position is now that Scotland would negotiate membership of the EU before leaving the United Kingdom. In this book we explain as much as we can about this issue, and the many others that animate current debate, but positions have changed during the campaign. So this second edition has been revised from start to finish.

Another international issue with wide ramifications is whether Scotland would be a member of NATO, and if so on what terms. In 2012, the SNP changed its policy from one of outright opposition to NATO membership in favour of membership on (nonnuclear) terms, and this is in the Scottish government White Paper. We do not know NATO's reaction to any proposition that the Scottish government may make after a Yes vote.

The referendum will be a straight updown Yes or No to the question, 'Should Scotland be an independent country?'. However, since the election of the first SNP government in 2007, there has been considerable discussion about some intermediate option, variously labelled 'devolutionplus', 'devomore', 'devolutionmax', 'full fiscal autonomy', and 'independence-light/lite'. The Scottish people cannot, however, reasonably be asked to vote for or against any of them until they have been adequately defined. Nevertheless, current poll evidence suggests that the most common constitutional preference among Scots is for more devolution than they have at present, but less than full independence. Therefore 'devolutionplus' or one of its cousins may come in front of voters at some stage. Accordingly, we put a lot of work in this book into showing the ways it might be defined.

This book falls into four parts:

- The first part – Chapter 1 – explores 'A referendum on independence' and sets out the positions of the two governments involved. Getting to a referendum meant both the Scottish government and the government of the UK negotiating the terms of the referendum.

Other state actors, especially the Electoral Commission, were also involved. Much of this is now water under the bridge. But the Scottish people need to know how the question, the date, the franchise, and the method of counting were decided. The Scottish government's proposals for independence are set out in the hundreds of pages of its White Paper published at the end of 2013. The UK government is producing a series of *Scotland Analysis* papers on the different issues. We summarise both in this chapter.

- Chapters 2 to 4 are the heart of the book. In these, we deal with what a Yes would entail (Chapter 2); what a No would entail (Chapter 3); and how 'devolutionplus' or one of its cognate terms might be brought to a state such that, if put to the people, they would know what they were voting on (Chapter 4).
- The third part of the book – Chapters 5 to 8 – gives more background on the three options, allowing us to explain some of the underlying issues at greater length. In Chapter 5 we explain the concept of a social union, and examine the evidence as to whether the people of the present UK want one. In Chapter 6 we explain the concept of fiscal federalism and present expert evidence about how best to design a tax system, not only for a federal country, but for any country with more than one tier of government. Chapter 7 is a detailed exploration of North Sea oil: whose oil it is, how it might be taxed, and whether the country off which it lies ought to set up a Sovereign Wealth Fund in order to cushion the blow that would otherwise strike when the oil revenue runs out. Oil revenue may run out before the oil runs out because companies have been allowed to offset their decommissioning costs against their tax liability. Chapter 8 charts Scottish debates about independence and devolution since 1689. It is not a full history of devolution, but we aim to explain how and why 1707 happened; what happened in the high era of Irish demands for home rule and British resistance to them, and the modern party politics of devolution and independence. The past is another country, to be sure, but it is a country whose landmarks and main features have not changed. We hope that they will also help to guide voters. Readers who are pressed for time should concentrate on Chapters 2 to 4; but we hope that most readers will be interested in exploring some of the background issues as well.
- Finally, Chapter 9 aims to explain what will happen after the vote, especially if Yes wins.

We hope we are a well-matched and well-qualified team. One of us is a resident Scot; one is an expat; one is English. The expat member of the team will be queuing for his Scottish passport if the answer is Yes (but for better or worse will probably continue to live in England). Two of us are fellows of the Royal Society of Edinburgh, Scotland's national academy, which has been carrying out its own investigation of the issues jointly with the British Academy in London. One of us is an academic; one works in a leading think tank; one is a former civil servant. Each of us has been observing devolution in the UK for at least ten years, and perhaps for as long as seventy or eighty years between us. Jim Gallagher is now connected with the Better Together campaign. Guy Lodge and Iain McLean have not taken positions. All policy judgments in this second edition are therefore the responsibility of Guy and Iain.

Since we have been writing about devolution for so long, some of our arguments are a matter of public record. Two of us – Guy Lodge and Iain McLean – have been writing for many years to the effect that the Barnett Formula, which currently determines the block grant from Westminster to the Scottish Parliament, is broken and cannot last much longer (we have been saying that for a long time; but the formula is still with us). One of us – Iain McLean – first became involved in the practical politics of devolution back in the 1970s, when he was an elected member and committee vicechair or chair of Tyne & Wear County Council. He argued vigorously, both as a councillor and as an academic, that the Scotland and Wales Bill (and later the two separate bills) of the then government would not have worked. He has not changed his mind, nor does he apologise for that view. Another – Jim Gallagher – has advised the UK government on this subject, and was very closely involved in the Calman Commission (which Iain McLean also helped advise); but the views here should not be taken to be advice that was given to Ministers of any administration, still less the policy of any government or indeed Campaign.

Nevertheless, this book would not be credible unless it aimed to be neutral between Yes and No (and, if it materialises, Up to a Point), as we endeavour to do. We do not attempt to tell the people of Scotland how to vote, and have tried not to nudge them in one direction or the other. In an effort to ensure that our text is fair to all points of view, we have circulated drafts of the following chapters very widely, and we thank all those who have responded. As some must remain anonymous, we prefer to leave them all anonymous. But thank you all very much. You know who you are.

This book was planned and written at Nuffield College, Oxford, of which we are all fellows. We are very grateful to the college for electing both Guy Lodge and Jim Gallagher as Gwilym Gibbon Fellows. Sir Ioan Gwilym Gibbon (1874–1948), the son of a colliery overman from Ystradyfodwg, Glamorgan, rose to become head of the local government division of the UK Ministry of Health. His biographer in the *Dictionary of National Biography* records that he 'believed passionately in the rigorous accumulation of facts and examination of policy options. On this basis he was both a controversial and an influential figure' (Bradbury 2004). He left money to Nuffield College to further the links between academics and public policy. We hope that this book honours that tradition.

Although this book has been produced without direct external funding, we are also glad to have an opportunity to acknowledge financial support for earlier and parallel projects from the Leverhulme Trust, the Economic & Social Research Council (grants RES–153–25–0060 and RES–201–25–0001), the Joseph Rowntree Charitable Trust, and what was at the time of the research the Office of the Deputy Prime Minister (now the Department of Communities and Local Government). We also record our thanks to the British Academy and the Royal Society of Edinburgh for their joint programme on 'Scotland and the Union' which has enabled us to try out themes from this book and speak to participants, such as experts on the dissolution of Czechoslovakia, whom we might not otherwise have met. They may recognise some of their thoughts, but the responsibility is ours.

Finally, a note about how we have gone about updating this book. When we wrote the first edition, we complained that people had been taking too little notice of the referendum. Now, our problem is the opposite. Everybody has sat up and taken notice. The newspapers and airwaves are full of the opinions of members of the chattering classes in London and Edinburgh. Most of these, however deeply felt, are of no value to readers. Readers need to make up their own minds, and the fact that a given poet will vote Yes and a given sportsman will vote No should be of no importance to them. Many statements by politicians likewise add no information: we already knew what they thought before they opened their mouths.

Therefore, in adding new references for this edition we have restricted ourselves to government and parliamentary documents issued by the London or Edinburgh governments and parliaments, plus statements by officials responsible for implementing the outcome of the referendum. To show how we have operated this principle, we illustrate how we treat, in this edition, statements made by several prominent people about Scottish independence in early 2014.

On 29 January the Governor of the Bank of England, Mark Carney, made a widely reported speech in Edinburgh (available from http://www.bankofengland.co.uk/publications/pages/speeches/2014/7 06.aspx). The Governor insisted that he and the bank were not taking sides in the debate, and would implement whatever monetary regime the two governments jointly agreed on after a Yes vote. He went on to explain the difficulties and opportunities offered by a currency union between independent states, and the necessary conditions to make one work.

Two weeks later, Chancellor George Osborne also made a widely reported speech in Edinburgh (available at https://www.gov.uk/ government/speeches/chancellor-on-the-prospect-of-a-currency-union -with-an-independent-scotland). In this he announced that the current UK Government would not accept a currency union with Scotland, on the grounds that it would not be in the interests of rUK, which would be Scotland's bargaining partner after a Yes vote, 'or indeed of Scotland'. Chief Secretary of the Treasury Danny Alexander (a Liberal Democrat) and shadow chancellor Ed Balls (Labour) announced on the same day that their parties would also refuse to enter a currency union with an independent Scotland. The Chancellor's speech accompanied publication of a UK Treasury document on currency unions, and, very unusually, the Treasury Permanent Secretary Sir Nicholas Macpherson also published his formal advice to Ministers (https://www.gov. uk/government/uploads/system/uploads/attachment_data/file/279460/ Sir_Nicholas_Macpherson_-_Scotland_and_a_currency_union.pdf). This stated in forthright terms that Treasury civil servants advised Ministers against entering a currency union with an independent Scotland.

The following day, the President of the European Commission, José Manuel Barroso, told the BBC that it would be 'extremely difficult, if not impossible' for an independent Scotland to join the European Union.

Scottish Ministers immediately said that the statements by Osborne, Alexander, Balls, and Barroso were no more than 'bluff, bluster, and bullying', and that they would sing a different song after the Scots had actually voted Yes.

In this book we treat the Barroso statement and the other three differently, for the following reasons. Mr Barroso appeared to be predicting the approach of member states and he himself will not be at the table when an independent Scotland seeks to enter, or remain in, the EU. Scotland's main counterparty will be, not the Commission, but the European Council: that is, the governments of the 28 member states who will have to decide on the application.

As to the three UK politicians, one of them will probably be the Chancellor with whom the Scots have to negotiate after a Yes. Their views carry more weight than do Barroso's. However, the Scottish government insist that a Chancellor in post would take a different view after Scotland had actually voted Yes. So we devote more attention to the views of Governor Carney, Permanent Secretary Macpherson, and their supporting documents. They constitute official advice to governments, backed up by evidence, and readers need to know what we think of them. They are discussed in later chapters.

1

A Referendum on Independence

THE SCOTTISH REFERENDUM will take place on 18 September 2014, a Thursday. The question, approved by the Electoral Commission, will be *Should Scotland be an independent country?* The UK and Scottish governments have agreed to abide by the result. In this chapter we discuss the constitutional significance of a referendum, and the legal issues about holding one on independence, initially controversial but now settled. We explain why the referendum does not propose more than two options. We look at the detailed administration and oversight of a poll to ensure fairness and neutrality. We then go on to give an account of the Scottish government's Independence White Paper, and the Scotland Analysis papers so far published by the UK government.

Referendums in the United Kingdom

In some places referendums are used quite regularly to decide individual questions of public policy. Far and away the biggest user of referendums is Switzerland. It has held more national referendums than all other countries combined. There has since the nineteenth century been a constitutional procedure for voters to demand a referendum on a proposal to change the law or the constitution. There have been hundreds of these initiatives leading to referendums, in individual Swiss cantons as well at the Federal level. At the Federal level it takes 100,000 voters to require a referendum to be held on a change in the law. The government and Parliament have to consider it and may offer a counterproposal. Only about 10% of initiatives however succeed in changing the law (Kobach 1993). In March 2012, for instance, one of the proposals put to vote was that there should be a legal requirement that all workers should have six weeks' holiday a year. It was defeated by two to one in a 44% turnout (BBC News 2012). This form of direct democracy is used in other places, including some US states, notably

California where citizens can take the initiative to have propositions put to the vote. Since 1910 there have been over 1200 proposals there on legal changes, public finance, or the state constitution.

Other countries have rules which require a referendum before making a change to the constitution. This is more common. Ireland is an example. Any bill to change the constitution requires a referendum before it becomes effective (Irish Constitution, Articles 46 and 47). There have been thirty-four referendums in Ireland since the Constitution was drafted in 1937, on matters such as joining the EU, ratifying EU treaties, divorce law, or the rules determining Irish citizenship. The most recent was in 2012. The Australian constitution has a similar rule[1]; since 1906 there have been forty-two referendums, of which only eight have been carried (Australian Electoral Commission 2011). In 1999 for example Australians voted against becoming a republic.

The British political system is wedded to representative rather than direct democracy. Elected representatives rather than voters directly decide policy questions. National referendums were unknown until the 1970s and have been seen by some as alien to that approach, and contrary to the doctrine of Parliamentary sovereignty.[2] They have not been used to decide day-to-day policy questions. The only exceptions were ballots in Scotland and Wales to decide whether licences to sell alcohol could be granted in individual areas or wards. These were abolished in the 1970s. Similarly the UK does not have a codified constitution and no formal procedure for amending it, and so there is no formal requirement for constitutional referendums. Nevertheless the practice of holding referendums on important constitutional issues has become well established in the UK since the first UK-wide referendum on membership of what was then the Common Market in 1975.

Table 1.1 shows all of the referendums which have been held across the UK since 1975. (It excludes the 1973 'border poll' in Northern Ireland, and referendums on local mayors in England.)

There is no constitutional rule which says when there should or should not be a referendum, and governments are sometimes criticised for using a referendum as a political manoeuvre. In 1975, for example, Harold Wilson presided over a Labour government which was divided over Europe, and a referendum on EU membership took that decision out of the government's hands and passed it to the people. Similarly the present coalition parties in the UK government have different policies on electoral reform, and the 2011 Alternative Vote referendum also gave that choice to the electorate.

Nevertheless the practice of putting proposals for constitutional change to the electorate for decision has become well established in Britain. This is notably true for 'national' questions such as devolution. There have been referendums in Scotland, Wales and Northern Ireland on devolution. This signifies assent to the change and entrenches the position of the devolved bodies: the UK government or Parliament would find it difficult to abolish the devolved bodies or change their powers very radically without the authority of a further referendum.

A referendum on independence for Scotland

Nations have become independent without a referendum. On 1 January 1993, for example, Czechoslovakia split into the two new states of the Czech Republic and Slovakia. The deal was negotiated between the political leaderships of two parts of the Federal republic without holding a referendum in either of them. Indeed as late as July 1992, support in public opinion polls for splitting Czechoslovakia into two wholly independent states was as low as 16% in both parts of the country, so a referendum might well have been lost (Wolchik 1995, Table 12.3). Support for greater autonomy was however higher in Slovakia, and there was a risk that a referendum might have produced different outcomes in each part of the country.

In general however referendums have been used as the way of deciding 'national' questions such as independence or territorial autonomy. It has been suggested (for example, Bogdanor 1994) that a referendum is suitable for a question like this, which might cut across normal party alignments. There are certainly examples where a referendum has been chosen as the constitutional route to independence for a country that is separating from a larger union or federation. Examples include Norway in 1905, which held a plebiscite on the 'dissolution of the union' with Sweden. (Only men were allowed to vote, and the Swedes accepted the result after negotiations, though their government initially opposed the plan.) More recently, in 2006, the Republic of Montenegro held a referendum on leaving its union with Serbia, as the Yugoslav republic finally broke up. In 2011, South Sudan left Sudan after a referendum held under UN supervision (UN 2011). (Sudan announced it would accept the result but armed conflict persists on the borders of the two countries and, sadly, within South Sudan.)

Table 1.1 Referendums in the UK since 1975

Event, location, date	Referendum question	'Yes' vote	'No' vote	Turnout	Result
Membership of the European Community, UK, June 1975	Do you think that the United Kingdom should stay in the European Community (the Common Market)?	67.2%	32.8%	64.0%	The UK remained in the European Community.
Devolution to Scotland, March 1979	Do you want the provisions of the Scotland Act 1978 to be put into effect?	51.6%	48.4%	63.6%	Devolution did not proceed as the threshold requirement that not less than 40% of the total electorate had to vote 'yes' for devolution was not met – only 32.8% voted 'yes'.
Devolution to Wales, March 1979	Do you want the provisions of the Wales Act 1978 to be put into effect?	20.3%	79.7%	58.8%	Devolution did not proceed.
Devolution to Scotland, September 1997	I agree that there should be a Scottish Parliament or I do not agree that there should be a Scottish Parliament.	Agree: 74.3%	Do not agree: 25.7%	60.2%	The Scottish Parliament was established.
As above	I agree that a Scottish Parliament should have tax-varying powers or I do not agree that a Scottish Parliament should have tax-varying powers.	Agree: 63.5%	Do not agree: 36.55%	60.2%	The Scottish Parliament was given tax-raising powers.
Devolution to Wales, September 1997	I agree that there should be a Welsh Assembly or I do not agree that there should be a Welsh Assembly.	Agree: 50.3%	Do not agree: 49.7%	50.1%	The Welsh Assembly was established.
Greater London Authority, London, May 1998	Are you in favour of the Government's proposals for a Greater London Authority, made up of an elected mayor and a separately elected assembly?	72.0%	28.0%	34.0%	The Greater London Authority was established.

Event, location, date	Referendum question	'Yes' vote	'No' vote	Turnout	Result
Belfast Agreement, Northern Ireland, May 1998	Do you support the Agreement reached at the Multi-Party Talks in Northern Ireland and set out in Command Paper 3883?	71.1%	28.9%	81.0%	Community consent for continuation of the Northern Ireland peace process on the basis of the Belfast Agreement was given.
Elected Regional Assembly, North East of England, November 2004	Should there be an elected assembly for the North East region?	22.1%	77.9%	47.1%	The Elected Regional Assembly for the North East was not established.
Legislative powers for Welsh Assembly, March 2011	Do you want the Assembly now to be able to make laws on all matters in the 20 subject areas it has powers for?	63.5%	36.7%	35.6%	The Welsh Assembly gained new law-making powers.
Alternative Vote referendum, May 2011	At present, the UK uses the 'first past the post' system to elect MPs to the House of Commons. Should the 'alternative vote' system be used instead?	32.1%	67.9%	42.1%	The parliamentary voting system was not changed.

Source: House of Lords Constitution Committee – Twelfth Report: *Referendums in the United Kingdom*, 17 March 2010, amended and extended

Sometimes there are added rules. For example in Montenegro there was a requirement for 55% support before independence. On other occasions there have been minimum turnout requirements such as the 40% rule applied in the 1978 Scottish devolution referendum. No such ideas have been proposed for the independence referendum.

The Scottish National Party (SNP) adopted the policy of a referendum as the constitutional route to independence, following the advice of the jurist Sir Neil MacCormick and others. (See for example, MacCormick 1999). The SNP Manifestos for both the 2007 and 2011 Scottish Parliament elections contained a pledge to put the issue of independence to the people of Scotland in a referendum. They formed a minority government in 2007 but, although they drafted a Bill, they did not try to legislate for a referendum. The opposition parties who formed the majority would very likely have defeated any Bill. In the 2011 campaign they announced an intention, if elected, to introduce a referendum Bill in the second half of the Parliament. Having, against expectations, secured an overall majority, the SNP Scottish government could deliver a vote in the Scottish Parliament in support of a referendum Bill.

The legal power to hold a referendum

An overall majority and an electoral mandate did not however, of themselves, give the legal power to hold a referendum, even if they conferred a moral authority. Any referendum needs to be authorised by an Act of Parliament or, if it is on a devolved matter, by an Act of the Scottish Parliament. But while Scottish independence may be a Scottish matter, it is not a devolved one. When the Scotland Act 1998 (which sets out the legal powers of the Scottish Parliament) was drafted the intention was that an independence referendum should not be within the legislative competence of the Parliament. Ministers said this at several points during the parliamentary process.

What Ministers intended and what was achieved by the drafting might not however be the same, so it is necessary to examine what the legislation actually says. The Scotland Act 1998 gives the Scottish Parliament power to make laws on anything, except various matters which are reserved. A Bill of the Scottish Parliament which 'relates to' one of these reserved matters is not within its powers. The courts have made clear that 'relates to' means more than simply touches upon or has some effect on: it means something closer to 'is primarily about'. To decide whether a Bill relates to something which is reserved, the courts would look at its purpose and its effect 'in all the circumstances'.

One of the reserved matters is the union between Scotland and England and a referendum on independence whose effect would be to end that union clearly relates to that.

This problem of legal powers created an obvious difficulty for the Scottish government. The UK government proposed the way out of the problem. They recognised that the Scottish government had an electoral mandate to hold a referendum, and agreed that one should be held. Their view was that a referendum should be 'legal, fair and decisive'. To make it legal, they proposed that the gap in legislative powers should be remedied using an Order under section 30 of the Scotland Act 2012. An Order of this kind can give additional legislative competence to the Scottish Parliament.[3]

This is the route that was followed. The arrangements were confirmed in the 'Edinburgh Agreement' signed by First Minister Alex Salmond and Prime Minister David Cameron on 15 October 2012. The Agreement opens:

The United Kingdom Government and the Scottish Government have agreed to work together to ensure that a referendum on Scottish independence can take place. The governments are agreed that the referendum should:

- have a clear legal base;
- be legislated for by the Scottish Parliament;
- be conducted so as to command the confidence of parliaments, governments and people; and
- deliver a fair test and a decisive expression of the views of people in Scotland and a result that everyone will respect.

The governments have agreed to promote an Order in Council under Section 30 of the Scotland Act 1998 in the United Kingdom and Scottish Parliaments to allow a single-question referendum on Scottish independence to be held before the end of 2014. The Order will put it beyond doubt that the Scottish Parliament can legislate for that referendum.

It will then be for the Scottish government to promote legislation in the Scottish Parliament for a referendum on independence. The governments are agreed that the referendum should meet the highest standards of fairness, transparency and propriety, informed by consultation and independent expert advice. The referendum legislation will set out:

- the date of the referendum;
- the franchise;
- the wording of the question;
- rules on campaign financing; and
- other rules for the conduct of the referendum.

The agreement confirms that the referendum must take place before the end of 2014; must be regulated by the Electoral Commission, which has a right to recommend the wording of the question and nominate an umbrella campaign on each side which will have the right to a free mailshot to all voters; imposes restrictions on Ministers of both governments in the month preceding the vote; and, in its most important paragraph, concludes:

> 30. The United Kingdom and Scottish Governments are committed, through the Memorandum of Understanding between them and others, to working together on matters of mutual interest and to the principles of good communication and mutual respect. The two governments have reached this agreement in that spirit. They look forward to a referendum that is legal and fair producing a decisive and respected outcome. The two governments are committed to continue to work together constructively in the light of the outcome, whatever it is, in the best interests of the people of Scotland and of the rest of the United Kingdom.

The resultant Order was approved by the Scottish Parliament in December 2012, and by the House of Commons and House of Lords in January 2013. It was formally made by the Queen in February 2013, and enabled the Scottish Parliament to legislate for an independence referendum provided that there was only one question in the referendum and that it was asked before the end of 2014. The referendum was to be regulated by the Electoral Commission.

Subsequently, the Scottish government and the Electoral Commission agreed the wording of the question (see below) and the legislation has now been made. There were two Acts of the Scottish Parliament, one to provide for the referendum itself and one to set the franchise, i.e. who was allowed to vote in it. The referendum date is fixed for 18 September 2014. The franchise is to be the same as for local government elections, plus 16 and 17 year olds. (That means that EU citizens resident in Scotland can vote, if registered to do so, but not expatriate Scots.) The umbrella organisations for the Campaign have been chosen. They are Yes Scotland (http://www.yesscotland.net) and Better Together (http://bettertogether.net/). Both have been campaigning hard, though they are not formally regulated until sixteen weeks before the vote, when limits will be applied to their spending.

Why does the referendum not offer more than two choices?

The opinion poll data on Scots' constitutional preferences is reviewed in later chapters. It shows that they have been steady for decades. A minority of Scots prefer independence. A majority would prefer more autonomy than (what they perceive) they have, but less than independence. It may seem perverse that the Scots will not be able to vote on the option most of them seem to prefer.

Referendums however almost always offer voters a choice between two possibilities. In the UK that has typically been the status quo and a constitutional change – for example in 2011 a choice between the present 'first past the post' Parliamentary voting system and the Alternative Vote, or in 1975 whether to stay in the European Economic Community or leave it. A binary referendum of this sort has advantages of simplicity, clarity and decisiveness. A question is asked and the majority of voters answer 'yes' or 'no', and that is enough to determine the matter authoritatively. This is what an independence referendum will do.

An exception to this was the Scottish devolution referendum of 1997. It asked voters two questions: did they want a Scottish Parliament, and should it have tax-varying powers? In effect, the electorate had to choose between three options: the status quo, a Scottish Parliament with no tax powers, and a Scottish Parliament with certain defined tax-varying powers. If there are three options there are good grounds of principle why more than two questions should be asked so as to make a decision based on full information about the preferences of the electorate. In the event of course the last option secured substantial support and the referendum was decisive.

Some (including one of the present authors) have argued that Scotland's relationship with the UK is not something that is suitable

9

for a binary choice: there is a range of possibilities from complete independence at one end to the status quo (or perhaps less devolution) at the other. The majority of Scottish opinion seems to favour more devolution than at present, though only a minority supports independence. To polarise the options to independence or not appears to rule out the ground on which a majority of Scots would be prepared to compromise. Accordingly, it has been argued, there should have been a third option of more devolution on the ballot paper. The choices might have been: the status quo (however defined), a proposal for more devolution, and independence. Since it is likely that more devolution would be the second preference of many supporters of independence as well as the first choice of others, then such an option might secure majority support. The Scottish government initially said that they might be open to this possibility, and appeared at one point to be likely to support it.[4]

This approach however was subject to some formidable challenges. The first was political. The Scottish government's manifesto commitment was to a referendum on independence, and although they had said that they might be open to adding a third option, they have legislated for a single question. The UK government appeared to take the view that the SNP's mandate was for an independence referendum. They were willing to make legal provision for that, but not for a three-option referendum.

The second challenge was more complex. What option could be put to the voters? The choice in a binary referendum is not in fact between the 'status quo' and independence because the 'status quo' is not a Scottish Parliament with the powers it has today. Both the Westminster and the Scottish Parliaments have now agreed the Scotland Act 2012. It extends the Scottish Parliament's tax and borrowing powers, and provides for them to be extended further in future (its effects are more fully explained in Chapter 3). So the alternative offered to independence is already 'more devolution'. (Indeed since opinion polls suggest that about one third of Scots are satisfied with the status quo without the Scotland Act, perhaps that option should be on the ballot paper. This illustrates the difficulty of choosing what alternatives to independence could or should be offered.)

At present no firm proposals exist for more radical devolution than that in the Scotland Act that could be put to the vote. Although political parties have developed plans for more powers, none have been agreed between governments, so that if they were put to the ballot and supported by the voters, they would be sure to be put into practice. A scheme of more powers that was not agreed by the Scottish Parliament could not be implemented; similarly one cannot be decided upon without UK agreement, as the rUK has a legitimate interest in what powers are devolved because of the potential effect on it.

A third argument is that independence and more devolution are qualitatively different things, and should be decided in different ways. Independence means no longer being part of the UK, while more devolution means a different relationship within it. Independence is a unilateral choice: the Scottish electorate can at the end of the day make a decision to become independent from the UK and then negotiate the terms of separation; but proposals for more devolution within the UK need to be agreed with the UK (as the Scotland Act was) so that the voters could vote in the knowledge that the plan will be implemented if they support it.

Nevertheless, on the face of it, many in Scotland might welcome markedly more devolution than the Scotland Act provides, perhaps devolving responsibility for social security or even all taxation powers. Chapter 4 explores what the range of possibilities might be, including the ideas now proposed by two of the main political parties.

Could there be a three-option referendum?

The Scottish and UK governments have agreed on a binary referendum. But it is in principle possible to run a three-option referendum, if certain conditions are met. There would have to be three valid options to be put to the voters and, presumably, three sets of campaigners to argue for them. Agreement would be needed on how the questions would be put, and how the votes counted. The last point leads down some complex byways but in any event, these conditions will not be met in Scotland in 2014. Certainly three-option referendums dealing with national questions are rare internationally. One place where they have been tried, repeatedly, is in Puerto Rico. It is an 'unincorporated territory' of the United States of America. Its inhabitants are US citizens but cannot vote in US Presidential elections, though the US Congress can legislate for the territory. There have been several multi-option referendums on its status: in 1967 (three options offered); in 1993 (three options offered); in 1998 (five options offered – including 'none of the above', which secured an absolute majority of votes). None of these was decisive about the territory's future, so a further referendum was held in November 2012. Voters were first asked the gateway question, whether or not they wished to retain the territory's present status; 54% of those voting said no. They were then invited to choose between three options, and 60% of those who expressed a view supported becoming a state within the United States. This now seems likely to happen.

Regulation of referendums

There is now a standard regulatory framework for referendums held in the UK. It was created in 2000 and drew on experience of the European referendum in 1975 and the devolution referendums of 1997. Under this legislation the Electoral Commission, which regulates political parties and elections, also deals with referendums. The main parts of the regulatory framework are supervision of the question to be asked, of the participants in the referendum campaign, and of public support (if any) for referendum campaigns, and limits on spending in the campaign.

These controls have been applied in recent referendums – to the referendum on whether there should be a Regional Assembly in the northeast of England, the referendum on further devolution for Wales, and the referendum on whether or not to change the parliamentary voting system. If the UK Parliament had passed the Act to have a referendum on Scottish independence then it would automatically have been regulated by the Electoral Commission. The regulatory framework does not, however, automatically apply to referendums promoted by an Act of the Scottish Parliament.

In their initial proposals for an independence referendum, the Scottish government proposed that there should be a specially created Scottish referendum commission, reporting to the Scottish Parliament, to regulate an independence referendum. That view, however, has now changed, and they have accepted that the Electoral Commission should have this responsibility. The necessary legal changes are included in the Section 30 Order discussed above.

The first task which faced the Electoral Commission was giving advice on, or in effect deciding upon, the wording of the question to be asked. That wording was the subject of heated debate between the political parties. The Commission's statutory duty is to decide whether the question is 'intelligible', but in practice they interpret this to mean whether the question is both clear and, so far as possible, unbiased. The proposals of the Scottish government in 2010 were for a rather convoluted question: 'Do you agree that the powers of the Scottish Parliament should be extended to enable independence to be achieved?'. It was drafted in this way because the Scottish Parliament did not have the legal competence to ask a more direct question. In 2012 however, once the United Kingdom government had proposed removing the legal obstacles, the Scottish government proposed a simpler and more direct question: 'Do you agree that Scotland should be an independent country?'.

Even this question, however, was subject to criticism (Scottish Affairs Committee 2012a). It is argued that any question beginning 'do you agree' is a leading question, and biases respondents towards the answer 'yes'. While such an effect may be small, if it exists at all, it could cause the losing side in a referendum argument to question the validity of the result. (Whatever the result is, that is clearly undesirable: but it would obviously be very difficult if Scotland became an independent country on the basis of a referendum whose legitimacy was contested.)

The Electoral Commission examined the question proposed by the Scottish government. The Commission concluded that the words 'be an independent country' were sufficiently clear but that beginning the question with 'do you agree' was leading, and should be dropped. (Electoral Commission 2013a) The Scottish government accepted this advice.

The Commission also has powers to regulate referendum campaigns, and in particular the amount of spending by campaign organisations. This is intended to ensure that the campaign is as fair as possible, and in particular that there is a degree of 'equality of arms' between the two sides in a campaign. There is also provision for public funding of campaign organisations, though the Scottish government does not plan to offer any. The Commission has now recommended spending limits for the two campaigns and for the political parties and others involved (Electoral Commission 2013b). Each campaign will be able to spend £1.5 million during the regulated period.

There are potential difficulties with this form of regulation for an independence referendum. The main one is that, in the past, referendum campaigns have been relatively short: there is a formal campaign period of perhaps six weeks before the actual vote, and on other occasions the campaign has only really been kicked off by the referendum legislation itself. This is a difficulty because the two campaigns were effectively launched in May and June 2012: more than two years before the referendum. Because the legislation was not then passed, the rules for campaign spending, campaign donations (including foreign donations) and so on did not apply to them. Under the legislation now passed, the regulated period will be no longer than sixteen weeks. A voluntary scheme of disclosure can apply before then and some guidance has been given on this by the Electoral Commission.[5]

In other countries some government agency similar to the Electoral Commission has the task of producing neutral and unbiased information to inform the electorate about the choice that faces them. This is not part of the job of the UK Electoral Commission, though some have argued that it should be. The Commission has suggested that the two governments should agree the terms of information about what happens after a referendum, which the Commission would then distribute to the public. At the time of writing the governments have not agreed this material, and they certainly will not agree that it should set out all the arguments for and against independence. In a question which is as emotive as national identity or sovereignty, an unbiased presentation of the issues is very important, but also very difficult (as we have discovered in writing this book). The best a neutral assessment can hope for is to be criticised by both sides. We now proceed to summarise the main documents issued by the Scottish and UK governments since they signed the Edinburgh Agreement.

Should Scotland be an independent country?

The question appears deceptively simple. It is the question that the people of Scotland will decide on 18 September. If they decide Yes, Scotland will become an independent country shortly after that. The current Scottish government hopes that Independence Day will be in March 2016. If they decide No, then Scotland will not become an independent country.

But what exactly *is* an independent country? As the Scottish and UK governments have been setting out their rival visions during 2013, an odd paradox has arisen. The Scottish government is run by the Scottish National Party (SNP), which holds more than half of the seats in the 2011–16 Scottish Parliament. The UK government from 2010 to 2015 is a Conservative-Liberal coalition. Its dominant member, the Conservative Party, was until recently officially known as the Conservative *and Unionist* Party. And yet the SNP downplays how independent an independent Scotland will be, and the UK government emphasises the scope of separation.

The Scottish government published its independence prospectus in November 2013. Entitled *Scotland's future: your guide to an independent*

Scotland (Scottish Government 2013a), it runs to 670 pages. It is really a combination of independence prospectus and election manifesto. In some places, it distinguishes between the two roles. For instance, in the summary there are two lists: *Gains from independence – whichever party is elected,* and *Gains from independence – if we are the first government of an independent Scotland* (Scottish Government 2013, pp. xii–xiii). But the distinction is not maintained consistently. Some of the more eye-catching promises in the White Paper are straightforward election promises, whose implementation does not seem to be affected either way by independence, as they are in policy domains that are already controlled by the Scottish Parliament.

In the next sections we analyse the main promises made by the White Paper. Readers who want more than we offer here but less than 670 pages should note that all of its main points are in the Introduction and Summary at the start, and much of the detail is in the '650 questions about independence that have been asked of us', beginning on p. 373. The questions are remarkably wide ranging. They include:

- *Regulation of Outer Space Activity in an Independent Scotland* (QQ105–6; summary: there will be no change, to the great relief no doubt of the population of Jupiter);
- *If I buy a … season ticket before independence that continues into independence will it be valid …?* (Q121: yes).
- *Will independence affect who can play for the Scottish rugby and football teams?* (Q219: no, unfortunately).

Many of the proposals in the White Paper are designed to soothe. Readers are again and again assured that nothing much will change (although as we shall see some of these assurances depend on third parties not under the control of the Scottish government). In other areas, radical change is promised – these being the parts of the White Paper that are largely manifesto promises rather than details of the independence process. We look in turn at constitutional, international, and domestic matters.

Constitutional matters

In brief: Scotland will become a constitutional monarchy. The existing Scottish Parliament will continue to be the unicameral parliament of independent Scotland. A Constitutional Convention will draw up a constitution based on the principle of popular (not parliamentary) sovereignty.

As to the monarchy, Queen Elizabeth and her heirs and successors will become (once again, as the Stuarts were between 1603 and 1707) monarchs of Scotland in their own right. Scotland will (re-)join the sixteen existing Commonwealth 'Realms' that have the Hanoverian dynasty as heads of state. The Scottish government notes with pleasure that gender discrimination in the line of succession has been removed, and will lobby the other 'Realms' in the hope of removing the religious discrimination in the succession rules against Roman Catholics. Honours will continue, but 'We will agree with the Royal Household any amendments to the Honours system to reflect Scotland's independence' (Q584). Scotland's flag will remain the St Andrew's Cross. It will be for the rest of the UK to decide what flag it should adopt.

As to the Scottish Parliament, it will continue at its present location and with its present electoral and internal arrangements. Thus it will continue to have 129 members, elected under the mixed-member system of proportional representation that it has had since it restarted in 1999. It will remain (ironically) a 'Westminster' system in the sense that the executive and legislature are fused. The government will continue to be formed by the party/parties that control the Parliament, and all ministers will be answerable to it. The present arrangements for fixed-term parliaments and for scrutiny of bills and actions will continue. The next election will be, as already determined, in 2016. The devolved Parliament then elected will become the first Parliament of independent Scotland. As the next UK election falls before the next Scottish election, the White Paper envisages that Scottish MPs will be elected to Westminster at that election (in 2015) and will drop out on Independence Day in 2016.

A Constitutional Convention will start work immediately on independence. The White Paper is very prescriptive on some matters and rather vague on others. The government will propose to the convention that the constitution should guarantee some rights and obligations, including:

- 'equality of opportunity and entitlement to live free of discrimination and prejudice';
- 'entitlement to public services and to a standard of living that, as a minimum, secures dignity and self-respect';
- 'a ban on nuclear weapons being based in Scotland'; and
- 'children's rights' (Scottish Government 2013, p. 353).

Some of these rights impose duties on providers of public services. The White Paper says little about how the constitutional convention will operate (it draws attention to the recent conventions in Ontario, British Columbia, and the current one in Ireland, of which the two Canadian cases were not ratified). It does not mention any ratification procedure. However, the procedure must reflect 'the fundamental constitutional truth – that the people, rather than politicians or state institutions, are the sovereign authority in Scotland' (p. 351). But it will not be invited to consider, among other things, the option of a republic rather than a constitutional monarchy, the electoral system, the number of MSPs, or a second chamber.

A constitution that offers rights and imposes duties requires a constitutional court. The White Paper says nothing explicit about this. However, it does state that the Inner House of the Court of Session and the High Court of Justiciary will collectively comprise Scotland's Supreme Court. As well as constitutional interpretation, that court will have the task of enforcing the legal obligations imposed by European Union law and the European Court of Human Rights. Scotland is already, under devolution, required to be compliant with the European Convention on Human Rights, and the White Paper confirms that this will continue under independence.

The rules on citizenship are set out at pp. 271–2:

> British citizens habitually resident in Scotland on independence will be considered Scottish citizens ... Scottish-born British citizens currently living outside of Scotland will also be considered Scottish citizens. Following independence, ... citizenship by descent will be available to those who have a parent or grandparent who qualifies for Scottish citizenship. Those who have a demonstrable connection to Scotland and have spent at least ten years living here at some stage ... will also have the opportunity to apply for citizenship.

A long but confusing and circular footnote states that 'habitually resident' means the same as does 'ordinarily resident' in current UK law: *the test for ordinary residence is satisfied where the person has habitually and normally resided for a settled purpose apart from temporary or occasional absences*' (pp. 640–1, no. 296). The definition of 'settled purpose' is itself circular, but non-lawyers may have lost the will to live at this point.[6] Scotland will permit dual citizenship and it envisages that the rest of the UK will do the same. As long as Scotland and the rest of the UK are both EU member states, it should make no difference to someone qualified to hold a Scottish passport whether she does that or retains a UK passport. It is therefore quite likely that an independent Scotland would contain a high proportion of people holding dual citizenship and UK passports.

International matters

The White Paper proposes that an independent Scotland will remain in the EU; will apply to join NATO and many other organisations; will create a foreign service, while hoping to share some consular services with the rest of the UK; and will negotiate agreements with the rest of the UK in a wide range of areas which will become cross-border on independence.

The carefully-worded section on EU membership runs:

> Following a vote for independence, the Scottish Government will immediately enter into negotiations with Westminster and EU member states to ensure that an independent Scotland achieves a smooth and timely transition to independent membership of the EU. Scotland will negotiate the terms of membership of the EU during the period we are still part of the UK and, therefore, part of the EU. There is, within the EU Treaties, a legal framework by which Scotland, a country that has been an integral part of the EU for 40 years, may make the transition to independent EU membership in the period between the referendum and the date on which Scotland becomes an independent state. Article 48 provides a suitable legal route to facilitate the transition process, by allowing the EU Treaties to be amended through ordinary revision procedure before Scotland becomes independent, to enable it to become a member state at the point of independence ... The terms of Scotland's membership will be agreed with the EU and the necessary Treaty amendments will be taken forward with the agreement of member states. (QQ256, 264)

Although Scotland would remain in the EU, the Scottish government say that it would not be forced to join the Eurozone, because that would require a prior application to join the Exchange Rate Mechanism, which the Scottish government does not plan to do. Scotland's independent membership of the EU would entitle it to more

MEPs than at present, to a block vote in the European Council and Council of Ministers of the same weight as in other member states with similar populations, and probably to a European Commissioner. Although the White Paper does not give the numbers, Scotland's population of around 5 million would give it the same weight as Denmark, Finland, and Slovakia, which each currently have thirteen MEPs and seven weighted votes in the Council.[7]

The White Paper goes into considerable depth on what an independent Scotland might expect from the Common Agricultural Policy (CAP) (pp. 281–4; 522–6). In one respect this is surprising, as agriculture and fishing are a tiny part of the Scottish economy. On the other hand, CAP, while diminishing, remains the largest distributive programme of the EU.

Other EU issues will be knottier after independence. Two of the less obvious ones are cross-border pension arrangements and student support. EU law requires cross-border defined-benefit pension schemes to be fully funded. Most current UK schemes have fallen far short of that since the financial crisis began in 2008. On the face of it, on a vote for Scottish independence, these schemes would have either to have a massive cash injection from employers and employees alike, in order to become fully funded, or else to be wound up. This would have serious implications for every member in the rest of the UK as well as in Scotland. The numbers affected greatly exceed the numbers of farmers and fishermen in Scotland. The White Paper is optimistic that a deal can be reached on independence:

Specific requirements apply under EU law to pension schemes that operate across different member states. However, the cross-border rules allow member states a degree of flexibility. Transitional arrangements were put in place by the Westminster Government and Ireland when these rules were introduced and we consider that it will be possible to agree transitional arrangements for existing UK-wide schemes. The Scottish Government is keen to start discussions with the Westminster Government and the European Commission as soon as possible, with a view to reaching agreement in the interests of employers and pension schemes across the UK. (Q195)

Currently, the Scottish government does not levy tuition fees on Scottish students at Scottish universities, but requires students from the rest of the UK to pay the same tuition fees as if they attended a university in their home part of the UK. Under existing EU law, non-UK EU students in Scotland must pay the same fee, i.e. zero, as Scottish students. But what happens after independence, when the rest of the UK becomes a member state like any other? The following paragraphs (QQ 237–40) look as if they have been carefully drafted by government or university lawyers:

237. Would Scotland still charge students from the rest of the UK tuition fees? Yes. The divergence in funding policy between Scotland and England and the resulting disparity in the cost of a university education creates a huge financial incentive for students from England to study in Scotland. In that context, and to ensure Scottish students remain able to study at Scottish Higher Education Institutions, we propose maintaining the status quo by continuing our policy of allowing Scottish Higher Education Institutions to set their own annual tuition fees for students from the rest of the UK at a rate no higher than the maximum annual tuition fee rate chargeable to such students by universities in the rest of the UK.

238. Would charging students from the rest of the UK tuition fees in an independent Scotland be compatible with EU law? We believe that the unique and unprecedented position of a post-independent Scotland will enable us to continue our current policy in a way which is consistent with the principles of free movement across the EU as a whole and which is compatible with EU requirements.

239. Are you confident that the Court of Justice of the EU will support this position? Each member state is free to adopt its own domestic policies, consistent with the objectives of the EU. We believe that our fees policies contribute to student mobility across the wider EU, while addressing the consequences of the unique situation of Scottish independence. In these circumstances we believe that it will be possible to deliver our policy in a way which is compatible with EU requirements.

240. Will students from parts of the EU other than the rest of the UK pay tuition fees? Students from other parts of the EU have the same right of access to education as home students. This means EU applicants are considered for entry on the same academic basis as home students and pay the same. This will remain the case with independence.

It is not clear that such a plan would be consistent with EU law. The Scottish government has not published any legal advice on the issue (governments seldom do) but have referred to advice obtained by Universities Scotland, the umbrella body for Scottish Universities (at www.universities-scotland.ac.uk), which suggested some sort of residency requirement for free university tuition might be legally possible, but did not suggest charging fees to rUK students, while exempting other EU students.

The other international body that generates interesting questions is NATO. In 2012, the SNP leader at Westminster, Angus Robertson, persuaded his party to drop their opposition to NATO membership, a policy position the SNP had held since it first became an electorally credible party in the 1960s. Now, the position in the White Paper is:

> Following a vote for independence in 2014, the Scottish Government will notify NATO of our intention to join the alliance and will negotiate our transition from being a NATO member as part of the UK to becoming an independent member of the alliance. Scotland would take our place as one of the many non-nuclear members of NATO.

However, as noted, it also proposes not only to expel the UK's nuclear-armed submarine fleet from its base at Faslane on the Gare Loch and the warhead store at Coulport on the neighbouring Loch Long, it also wishes to write a ban on basing nuclear weapons in Scotland into the constitution. An independent Scotland would sign the Nuclear Non-Proliferation Treaty. It would negotiate with the rest of the UK 'with a view to the removal of Trident within the first term of the Scottish Parliament following independence' [i.e. by 2020; Q315]. What then about other NATO members' nuclear-armed ships entering Scottish waters? The White Paper's reply is interesting:

> It is our firm position that an independent Scotland should not host nuclear weapons and we would only join NATO on that basis.
> While the presence of nuclear weapons on a particular vessel is never confirmed by any country, we would expect any visiting vessel to respect the rules that are laid down by the government of an independent Scotland.
> While they are both strong advocates for nuclear disarmament, both Norway and Denmark allow NATO vessels to visit their ports

without confirming or denying whether they carry nuclear weapons. We intend that Scotland will adopt a similar approach as Denmark and Norway in this respect. (Q282)

This reply suggests that independent Scotland's policy towards other NATO member states' ships will be 'Don't ask, don't tell'.

Scotland would apply to join the United Nations. It would not expect to join the Security Council except in an occasional rotation, but would support the rest of the UK's remaining a permanent member of the Security Council. It would set up a network of embassies and consulates 'comparable to that of other nations of a comparable size' (Q288), while seeking to share some overseas services with the UK or other allies. A list of overseas posts includes the capitals of the major world and European nations 'and in view of the close historical and co-operation ties with Malawi, Lilongwe'. (p. 229)[8]

For many readers the most important international relationship will be that with the rest of the UK. In keeping with its theme of minimising the disruption which it anticipates independence will cause, the White Paper envisages extensive cross-border cooperation with the rest of the UK. This ranges from the cultural and symbolic:

We propose . . . a joint venture, where the SBS [Scottish Broadcasting Service] will continue to supply the BBC network with the same level of programming, in return for ongoing access to BBC services in Scotland. Through this new relationship between the SBS and the BBC, existing BBC services will continue . . . Current program-ming like *EastEnders*, *Doctor Who*, and *Strictly Come Dancing* and channels like CBeebies, will still be available in Scotland (pp. 318–19)

. . . to much larger and more problematic issues:

Will an independent Scotland continue to use the Bank of England? Yes. The Bank of England is the central bank for Scotland, as well as for England, Wales and Northern Ireland. It was formally nationalised in 1946 and is therefore an institution and asset owned both by Scotland and the rest of the UK. (Q7)

There are no circumstances in which the Scottish Government would countenance any measure being taken that jeopardized the ability of citizens across the rest of the UK and Ireland to move freely across our borders as they are presently able to do. It is for this reason that following independence Scotland will remain part of the Common Travel Area (CTA), which dates back to the 1920s. (p. 223)

This latter promise must presumably hold even if the rest of the UK leaves the EU. It certainly is intended to hold, even though the White Paper signals that an independent Scotland would be much more welcoming to immigrants than is the present UK.

Domestic matters

Much of the White Paper is concerned with day-to-day issues affecting life in Scotland, many of them in policy areas already under the control of the Scottish Parliament. Most notably, the White Paper states that independence will allow Scottish governments to do specific things like improve childcare, make the tax system fairer, cut energy bills and scrap the 'bedroom tax'. (Q2)

We do not discuss the details of these pledges, as we do not see them as relevant to the vote in September 2014. When pressed by the leader of the Liberal Democrats, Willie Rennie, as to why the White Paper contains an extensive discussion of childcare, which is already devolved, Deputy First Minister Nicola Sturgeon replied:

> If Willie Rennie has been listening to this session so far – I am sure that he has – he will know that we need the powers of independence to provide that policy, grow revenues and allow those revenues to make that policy sustainable and affordable. (*Official Report* 26.11.2013, col. 24863)

To paraphrase: every policy requires taxing and spending. Only independence gives the Scottish Parliament full control over tax-and-spend. Therefore, only with independence can a government make the list of domestic spending pledges that appears in the White Paper.

However, although the individual domestic policies to be pursued by a government are not relevant to citizens deciding how to vote in the referendum, their affordability is. Even if the vote is No, the Scottish Parliament will be forced to take greater fiscal responsibility than at present, as we explain elsewhere in this book. Fiscal responsibility means balancing spending (nice) against taxing (nasty). If the vote is Yes, the Scottish Parliament will have full fiscal responsibility from independence day.

The White Paper does not say much about this. It offers an analysis (Annex C), which says that Scotland's fiscal balance, although negative, is, when calculated with the assignment of Scotland's share of North Sea receipts to Scotland, more favourable than the UK's.

The numbers in the White Paper are a snapshot based on a Scottish government statistical series called *Government Expenditure and Revenue in Scotland (GERS* to its friends, who are mostly not football fans). When the succeeding edition of *GERS* was published in March 2014, the numbers no longer bore out the claims in the White Paper:

In 2012–13, total Scottish non-North Sea public sector revenue was estimated at £47.6 billion, (8.2% of total UK non-North Sea revenue) . . . When an illustrative geographical share of North Sea revenue is included, total Scottish public sector revenue was estimated at £53.1 billion (9.1% of UK total public sector revenue).

In 2012–13, total public sector expenditure for the benefit of Scotland by the UK Government, Scottish Government and all other parts of the public sector, plus a per capita share of UK debt interest payments, was £65.2 billion. This is equivalent to 9.3% of total UK public sector expenditure.

In 2012–13, the estimated current budget balance for the public sector in Scotland was a deficit of £14.2 billion (11.2% of GDP) excluding North Sea revenue, . . . or a deficit of £8.6 billion (5.9% of GDP) including an illustrative geographical share of North Sea revenue. (*GERS* 2012–13, Summary, at http://www.scotland.gov.uk/Publications/2014/03/7888)

The projections in the White Paper are for 2016–17, which the Scottish government hope will be the first year of independence. They suggest that Scotland's deficit will be proportionately less than the UK's in that year. This depends on a number of assumptions: the level of oil revenues is the critical one. These are put at £6.8–7.9bn. Oil revenues however have been falling and are projected to fall further. In 2012–13 the amount was £5.6bn and the forecast for the UK in the most recent budget was £3.2bn, of which about £2.9 might be Scotland's. Therefore citizens who wish to know whether the existing level of public expenditure is sustainable at the existing level of tax, or whether the spending cuts (e.g. on defence) and increases (e.g. on childcare and pensions) announced in the White Paper make fiscal balance easier or harder to achieve have to look elsewhere. We discuss this further in Chapters 2 and 8.

The Scotland Analysis *series*

While the Scottish government has concentrated most of its effort on a doorstop of a White Paper, the UK government has taken a different approach. It has been producing a series of documents, under the banner *Scotland Analysis*, dealing with issues connected with the referendum and independence. The papers are intended to 'inform the debate' and set out the arguments for Scotland remaining inside the United Kingdom, but are analytical in style and some are very technical indeed. A series of short pamphlets summarising each of them has also been issued.[9] The first paper was issued in February 2013 and by April 2014, there were thirteen. More are expected while this book is in press. Table 1.2 lists each of the papers at the time of writing.

Taken together, these papers form a substantial, but not yet comprehensive, set of arguments from the UK government on why continued union, with devolution, is better for Scotland than forming a separate, independent state. Whether the arguments are persuasive, of course, is something voters will judge.

The legal analysis of the first paper influences many of the others. It contains formal legal advice to the government from two eminent lawyers that if Scotland became independent it would be a new state, and the UK would be 'continuing'. So the UK would remain, for example, a member of the UN Security Council and the European Union. A conclusion drawn from this is that the existing UK institutions – everything from the Bank of England and the BBC to UK government departments – would serve the continuing UK, and Scotland would have to set up its own new institutions. It is, however, acknowledged by the UK government that the assets and liabilities, as opposed to the institutions, of the United Kingdom would in the event of independence have to be shared on an equitable basis between the two states. This would be an issue for the negotiations we discuss in Chapter 9, but the legal framework would guide those negotiations.

Table 1.2 The *Scotland Analysis* Series, HM Government, (2013, 2014)

Date	Title	Coverage
February 2013	Devolution and the implications of Scottish independence	The case for devolution, and the legal analysis that an independent Scotland would be a new state.
April 2013	Currency and monetary policy	How the UK currency union works and the currency options for an independent Scotland.
May 2013	Financial services and banking	How the UK financial services and banking industry operates, its importance for Scotland, and how independence might affect it.
July 2013	Business and micro economic framework	How Scotland is integrated into the UK economy, and the potential implications of independence for that.
September 2013	Macro economic and fiscal performance	How Scotland performs economically in the UK, potential border effects and long-term fiscal issues arising from independence.
October 2013	Security	The UK's approach to security and how it might be affected by independence.
November 2013	Science and research	How science and research are supported and funded in the UK, and the implications of independence for that.
January 2014	EU and international issues	The UK approach to European Union and foreign policy, how this deals with Scottish interests, and the potential effects of independence, including on EU budgets.
January 2014	Borders and citizenship	The implications for borders and citizenship of independence, compared with the present arrangements.
February 2014	Defence	The UK's approach to defence, and implications of independence for it, and the defence industry, if Scotland were to be a separate state.
February 2014	Assessment of a sterling currency union	The arguments against a sterling currency union after independence, together with the advice of the permanent secretary to the Treasury.
April 2014	Energy	Makes the case for a single British energy market, and argues it would not continue unchanged after independence so that additional costs would fall on Scottish consumers and increase energy bills.
April 2014	Pensions and welfare	Analyses UK pensions and welfare spending, and argues that it is in Scotland's interest to pool risks such as an ageing population and the costs of running welfare with the rest of the country.

This paper also argues that being part of the UK but having a Scottish Parliament with wide and increasing powers means that Scotland gets the 'best of both worlds'.

The three papers on defence, security and EU and international issues make the argument that Scotland is better served by being part of a larger nation state, with more international influence, and much greater military and security capability than Scotland could manage on its own. Scotland would have to set up its own armed forces and security services as well as manage its own international relations. The UK government argues that not only is Scotland better represented internationally and in the EU, but that it would also lose advantages in EU funding, notably the British rebate, if it were an independent state.[10] On borders and citizenship, the UK argues that a single immigration policy, allied with the Common Travel Area, which applies between the UK, the Republic of Ireland and the Channel Islands, works to Scotland's advantage. Keeping a Common Travel Area means there are no internal borders in Britain.

Some similar issues arise in relation to the paper on research and universities. While the Scottish government's White Paper argues for a continued UK-wide research funding agreement after independence, the UK government doubts that this is practicable. Instead it emphasises how successful the Scottish university sector is in attracting research funding from the UK research councils (it is otherwise supported by the Scottish Parliament) and how border effects might reduce cooperation and make it unlikely that Scottish universities would be funded by UK bodies.

The centre of gravity of the papers, however, is firmly on economic issues. Throughout them, the United Kingdom government argues that the UK is an economic and political union, and that splitting the political union would have negative economic consequences for Scotland. The Macroeconomic and Fiscal paper argues that Scotland does economically relatively well inside the UK – being one of the better-off regions of the country, having enjoyed higher per capita economic growth than the rest of the UK for some decades. It and the Microeconomic Analysis paper set out the argument why an international border would tend to reduce trade (through 'border effects', which are assessed in an unusually dense piece of economic analysis) and so reduce economic integration, and the benefits which currently come to Scotland from the unhindered movement of trade, capital and workers.

The Macroeconomic analysis paper addresses the fiscal risk to an independent Scotland from the likely reduction in oil revenues. It points out that Scottish public spending is higher than the UK average. While this might in recent decades have been offset by oil revenues in addition to Scottish domestic taxation, that advantage is a volatile one, and reduces as oil revenues gradually decline. A subsequent update[11] using the most recent data very directly challenges the Scottish government's White Paper estimate of Scotland's fiscal balance in the proposed year of independence. The Scottish government say this would be a deficit of 3.2% of GDP, and so more favourable than the UK position. HM Treasury puts Scotland's deficit at 5.3 % of GDP, and quote other independent forecasters who put it between 5.1% and 5.4%, worse then the UK's. These substantial differences principally reflect the recent drop in oil revenues and further forecast reductions and are highly significant for Scotland's future taxes and public spending: if the UK government and independent forecasters are right, independence implies big tax rises and spending cuts.

The most significant economic issue addressed in the papers is however the question of currency. Two substantial papers look at the issue. The first, of April 2013, explains how currency union currently operates inside the UK, and sets out the options for the currency were Scotland to become independent. It looks at the scope for currency union, the possibility of joining the euro, and the idea of a separate Scottish currency. The second paper of February 2014 is much more focused. It sets out very firm arguments why a currency union would not be in the interests of the UK (or Scotland) after Scottish independence. In a striking development, the paper was published alongside direct advice from the permanent secretary to the Treasury to the Chancellor, which advises strongly against a currency union.

Sir Nicholas Macpherson describes currency unions between sovereign states as 'fraught with difficulty'. They are only stable, he says, if they are seen as irreversible, and the Scottish government's position is that they might choose to leave a union at a later date; he also argues that the size of the Scottish banking sector in relation to the economy means that the rest of the UK would end up bearing most of the liquidity and solvency risk from it. Because the two countries are so different in size, it is plausible to imagine that the rest of the UK could bail out Scotland, but not the other way around.

The publication of advice of this sort is most unusual, if not unprecedented. It is clear that the UK government want to state as firmly as they can their opposition to the Sterling currency union promised in the Scottish government's White Paper so that voters should not, therefore, assume it will be delivered in the event of independence.

The Energy paper makes the case for a single energy market in Great Britain, essentially that the costs of transmitting electricity and gas and support for low carbon energy such as wind farms are shared across a much larger number of consumers. Scotland is a net exporter of electricity to the rest of Britain, and generates a disproportionate share of Britain's green energy, which is subsidised by consumers across the whole of the country, as a result the paper argues that Scottish household energy bills are lower in the UK than they would be in an independent Scotland, by anything from £38 to £189 a year. (The Scottish government say the opposite: that they would cut bills by paying for energy efficiency measures from taxation and not via energy bills, and that the rest of Britain would rely on Scotland to keep the lights on.)

The paper on welfare and pensions sets out the case for what we have called in Chapter 5 of this book a 'social union'. It describes how the UK pension and social security system allocates resources in response to need, rather than population or where taxable income is generated, and as a result welfare spending in Scotland is £60 per head higher than in the UK as a whole. The paper lays great emphasis on pensions, by far the largest part of the social security budget. It estimates that today each working-age adult in an independent Scotland would require to contribute £80 a year more to support pensions than they do in the UK. Because the proportion of older people in Scotland grows more steeply than in England, this number rises markedly, to £200 a head in a few decades. The UK government argues that this burden sharing across the whole UK is in Scotland's interest. We explore this issue in detail in Chapter 5.

Further papers in this series are likely. Collectively they give a very full account of the arguments that might be made for important aspects of the union between Scotland and the rest of the UK, and so they do indeed inform the debate. Even their authors, however, might hesitate to argue that they present a case in language which is readily accessible to the ordinary voter.

Competing visions

So voters are faced with two competing visions from two different governments, as well as from two sets of referendum campaigners.

The SNP argue that independence means Scots would run their own country, and that it would be wealthier and fairer as a result. On the other side, supporters of the union argue that the SNP's vision is flawed, especially on economic issues: being in the UK offers security and stability, in contrast to economic risk, as well as the opportunities from a devolved Scottish Parliament, whose powers are planned to increase. These are the arguments that voters must weigh up, and in the following chapters of this book we try to help them do so.

Notes

1. Section 128 of the Australian Constitution provides that both a majority of voters overall in a majority of states have to approve a constitutional change.
2. Ironically the great advocate of parliamentary sovereignty, A. V. Dicey, came to favour referendums as he argued they could stop Parliament passing a law of which the majority of voters disapproved – he had Irish Home Rule in mind. (He was against it.)
3. For example in 2002 a Section 30 Order was used to give the Scottish Executive power over railways in Scotland (SI 2002 No 1629); in 2009 (SI 2009 No 1380) another gave the Scottish Parliament the power to legislate to limit its liabilities to pay compensation to prisoners for breaches of human rights following the case of *Somerville* v. *Scottish Ministers* [2007] UKHL 44.
4. The First Minister was quoted in July 2012 saying that Scotland had a 'right to decide' on full tax powers (Gordon 2012).
5. The Commission offered this idea in evidence to the Scottish Affairs Committee. It can be found at <www.electoralcommission.org.uk/__data/assets/pdf_file/0007/149749/SAC-Voluntary-arrangement.pdf> (last accessed 16 November 2012). Some disclosures have been made under it.
6. In fairness to the Scottish government, this vicious circularity is in the existing UK rules.
7. The system of voting weights is to be replaced in late 2014 by a rule requiring proposals to have a qualified majority both of states and populations.
8. Scottish Presbyterian missionaries in the footsteps of David Livingstone converted many citizens of Malawi (then Nyasaland) to Christianity in the nineteenth century. The commercial capital of Malawi is not Lilongwe, but Blantyre, which is named after Livingstone's home village in Lanarkshire. The connection has been more recently revived by devolved Scottish administrations.
9. Accessible at www.gov.uk/collections/Scotland-analysis-papers-summary-leaflets>.
10. Indeed it is even suggested that an independent Scotland, like all other member states, might actually have to contribute to a continuing UK rebate.
11. *Further HM Treasury Analysis on Scotland: forecasts for the Scottish deficit in 2016–17*, <www.gov.uk/government/publications/further-hm-treasury-analysis-on-scotland-forecasts-for-the-scottish-deficit-in-2016-17>.

2

Independence for Scotland:
What would it Mean in Practice?

THERE IS NO doubt that Scotland could become an independent
country, no longer part of the UK. That is the question the referendum will decide. So in this chapter we look at:

- What political independence means
- Important choices facing an independent country about its international status, defence policy and, notably, membership of the EU
- The economic implications of independence and the options for
  monetary policy and the currency, banking and financial institutions
- Other major choices, and how many of them can be known about or
  decided before a referendum vote
- Whether there are different forms of independence, such as
  'independence-light'

Chapter 9 considers in more detail what would happen after a vote for
independence and the negotiations that would have to take place with
the rUK, the EU and others; what issues would have to be covered,
what leverage Scotland would have in the process, and the possible
outcomes.

Scotland as a small independent country

It is universally accepted that Scotland could become an independent
state, separate from the rUK. Campaigning for it has been the *raison
d'être* of the Scottish National Party (SNP). The case that is made for
independence is that Scotland is already a nation, and should take on
the full rights and responsibilities of nationhood. As a sovereign state,
Scotland would take its 'normal' place in the world, and Scots, and Scots
only, would be responsible for all the decisions affecting Scotland. They

are best placed to take them. Scotland would be a small but wealthy nation, and could decide for itself what policies to follow, and what sort of country to become. Of course it would cooperate with other countries, especially England, but in the end it would be responsible for its own decisions. That would be a much healthier relationship than the present one, and the power and responsibility independence brings would make Scotland a more self confident place. Others, of course, disagree.

Scotland would be a small country, but by no means a tiny one. While it would be less than one tenth of the size of the major European countries like France, Germany, or the rest of the United Kingdom, it would be bigger than a number of EU member states such as Luxembourg or Ireland, and comparable in size to a country like Denmark.

Table 2.1 shows that, on 2010 population figures, Scotland would be the ninth-smallest (alternatively, the twentieth-largest) EU member state, coming in between Ireland and Finland. The rUK drops below Italy but remains above Spain in population terms. Scotland would thus be markedly bigger than some places which have the status of independent state, including for example Montenegro, which recently became independent from Serbia, but has well under one million people in its population. So it is not reasonable to argue that Scotland is too small to be an independent country. The question that faces the Scottish electorate is whether it is the right thing to do.

Political independence

Political independence means that Scotland would be recognised internally and externally as a sovereign state. It would have its own constitution and citizens, and the powers to make all the laws affecting the territory of the country. The land and sea boundaries of the country would be relatively easy to determine according to existing international law.[1] Scotland would enter into its own international agreements and relationships, join international organisations, issue its own passports, arrange for its own defence, and so on.

It is clear that the United Kingdom itself accepts that Scotland could be independent. Successive British governments have said that if Scotland did want to become independent then it should be able to do so. This is very significant. The UK is unusual in taking this approach, as many countries would strongly resist secession; today Spain opposes an independence referendum in Catalonia. In some cases force might be used and indeed many in the UK wanted to resist Irish independence

Table 2.1 Population and land areas of the member states of the European Union if Scotland becomes independent before any accessions

Member state	Population in 1,000s	Population % of EU	Area km^2	Area % of EU	Pop. density people/km^2
Malta	417.60	0.08	316	0.00	1,305.70
Luxembourg	511.80	0.10	2,586	0.10	190.10
Cyprus	804.40	0.16	9,250	0.20	86.60
Estonia	1,340.20	0.27	45,226	1.00	29.60
Slovenia	2,050.10	0.41	20,253	0.50	101.40
Latvia	2,229.60	0.44	64,589	1.50	35.00
Lithuania	3,244.60	0.65	65,200	1.50	51.40
Ireland	4,480.80	0.89	70,280	1.60	64.30
Scotland	5,222.10	1.04	78,772	1.78	66.29
Finland	5,375.30	1.07	337,030	7.60	15.80
Slovakia	5,435.30	1.08	48,845	1.10	110.80
Denmark	5,560.60	1.10	43,094	1.00	128.10
Bulgaria	7,504.90	1.49	110,912	2.50	68.50
Austria	8,404.20	1.67	83,858	1.90	99.70
Sweden	9,415.60	1.87	449,964	10.20	20.60
Hungary	9,985.70	1.99	93,030	2.10	107.80
Czech Republic	10,532.80	2.10	78,866	1.80	132.80
Portugal	10,636.90	2.12	92,931	2.10	114.40
Belgium	10,951.70	2.15	30,510	0.70	352.00
Greece	11,325.90	2.25	131,940	3.00	85.40
Netherlands	16,655.80	3.30	41,526	0.90	396.90
Romania	21,413.80	4.26	238,391	5.40	90.20
Poland	38,200.00	7.60	312,685	7.10	121.90
Spain	47,190.40	9.18	504,782	11.40	93.40
United Kingdom less Scotland	57,213.60	11.36	166,048	3.75	344.56
Italy	60,626.40	12.06	301,320	6.80	200.40
France	65,075.30	12.95	643,548	14.60	99.60
Germany	81,751.60	16.27	357,021	8.10	229.90

Source: Eurostat; Scottish Government. Scottish population: mid-2010 estimate

by force between 1912 and 1921. There is absolutely no suggestion of that now vis-à-vis Scotland. Whether other countries recognise Scotland as an independent state is up to them, but because the UK is willing to do so, it is likely that other nations would do the same.

This would be an exercise of self-determination, acknowledged by other states. Exactly which territories or groups of people can exercise that right is not always clear. Not all parts of the UK are likely to be able to do the same.[2] It is however clear that because Scotland has its own distinct history, institutions and national identity, it is likely to be widely recognised as a nation having that right. After all, Scotland was an independent country until 1707, has always retained its own legal system, and now has a devolved Parliament. Although it shares a language, it has a cultural identity in some respects distinct from the other parts of the UK. Self-determination is likely to apply to the whole territory of Scotland, and it seems unlikely that parts of Scotland would have the right under international law to secede from Scotland, or to choose to remain within the United Kingdom. There has been some speculation about what would happen should Orkney or Shetland vote No while the rest of Scotland voted Yes. The SNP has been willing to concede some autonomy to the Northern Isles and an independent Scotland might decide to offer the islands some special status, and indeed the three Island authorities (including the Western as well as Northern Isles) have in recent months been running a campaign for more autonomy within the UK. The idea of the Northern Isles remaining part of the UK while the rest of Scotland became independent, although theoretically possible, is unlikely to happen in practice.

Scotland's constitutional status under political independence

The key thing about the Union of 1707 was that the old Scots Parliament and the English Parliament were abolished. Instead Scotland sent representatives to the new Union Parliament at Westminster. Although an independent Scotland might be able to negotiate with the rest of the United Kingdom to retain some common institutions, it could not elect MPs to the House of Commons or have representatives in the House of Lords (or whatever chamber eventually replaces it). Those bodies would look after the interests of the rUK only. That much is certain: in other respects, a newly independent Scotland would have to decide what sort of constitution it wanted. Obviously it should be a democracy, but should it continue to be a monarchy (as the SNP now propose)? What sort of Parliament should it have – one chamber or two, what electoral system should be used, and so on? It would also have to decide on the rules for citizenship of the new country. Would everyone living in Scotland on the day of independence automatically become a Scottish citizen, or might they be able to retain UK citizenship, and what about people born in Scotland but living elsewhere in the UK or the EU – or indeed anywhere in the world?

A newly independent country would be able to decide all these things for itself and it would have to codify them all in a written constitution.

The Scottish government's White Paper however makes some detailed commitments. Although there would be a constitutional convention to draft a written constitution, it is proposed that Scotland should be a constitutional monarchy, with a single chamber Parliament elected by the same list system as the devolved Parliament today, with the same number of members. The Scottish government's position appears to be that it is the Scottish Parliament which would adopt the new constitution rather than the Scottish people through another referendum.

International issues

An independent Scotland would be a new country with its own international legal personality, separate from the rUK. Scotland could make treaties with other countries, join international organisations, and so on. Because Scotland would be leaving the UK, it is likely that it would be seen as a new state with the rUK as the 'continuing' state (House of Commons Library 2011, Secretary of State for Scotland, 2013). Indeed this view has been set out by the UK government in their Scotland Analysis papers and it appears to be accepted by the Scottish government, although they may dissent from some of the conclusions drawn from it. Whether Scotland acceded to membership of international bodies would depend on their rules. It would have to apply for membership of bodies like the United Nations (UN), the Commonwealth, the Council of Europe, the EU, NATO and no doubt many others. In some cases, such as the UN or the Council of Europe, application is likely to be little more than a formality, with no substantial conditions attached. Scotland will already meet any membership conditions there are: for example membership of the Council of Europe requires signing up to the European Convention on Human Rights, and members accept the jurisdiction of the Human Rights Court in Strasbourg, which as part of the UK Scotland already does. In others, there may be conditions of membership. This will be particularly important for NATO and the EU, which are discussed below.[3]

Defence and foreign affairs

An independent Scotland would have to conduct its own foreign relations, and be responsible for its own defence, though in each case, of course, it might seek to enter into arrangements with other countries, especially the rUK, as that will remain Scotland's most important social and economic partner. So far as foreign relations are concerned, Scotland would have to have representation in the international organ- isations to which it belonged such as the UN (and the EU, discussed below) and would almost certainly want to have representation in the capitals of some other major countries, most notably London. But it might hope (subject to agreement) to share such matters as consular representation across the world with the rUK.

An independent Scotland would also have to adopt a defence policy. This is more complex than it sounds, and there are a number of choices. Scotland could, for example, choose a policy of neutrality. That would mean not joining any alliances, such as NATO. A neutral country can choose to have relatively small armed forces, like Ireland, or alterna- tively to be quite heavily armed, like Switzerland. One possible con- figuration for the Armed Forces of an independent Scotland is given in Crawford and Marsh 2012. The principal choice, however, facing Scotland would be whether to be a member of NATO, as the UK is at present. NATO is an alliance of twenty-eight countries, having grown from the twelve countries which banded together after World War II to provide mutual defence,[4] and now includes some very small countries, such as Albania and Croatia, as well as big powers like the US, the UK and Germany. Scotland could conceivably try to negotiate a defence agreement with the rUK outside of NATO, but it seems likely that the UK would wish any agreement to be within a NATO framework as it will remain a NATO member.

NATO is a nuclear alliance, and membership is closely linked with the continuation of the UK's nuclear deterrent, based at Faslane and Coulport in the West of Scotland. It is highly unlikely that an independ- ent Scotland would be able, or would choose, to be a nuclear weapons power. There are obvious reasons for this: first, it is an extremely expen- sive undertaking, which a country of five million people would struggle to afford; and it might well be that public opinion in an independent Scotland was opposed to nuclear weapons. Finally, the international treaties on the non-proliferation of nuclear weapons would forbid a country like Scotland from having them. Nonetheless an independ- ent Scotland would have to deal with the fact that the UK has a major nuclear weapons base within its territory.

The future of that base would have to be determined by negotia- tion between Scotland and the UK. Scotland could, as an independent country, decide that it wished to have no nuclear weapons on its soil, and negotiate with the rUK as to how they would be removed. Alternatively it could decide to regard Faslane and Coulport as important cards in the negotiations on the terms of separation (there is a full discussion, though now out of date, in Chalmers and Walker 2001 and a view of the choices is given in Scottish Affairs Committee 2012c). As we discuss in Chapter 9, there will be many very difficult issues to be negotiated, and Scotland might not be in a strong position in relation to all of them: however, all parties would know that it would be difficult to move the Trident base, especially the nuclear-weapon store at Coulport, to anywhere in the rUK that was operationally as suitable and that local public opinion would support.

Those negotiations would be heavily influenced by possible NATO membership and its terms. If Scotland were not a member of NATO, it might agree with the rUK for the base to remain in operation, either as some sort of continuing UK territory or leased to it, perhaps for a defined period. If Scotland were a member of NATO, then it would be easy to allow a NATO country to retain a base on Scottish territory, as the UK currently does with the US, such as bases like RAF Lakenheath, which is home to the US Air Force 48th Fighter Wing. The Scottish government's White Paper however proposes that Scotland should be a non-nuclear member of NATO (as a number of NATO members are) but that UK nuclear weapons should be removed – indeed constitutionally forbidden.

The other members of NATO might agree to Scottish member-ship, but they might want a resolution of the nuclear issue first, and might not be willing to agree to one member simply ejecting another's nuclear forces. These would be very major decisions, and matters of great importance to the UK as well as to Scotland. The nuclear sub-marine base at Faslane is undoubtedly a key UK strategic asset. Many people hold very strong views on nuclear weapons, and some might see getting rid of them as an argument for independence. In advance of a referendum, however, and before the negotiations which would have to be undertaken and the decisions made, it is not possible to say with certainty how this would turn out.[5]

Membership of the EU

Perhaps the most significant other relationship which an independ-ent Scotland would have is with the EU. An independent Scotland is under no obligation to join the EU, but many, including the present SNP Scottish government, would say that continued EU membership would be in Scotland's best interest. Indeed at one point the Scottish government argued Scotland would automatically become a member of the EU. They now take a different view.

There has been much discussion about whether and how Scotland might become an EU member state. The European Union was created by treaties, and those treaties do not make any provision for secession from a member state, or the break up of one. (Hardly surprising: the states entering into the treaties would not have wanted to plan for their own disintegration.)

So there is no estblished procedure for how the EU would deal with Scottish independence. The member states, and the European institutions – that is to say the European Commission, the European Court of Justice, and the European Parliament – would have to find a way of addressing the matter. In the past, the EU has shown a good deal of pragmatic flexibility when dealing with issues that have arisen that were not necessarily envisaged in the original treaties. The accession of new member states, the reunification of Germany, the creation of the Euro, the departure of Greenland: all show how a complex multinational organisation copes with unforeseen developments.

There are a number of ways in which Scotland's position might be decided. What will actually happen will depend on the circumstances, and especially on the views of the larger member states: that in turn might depend on their own internal politics. Positions inside the EU are very often a matter of political negotiation, or horse-trading; dealing with Scottish independence is unlikely to be an exception. In those circumstances, member states can be expected to look after their own interests, and trade agreement on one subject for concessions on another.

In the end, EU decisions often come down to what political consensus can be reached. If the UK is, after Scotland leaves, the 'continuing' state it will retain its status as an EU member, and Scotland as a new state will not automatically become one (Armstrong, K. 2014).

So Scotland would (at least on paper) be a new state seeking membership. There is disagreement about the process by which Scotland might become a member. Both the Presidents of the European Commission and Council, and a number of EU member states, have said that Scotland should be an 'accession state', applying under article 49 of the treaties for admission to the European Union. The Scottish government, by contrast, have suggested that instead of a Scotland applying, the treaties could simply be amended under article 48 to provide for membership. Although one distinguished Scottish lawyer agrees with the Scottish government, most (see, e.g., Armstrong, K. 2014) seem to think the accession route is the more likely.

In the end this is a political rather than a legal decision. If the EU member states want Scotland to be a member, then an accession process can be made to work. Scotland would have to aim for membership to be agreed on an accelerated basis. An accelerated accession process would have obvious practical advantages for Scotland. If the accession negotiations could be done quickly then an independent Scotland might avoid or minimise any period during which it was outside the EU. The EU might then avoid the risk of ejecting EU citizens, even temporarily, from the union. In principle, that would require border controls, tariffs on Scottish produce entering the EU, and a host of other requirements which apply to non-EU members. That would clearly be undesirable if it were obvious that an independent Scotland was going to join the EU. (If, on the other hand, there was genuine uncertainty about Scottish intentions – say if there were to be a referendum on the subject – then matters become more complex.)

There is no reason to suppose that existing member states, or any of the European institutions, would regard Scotland as unsuitable for membership of the EU, though some members such as Spain or Cyprus would have their own domestic issues to consider. The Spanish Prime Minister, concerned about independence movements in his own country, has already suggested that a new state would find accession difficult, and may have little incentive to make it easy or quick for Scotland.

Even apart from the politics, accession is far from simple. Extensive negotiations would be needed, most likely under considerable time pressure. Although Scotland already meets most EU requirements, a number of important practical questions would have to be decided. Some are discussed in Chapter 9: membership of the European Commission, number of MEPs, voting strength in the European Council and so on. These negotiations are not however just housekeeping as a number of difficult questions arise: who negotiates for Scotland and what mandate would they have? and how could they commit a future, independent Scottish Parliament or government?

There are also some very important substantive questions. The first of these is which of the requirements which normally apply to accession countries would be applied to Scotland. These are called the Copenhagen criteria, because they were first set out at a European Council meeting there in 1993. Of course Scotland meets many of the

Copenhagen criteria without any difficulty: it is already part of the EU, and meets the requirements of having stable political and legal institutions, and a functioning market economy able to form part of the European single market. The Copenhagen criteria however include commitment to the aims of political, economic and monetary union, and this raises the important question of membership of the Euro.

Most EU member states are Euro members. The UK has a formal opt-out from the relevant treaty, as does Denmark; Sweden voted against Euro membership and does not implement the treaty. Some countries which joined more recently are committed to join at later dates[6] and new accession countries are expected to commit in principle to Euro membership. Of course the Euro is under a great deal of economic and political stress at present, and economic or even monetary conditions could change before Scotland might join. So the circumstances of any negotiations are not certain. It seems unlikely, however, given present circumstances that the European institutions or other member states would insist on immediate Euro membership for Scotland. One possibility is that an independent Scotland might have to commit, as other countries have, to eventual membership, when economic circumstances were appropriate. That would have implications for the currency options for an independent country.

Of more immediate practical concern are the other opt-outs which the UK has negotiated from broader European requirements, and how these would apply to Scotland. These relate not just to the Euro, but to passport and border controls, and a number of EU regulations relating to justice and law enforcement and to the existence of a zero rate of VAT. Important amongst them is the so-called Schengen agreement. This allows for freedom to move within the EU without passport control. The UK is one of a few European countries which opted out of this arrangement. This is why it is still necessary to take a passport when going from the UK to, for example, France or Germany. At present, instead, the UK and the Republic of Ireland form a so-called Common Travel Area (which they have maintained in one form or another since 1923) so that passports are not needed to go from Glasgow to Dublin, or indeed to the Channel Islands or the Isle of Man.

If Scotland were required to adopt the Schengen rules, it would be possible to travel from Glasgow to Paris without a passport, but it would not be possible to cross the border to England without one. Practical common sense suggests that Scotland should not join the Schengen area, but this would require the agreement of other EU member states.

Scotland would also have to choose whether to opt wholly in to other EU justice rules.[7]

A further major issue is the UK rebate or 'abatement' from the EU budget negotiated in 1984 by Mrs Thatcher's government, because historically the UK tended to get back less from the European budget than other countries. This was down to the UK's relatively small farming industry and the fact that so much of EU spending was (and is) spent on farm subsidies. This abatement of the UK's net contribution to the EU budget is calculated according to a formula which takes account of payments made into the EU budget and amounts which flow back directly to the UK. It is worth around £3bn a year, leaving the UK the fourth largest net contributor to the EU budget, after Germany, France and Italy (HM Treasury 2011a). No Scottish figure is available as the calculation is done at a UK level. The Scottish government say in the White Paper that the rebate would continue, but the UK rebate is unpopular with other member states, as it was negotiated at a time when the UK (and indeed Scotland) was relatively poorer than it is now. It seems unlikely that any sort of rebate would be offered to an independent Scotland, and the UK government's Scotland Analysis paper calculates that the additional cost in European contributions for each household in Scotland would be between £750 and £1,470 a year. These numbers are disputed by SNP Ministers.[8]

It is difficult to predict quite how these negotiations would turn out or how long they would take. The rUK would play a big role in them, and its attitude would be critical, but neither the rUK nor Scotland can guarantee the result. The timetable will depend in part on the negotiations that will be needed between Scotland and the rUK. As we note in Chapter 9, these are complex and might prove difficult, but some aspects of them as least (e.g. currency) need to be settled before EU issues can be. On top of that, once the EU negotiations are completed the necessary Treaty changes will have to be ratified by each Member State. (Each State has its own rules about ratification. Some countries can require referendums though they might decide not to do so in this case.) It seems unlikely that this whole process can be completed by the Scottish government's target date of May 2016.[9]

Scotland as an EU member state

Assuming that these negotiations were successfully completed, Scotland would become one of the EU's smaller member states. It would probably be able to nominate a European Commissioner, and would be represented by perhaps twelve MEPs, like Denmark or Finland, as opposed to the present six. Scotland would, as now, be subject to EU treaty obligations. Most of these would simply confirm existing Scottish law and practice, because of the UK's existing EU membership. But some would be new to Scotland as an independent state. For example, unless special arrangements were made, Scotland would be obliged like other EU member states to have its own central bank, and its own regulatory system, notably in relation to financial services. The implications of this are discussed below.

Other international bodies

There are other international bodies which Scotland would almost certainly join if it became an independent country. It would apply for membership of the UN and, provided it was widely recognised by other countries, this would almost certainly be granted. Scotland is also very likely to join the Council of Europe. Signing up to that body would require Scotland to continue to accept the European Convention on Human Rights. If it were not a member of the EU, Scotland might seek to join the European Free Trade Area or the European Economic Area, which offer some of the single market benefits of EU membership though without some of the other obligations, though obviously without the capacity to influence EU policy directly.

The economic implications of independence

Independence is essentially a political concept, but it has important implications for the economy of a country. Indeed many of those who argue for independence do so because they think it would make Scotland more prosperous,[10] essentially because economic policies could be tailored to Scottish needs and not those of the whole UK (for example, UK interest rate decisions take account of the needs of London and the South East which may differ from those of Scotland). Prosperity however is also heavily influenced by relationships and trade with other countries, especially in a world in which the economy is highly globalised. It is important therefore to consider the potential effects of independence on Scotland's trading relationships.

Scotland is already part of two single markets within which it can trade: there is the UK domestic market, and the EU single market.

Britain has been a free trade area since 1707. That was one of the purposes of the union. Indeed it is now such an integrated and entirely open market that UK companies have long regarded it as a single domestic market. The EU has worked hard for decades to create a single European market but there remain, inevitably, some barriers to trade within it. Apart from the facts of geography, there are differences of language and culture and in the things which people want to buy, as well as more formal barriers to trade in, for example, financial services. Trade within Europe, however, has increased hugely since Britain joined what was then the Common Market in the 1970s, and since the development of the Single Market in the 1980s and 1990s.

Because it is a single domestic market, the UK is a highly integrated economy. The Scottish economy is part of it and, on most measures, typical of it. On the commonest measure of economic activity (Gross Value Added, which is more or less the same as Gross Domestic Product), Scotland has been close to the UK average, and getting closer to it over the last decade or so, as Table 2.2 shows. There are similar trends in other measures such as income.

The UK is also a monetary union in which Scotland is deeply embedded for trade and employment purposes. Most Scottish exports go to the rUK, rather than elsewhere in the EU. The Scottish government estimates that in 2010 exports to the rUK from Scotland were about £45 billion, and those to the 27 EU member states about £9.7 billion. Trade within the UK is more than twice Scotland's trade with all other countries (Scottish Government 2012b). This level of trade interconnectedness runs the other way too: the Scottish government estimates that Scotland is the UK's second largest trading partner. Scotland is also part of a common UK labour market, and Scots are able to travel to find work throughout the UK. There should also be no legal barriers to finding work elsewhere in the EU, though this is less common in practice for a variety of reasons.

The implications of a single market

The thrust of the idea of any single market is that by eliminating barriers to trade in the form of different regulations, tariffs or other taxes, economic growth is encouraged. This was an aim of the 1707 union, and of the EU single market. It has not been fully achieved in the EU, not least because of the incompleteness of the single currency, but significant non-tariff barriers remain especially in relation to services.

Table 2.2 Relative gross value added per head, nations and territories of the UK since 1999

GVA per head: Indices (UK less Extra Regio = 100)	1999	2000	2001	2002	2003	2004	2005	2006	2007	2008	2009	2010	2011	2012
United Kingdom	100	100	100	100	100	100.	100	100	100	100	100	100	100	100
England	102.6	102.7	102.7	102.7	102.7	102.7	102.6	102.5	102.5	102.5	102.5	102.4	103.0	103.0
Wales	76.7	76.3	76.3	75.9	75.7	75.6	75.6	75.2	74.7	73.9	73.3	74.0	71.9	72.3
Scotland	94.3	94.2	94.0	94.1	94.1	94.6	95.4	96.4	96.8	97.8	98.8	98.7	94.8	94.0
Northern Ireland	80.6	80.7	80.4	79.4	79.5	79.9	80.2	80.1	79.5	77.9	76.2	76.4	76.0	75.7

Source: HM Treasury; Office for National Statistics

The UK domestic single market is however well functioning: goods and services can be sold, workers can work, finance be transferred, without hindrance in any part of UK; legal, tariff or tax differences play little role in investment.

Scottish independence would inevitably have some effect on this, though it is hard to say how substantial. There would be scope for tax differentials, in corporate tax (the Scottish government propose to reduce this to attract industry, but Scotland could equally choose to tax more highly to provide more public services), income tax, or even a different rate of Value Added Tax (VAT). Although Scotland would be likely to remain within the EU, and so benefit from the EU single market rules, there is some risk that differences in regulation and taxation would make it more difficult for Scotland to trade with the rUK, say in financial services, where tax policy is very important[11] (indeed, if there were no differences in regulation or taxation at all, there would hardly be any point to independence).

The UK government has emphasised this risk, called a 'border effect' in economics jargon, in its Scotland Analysis series. They give examples of the barriers to trade across the Irish border and on the basis of a theoretical economic analysis they suggest the reduction in trade could over time reduce Scottish income by 4%. At a less theoretical level, a number of major Scottish companies, notably companies in the financial services sector such as Standard Life and Alliance Trust, have expressed concerns about the risk which independence would cause to their businesses, whose customers are primarily located in England. Several have announced plans to set up companies based in England rather than Scotland. Similar concerns have been expressed by defence contractors based in Scotland (see for example Scottish Affairs Committee 2014).

The single greatest advantage that any domestic market has, however, is that there is a single currency throughout. This enables individuals and companies to trade without any exchange rate costs or risks. This is a strong motivation behind the creation of a single European currency to match the single European market. Because Scotland is so much part of the UK economy, there is a powerful argument for having the same currency, so as not to disrupt trade. In the economists' jargon, Scotland and the rUK today meet the conditions for an optimal currency area: goods and services flow freely across the border, there are no big imbalances in economic activity and the Scottish and English economies move in broadly the same cycles.

This has of course been used as an argument against independence. But the Scottish government now say that an independent Scotland should retain the pound sterling in a monetary union with the rUK. (The SNP had previously argued for Euro membership for an independent Scotland.) This approach was endorsed by the fiscal commission working group of the Scottish government's Council of Economic Advisers (Scottish government 2013a). This has proved highly controversial and as we go on to consider the currency options open to Scotland as an independent country, we examine it in detail: could an independent Scotland really still be part of a monetary union with England?

Currency issues

The single most important economic decision that an independent Scotland would have to make is what currency to have. There are three options, in principle, for Scotland. There could be a new, independent, Scottish currency: the pound Scots, say. Alternatively, as a member of the EU, Scotland could join the Euro. Finally Scotland could find a way to keep the pound sterling and remain in a monetary union with the rUK. These options are fully explained by the National Institute for Economic Research. (See Armstrong and Ebell 2013.)

Having a new Scottish currency would be entirely possible. Other countries with economies of similar scale to Scotland do this quite successfully. A new currency could be launched by Scotland's central bank just as the Euro was. Deposits in Scottish banks would be redenominated in the new currency, as would the assets and liabilities of Scottish businesses, at least in the domestic market. The new currency would probably take time to settle at the right level of exchange with sterling and other currencies, and there is a risk that it might be volatile, as its exchange rate could be heavily influenced by the price of oil. The Scottish central bank would be responsible for Scottish monetary policy, managing inflation, the money supply and so on. It would also, almost certainly, have to regulate Scotland's banking and financial sector. (The implications of the currency options for that sector are discussed below.) The main risk of having a separate Scottish currency, and splitting up the currency union which has lasted since 1707, however, is disruption of trade with England, particularly if the exchange rate were made volatile by oil prices. Scotland would have to decide how to manage its currency – whether to allow it to float, or perhaps try to fix the rate of exchange with sterling by having a currency board, discussed below, or peg it by intervening in the markets to keep the exchange rate as level as possible. (To do so however means having large reserves of hard currency and implies running a tight fiscal policy to build them up.)

It would also be possible for Scotland to join the Euro, though this is an option the Scottish government have ruled out. As we discussed above, it is unlikely Scotland would be required to join the Euro immediately as a condition of continuing EU membership, though it might have to promise to do so in the future. Joining the Euro however is not straightforward. The rules which are applied are designed to ensure that a country joins at the correct level compared to its previous currency. For that reason, countries which wish to join the Euro are expected first to join the European Exchange Rate Mechanism and keep their own currencies stable against the Euro for a period of two years. Sterling, of course, is not part of the European Exchange Rate mechanism, and it is therefore unclear how Scotland could move into the Euro, unless it had its own currency for a period of time. In any event, there has recently been considerable uncertainty in the Euro area. So this might not be a good time for a new country to join the single European currency.

The third option is continuing with sterling as the currency of an independent Scotland. The crudest way of achieving that is what leads SNP ministers to say that the UK could not stop Scotland from using the pound sterling. Scotland could avoid having a currency and monetary policy of its own, but simply allow sterling to circulate in the country as a means of exchange. This is known, in the economics jargon, as 'dollarisation'. Some countries have done this, often after an economic crisis (Zimbabwe is an example). Although some economists have supported it, and it may be the Scottish government's 'Plan B', it is not generally considered as an option for a wealthy developed economy. (It is not consistent with EU treaty obligations, as member states are obliged to have a central bank, and a regulated financial services sector. Banks would find it very hard to operate from Scotland without a central bank to act as the lender of last resort. They would have to have very large reserves readily available to avoid any risk that they would run out of liquidity.)

Alternatively, Scotland could have a currency of its own but link it, pound for pound, to sterling. Such a 'pegged' currency would aim to have a fixed exchange rate relative to sterling. A pegged exchange rate is vulnerable to market speculation. If the markets think the rate is wrong, governments have to spend very large sums of foreign-exchange reserves in an attempt to maintain the rate. (Few developed countries are now able to apply rigorous exchange controls which stop individuals and businesses converting their money into foreign currency to prevent this happening.) This is similar to the problem which sterling itself faced during the period of its membership of the European Exchange Rate Mechanism. Under pressure the currency had to be allowed to float and fell swiftly in value.

The way British colonies used to maintain the link with sterling was to have a traditional currency board. They maintained reserves of sterling in their country exactly equivalent, pound for pound, to the amount of the domestic currency they allowed to circulate in their economies. Gibraltar still does this today and it, along with the Channel Islands and the Isle of Man, forms what is left of the sterling zone. In principle this can be done, but neither it nor a pegged currency allows Scotland any flexibility in monetary policy.

The policy of the Scottish government however remains that the UK should continue to be a full monetary union, with a single central bank (the Bank of England) and a single currency. If this were possible, it would certainly remove exchange rate risk, and so facilitate trade with England. Many economists would argue that today the UK including Scotland forms an 'optimal currency area' (see for example Hallwood and MacDonald 2009). This position was set out in full by the Scottish government's Council of Economic Advisers fiscal commission working group who argued that the best solution for both Scotland and the rest of the United Kingdom was a currency union (Scottish government 2013a).[12] There are however a number of difficulties with the proposal.[13]

First, and most obviously, maintaining a monetary union with the rest of the United Kingdom requires the rUK to agree to do so. Such a currency union would not simply be a continuation of the present arrangements, as the two countries would be politically independent and fiscally separate. The UK government (Secretary of State for Scotland 2013) has set out the legal view that the Bank of England would automatically be the central bank of the continuing UK and not of Scotland, so that an independent Scotland would have to seek UK agreement to a sterling currency union. Whatever the legal position, the government and Parliament of the rUK would be under an obligation to join a currency union only if they were sure it was in the best interests of those whom they represent. It is now very clear that the UK does not take this view.

In a blizzard of interventions in early 2014, various UK bodies, including the Treasury and the Governor of the Bank of England, set out the arguments against currency union. Then coordinated political statements from the Chancellor of the Exchequer and politicians from the other main parties ruled currency union out as an option. We concentrate here on the non-political analysis rather than whether or not the politicians are (as the Scottish government say) bluffing.

The Governor of the Bank of England gave a careful lecture in Edinburgh on the economics of currency unions, while stressing that the decision was a political one. In addition to the criteria for an optimal currency as discussed above, he added that experience from the Eurozone confirmed that a currency union needed also to have effective banking union, substantial fiscal union, and shared sovereignty. Effective banking union was needed because problems in the banking system anywhere in a monetary union needed to be dealt with decisively if confidence was to be maintained; fiscal union was needed because dealing with them required the commitment not just of central bank liquidity, but of taxpayer resources. In his view that meant a central authority with control of fiscal resources of 25% of GDP (roughly half of public spending) and that implied shared sovereignty.

This was followed by a further *Scotland Analysis* paper from HM Treasury 'Assessment of a Sterling Currency Union'. Unusually it was presented as the publication of civil service advice to Ministers. It set out arguments why a currency union would not be in the interests of the rest of the UK or an independent Scotland. Currency union would be in the interest of neither country, as the two economies would gradually diverge and each would end up with a currency that was not suitable. Fiscal and political union were essential for the success of a currency union. In the end it was taxpayers who had to stand behind banks which were being rescued or agree to other fiscal transfers from one part of the currency union to another. That required political union. If a currency union was not seen as permanent, e.g. because of a promise to join the Euro or, as said in the Scottish government White Paper, it might be subject to change at a later date, it would swiftly be undermined by the market (as in the Czech Slovak case below). Political union was needed to rule out that risk. Finally it noted that in the case of Scotland and the rUK the risks were asymmetric: an independent Scotland might plausibly look to the rUK to rescue its banks (which were large as a share of the Scottish economy) but the rUK could not plausibly assume the opposite.

These issues have of course been played out in the Euro area in recent years. Because there was a single currency, governments using it have been able to borrow at similarly low interest rates, even if they have little prospect of being able to pay the loans back from their own revenues. In order to avert pressure on the currency, and the problems for the countries concerned, the members of the European monetary union have had to commit to very substantial fiscal transfers and write-offs of debt for these countries. The process has been slow and painful, and at the time of writing, it is still not clear how this crisis will turn out. This is what leads people to say that a monetary union must also be a fiscal union as well. If monetary stability is to be maintained there has to be scope for fiscal transfers inside it to off-set monetary movements: the EU's problem at present is that the scope for fiscal union to allow those transfers to take place is limited. Independence would put Scotland and rUK into that position.

It is clear that an independent Scotland would have no say in the decisions of the rUK, and would be unable to require the UK to remain in a monetary union against its will, or on conditions to which it did not agree. The Scottish government however say that the UK position will change after a Yes vote, as it is simply a campaign tactic, because currency union would be in the rUK's interest. Most of the economic commentary does not accept this (e.g. Armstrong and Ebell, 2014) though some economists do (Muscatelli 2014). They therefore continue to say that there will be a sterling currency union after independence. Voters will have to make up their own minds whom they believe.

There have been examples of monetary unions between countries that are not political unions, and are also not fiscal unions – that is to say taxes and spending are not all shared across the area. The Euro is an example: there are some shared political institutions but national sovereignty is retained and there are only limited fiscal transfers between the countries. Another was the monetary union which followed the break up of Czechoslovakia: the two new countries agreed to share a common currency and had certain fiscal rules that allowed them to do so.

The history of the Czechoslovak monetary union is interesting for our purposes. Czechoslovakia was a country created after the First World War (1918) by the union of Slovakia and the Czech lands of Bohemia, Moravia and Silesia. All had previously been part of the Austro-Hungarian Empire. After World War II Czechoslovakia came under Communist control, and although it was nominally a federal state of two parts, real political power was exercised centrally by the Communist Party. After the fall of the Berlin Wall, the 'Velvet Revolution' replaced Communist rule, but there were political differences between the two parts of the country. In 1992, the governments of the two federal states agreed to split the country, creating the Czech Republic and Slovakia. The two new countries agreed initially however to retain a monetary union, as the economies were seemingly similar.

This monetary union came under immediate pressure. Because the currency was not internationally convertible, the pressure was not from international speculators, but from ordinary citizens and businesses who thought that the economies of the two parts of the monetary union were likely to diverge. It looked likely that the Czech Republic would outgrow its Slovak neighbour, leading individuals and businesses to keep cash in the Czech Republic rather than Slovakia. The financial systems seized up and the monetary union swiftly collapsed, lasting no more than five weeks in total, a large part of which was spent preparing for the mechanics of its dissolution. The dissolution was done remarkably successfully, in part because the economy was still under a set of tight controls inherited from the communist regime, including controls on the movement of cash both outside the country and across the Czech–Slovak border. Slovakia is now in the Euro; the Czech Republic has its own currency.

Scotland's situation is different from these countries, which were emerging from communism into market economies (at the very least, there would be no exchange controls on the Anglo-Scottish border in the event of a replay). What the story shows however is that a monetary union which is not underpinned by economic and fiscal unity sufficient to sustain the confidence of individuals and markets can swiftly disintegrate.

Financial system and regulated financial services

The question of the currency of an independent Scotland and its central banking arrangements are obviously closely connected to the future of its banking and financial services sector. Banking and financial services are very important to the Scottish economy and, despite problems in recent years, still employ proportionately more people in Scotland than in the rUK. Edinburgh is the biggest financial centre in Britain outside London. Financial services employment is distributed across Scotland in Glasgow, Dundee and elsewhere. Of all the parts of the UK, only London is more reliant than Scotland on finance for jobs. The majority of the customers of the Scottish financial companies services are of course elsewhere in the UK, and banking and financial services are therefore a very good example of the case for maintaining a UK monetary union so as not to disrupt trade.

The issues are however more complex. As mentioned above, any banking system needs an organisation which acts as a lender of last resort, and this is almost always the central bank of the country in question. Together with a scheme of deposit insurance (in the UK the Financial Services Compensation Scheme) this is necessary to secure stability in the banking system. Deposit insurance protects depositors (who might otherwise lose money if a bank was unable to meet its liabilities); a lender of last resort protects the banks themselves (and ultimately their customers) as it reduces the scope for a run on an individual bank with an immediate liquidity problem – if it is solvent but short of ready cash, it can always borrow money from the central bank. Since the central bank is responsible for creating money, it should always have the capacity to lend to other institutions. The resources of the state (i.e. taxpayers) stand behind each institution, to provide support if need be, as they have had to in the UK in the recent financial crisis. The Bank of England has been very active in creating liquidity in recent years through its policy of quantitative easing, but its interventions depend ultimately on taxpayer support from the UK government.

If Scotland had its own currency, it would have to have its own central bank which would be able to act as lender of last resort. The same would be true if Scotland had a pegged currency, though the central bank's capacity to create money would be heavily constrained by the need to maintain a fixed exchange rate. If there were a monetary union with the rUK, then the Bank of England could be asked to act as lender of last resort for Scottish banks also. But in order to do that without unacceptable risk to its own financial position, it would have to be satisfied that the banks in Scotland were regulated to at least as high a standard as those elsewhere in the UK. Indeed the UK government might, understandably, take the view that if the Bank of England were expected to lend to Scottish institutions, it should also regulate them in exactly the same way it does institutions elsewhere in the country. In order to achieve this result, Scotland and the rUK would have to agree with the other EU member states that the treaty requirement on each of them to have its own central bank and financial regulatory system should be relaxed so that they could share one. In the circumstances it might also make sense for the Financial Conduct Authority, which regulates other aspects of financial services alongside the Bank of England, to operate across the monetary union as well. The Scottish government has suggested mixed regulation, with prudential supervision done as it is today at the UK level and customers' interests looked after by a new Scottish body.

This would require an amendment to the EU treaties so that the regulator in one member state could supervise companies in another, but it would also require the rUK to agree to take on this responsibility on Scotland's behalf, and the UK government would have to be satisfied that it was in their people's interest to do so. The industry might welcome continuity in regulation, but in practice they may well achieve that for themselves by changing their domicile to England – where most of their customers are – and operating branches in Scotland.

The difficulty with a plan of this sort arises if the monetary union is not seen to be stable and permanent. This might be because Scotland had an obligation to adopt the Euro or because, as in the Czechoslovak case, the markets took the view that the currency union might split up for economic reasons. It would then strongly be in the interests of the banks and other financial institutions to minimise the risk to their activities by ensuring that they were conducted in that part of the currency union they thought would be more stable, which in the Czech–Slovak case was the Czech Republic (and, as in that case, such behaviour could be a self-fulfilling prophecy). It will certainly be in the interest of financial services companies, in any event, to minimise the risk of regulatory change, and take action to ensure that whatever currency option an independent Scotland follows, they will retain their present regulatory status (this is not necessarily because Scotland could not devise a better one, but to avoid uncertainty about what Scotland could or would devise). Several have announced that they will do so.

The implications of monetary questions for independence

No independent country is ever completely economically free. All are to a greater or lesser degree linked economically to their neighbours, and this is particularly true of small countries with open economies. But because Scotland is deeply economically integrated with the rUK, its scope to run a completely separate economic policy is especially limited. What happens elsewhere in the UK will continue to be very important for the Scottish economy. So there are obvious advantages for Scotland in remaining in a monetary union. It is now not clear that such a monetary union could be achieved. Even if the Scottish government are right and it can be agreed, it would almost inevitably require a degree of fiscal coordination which would markedly reduce an independent Scotland's capacity to decide its own tax and spending. This implies a single interest rate and monetary policy, and UK supervision of Scottish banks, thus removing from Scotland many of the economic levers that an independent country possesses.

The fiscal position of an independent Scotland

As an independent country, Scotland would have to raise its own taxes and be responsible for providing its own public services. An important question is whether the tax revenues available as an independent country would enable Scotland to provide the same, higher, or lower levels of public service to the population. Because the position of Scotland inside the UK has been the subject of debate, there is in fact a good deal of information about Scotland's fiscal position. The information has been published since the early 1990s in a series of national statistics under the title *Government Expenditure and Revenues in Scotland* (latest *GERS* 2012–13). Of course what these show is Scotland's position as it is inside the UK, rather than what it would be like as an independent country, as many things could change if separation happened, and the estimates of tax revenue in particular are subject to significant uncertainty for that reason.

Nevertheless it is possible to get a broad understanding of how Scotland's public finances might look if it were an independent country. Useful statistics that we have derived from earlier *GERS* are in the Tables in Chapter 6 of this book. The key aspects of the financial position are as follows:

- Public expenditure in Scotland is significantly higher than in the rest of the United Kingdom. (There is much argument as to why this is so, and whether it is right, which we do not go into here.) Expenditure on devolved services such as health, education, transport and so on is in total about 18% higher per head than the UK average. Expenditure on reserved services is managed by the UK government. The largest by far is social security; benefits spending is about 2% per head above the UK average. Overall Scottish public expenditure on 'identifiable' services is about 14% per head higher than the UK average. Scotland also has to make a contribution to what are called 'non-identifiable' services such as defence and foreign relations and debt interest, as part of the UK, and in estimating the country's fiscal balance, this is assumed to be allocated on a per capita basis (HM Treasury 2012a).

- Tax revenue in Scotland is (oil aside, for the moment) slightly lower than the UK average per head. If this was all there was to it, Scotland would be in some financial difficulty. It would run a much larger deficit than the UK as a whole, and would be unable to sustain the levels of public services which are presently provided without much higher taxation.
- The availability of oil revenues, however, changes the fiscal picture. On the assumption that an independent Scotland gets the benefit of most of the North Sea revenues, as seems likely, Scotland's deficit becomes a smaller one. Table 2.3 makes estimates for the deficit, in cash and in real terms, in each of the last ten years.

We discuss the significance of oil revenues more in Chapter 7. The important point for the purposes of this chapter is that an independent Scotland would have been able to maintain broadly the present level of public services in recent years on the basis of its share of oil revenues, provided it had spent them all its oil revenues in order to do so. The Institute for Fiscal Studies (IFS) came to the same conclusion in November 2012: an independent Scotland would initially, relying on oil revenues, be in broadly the same or a somewhat healthier fiscal position as the rest of the UK, but in the longer run as oil revenues decreased it would face tougher budgetary choices than the UK as a whole (Johnston and Phillips 2012). If on the other hand it wished to maintain an oil fund so that revenues were invested to be available for future generations, then spending levels would have to be reduced or other taxes increased immediately. The same point was made by the Scottish government's fiscal commission. Obviously as oil revenues decrease in the future, expenditure will have to be reduced unless alternative economic activity is developed to replace them. The options for an oil fund are discussed more fully in Chapter 7.

The most recent figures for oil revenues show a substantial drop, as the table shows. As a result, after many years of being in a more favourable fiscal position than the UK as a whole, Scotland is now in a worse one: its public spending is higher than the UK's and its tax revenues lower. Oil is a volatile revenue source and may go up and down, but it

Table 2.3 Scotland's estimated fiscal balance 2002–13 in real terms, £bn, 2012–13 prices

	2002–3	2003–4	2004–5	2005–6	2006–7	2007–8	2008–9	2009–10	2010–11	2011–12	2012–13
Expenditure	38,912	42,360	44,518	49,962	52,810	55,925	59,440	62,087	64,095	64,869	65,205
Non-oil income	32,664	35,022	36,983	39,839	42,272	44,815	43,772	42,054	44,318	46,315	47,566
Oil income	4,232	3,521	4,532	8,017	7,504	7,112	11,577	5,679	7,455	10,000	5,581
Deficit before oil	−6,248	−7,338	−7,535	−10,123	−10,538	−11,110	−15,668	−20,033	−19,777	−18,554	−17,639
At 2012–13 prices	−7,934	−9,141	−9,134	−12,051	−12,195	−12,541	−17,201	−21,406	−20,595	−18,882	−17,639
Average deficit not including oil since 2002–3 at 2012–13 prices											−14,429
Deficit after oil	−2,016	−3,817	−3,003	−2,106	−3,034	−3,998	−4,091	−14,354	−12,322	−8,554	−12,058
At 2012–13 prices	−2,560	−4,755	−3,640	−2,507	−3,511	−4,513	−4,491	−15,338	−12,831	−8,705	−12,058
Average deficit including oil since 2002–3 at 2012–13 prices											−6,810

Source: Scottish Government (2014), Scotland Office (2010), authors' calculations

is projected to keep declining as the North Sea gives up the last of its wealth. This has profound implications for spending and taxation in an independent Scotland. Projections of the potential effect were done by the IFS (see Amior et al. 2013) and show very clearly that significant corrective action – to cut spending or raise tax income markedly – would be essential. To illustrate the scale of the fiscal challenge the IFS noted that to get to the same long term position as the UK as a whole by altering income tax Scotland would have to increase the basic rate by 9 pence. This is clearly not practical politics, but shows the scale of the change to tax and spending that would be needed. A similar analysis by the NIESR of Scotland's fiscal prospects compared with the UK as a whole over the next fifty years (Crawford and Tetlow, 2014) also makes for sobering reading. To get to what is seen as a stable debt to GDP ratio of 60% over that period, the UK needs to make a 'fiscal adjustment' (lower spending or higher taxes) of 0.4% of GDP. Scotland's challenge on its own would be much greater: they estimate from 1.5% to 5.9% of GDP, implying very large tax rises or spending cuts.

Even if it spent all its oil revenues, Scotland would still run a deficit, and would have to borrow money to finance it. Of course most countries do this, except typically those that are running surpluses from oil or other natural resource revenues (and putting them into an oil fund). So Scotland would have to establish a track record with lenders, in the form of a credit rating. The UK has a high, though not at present the highest, credit rating and pays very low interest rates. Scotland is unlikely to inherit the rating (one agency has suggested it would be two notches lower), so establishing a record of servicing payments on the share of the UK's debt it is likely to inherit would be important. Until a record had been established, Scotland would probably not be able to borrow at the very low rates the UK now does. Various estimates have been made of the interest rate 'premium' Scotland would have to pay, but this is hard to estimate at all accurately. All estimates however suggest added budgetary pressure.

So what would independence mean for the Scottish economy?

Scotland is at present a wealthy country, perhaps the third richest region of the UK.[14] Separating from the UK would certainly have economic effects, but it is not at all clear what they would be in the long run. Supporters of independence of course argue that it would unleash Scotland's economic potential, and make everyone better off.

Alternatively, if an independent Scotland could remain tied into a monetary and fiscal union with the rUK, that could mean less change in the economy than expected. On the other side of the balance, separation could make trade harder, and reduce Scotland's access to important United Kingdom markets, such as those for financial services, or for warships or other defence technology. With so many uncertainties, it is simply not possible to say, one way or another, what the long term economic effect of political independence would be: there might be opportunities, but there are also significant risks and some transitional disruption and cost is inevitable.

Other major issues affecting independence

In Chapter 9 we describe the process that would have to be gone through if there were a vote for Scotland to become independent. This includes extensive negotiations with the rUK about the terms of independence. As well as issues such as EU membership, defence, and the currency, many other important questions will have to be agreed. These include splitting up the armed forces, allocating the UK national debt, and responsibility for pension liabilities (in relation to old-age pensions, public service pensions, and the regulation of private sector pensions); the myriad of UK institutions and common services, from the BBC to the DVLA, which would have to be disaggregated and arrangements made to provide them in or for an independent Scotland. While it might be possible to speculate on how these negotiations might come out, it is inevitable that significant uncertainty about most of them will remain until the process of negotiation is completed.

Are there different forms of independence?

No country is ever completely independent, and all are to a greater or lesser degree interdependent with other nations. This is seen in cultural, economic and trade links, membership of international political organisations, like the EU, and defence alliances such as NATO. Independence does not mean complete self-sufficiency; so it is reasonable to ask whether other forms of independence that involve more sharing of power with other countries than most nation states do, are possible for Scotland. Does an independent country, for example, really need its own army or international representation? Could it not share many services with its neighbours? At a simple practical level, for example, why have a Scottish vehicle licensing agency, when Scotland could share one with the rUK? (For some reason, this is one body the Scottish government does not wish to share with the UK.)

It is certainly possible to conceive of such arrangements, which have gone under the label of 'independence-light'. It is conceivable, for example, that Scotland could form a Confederation with the rUK responsible for defence and foreign affairs matters, but left domestic Scottish matters to Edinburgh. In many respects the Scottish government's White Paper is a bit like this. It is much more difficult to envisage how it would be put into practice. The example of maintaining a currency union after independence illustrates some of the issues: first, it requires agreement from the rUK, which looks at best uncertain, and the terms on which it would be obtainable might well have wider impacts. The position of the Channel Islands also illustrates this dilemma. They are not part of the UK, but they could be described as in confederation with it. They deal with all domestic issues but the UK runs defence and foreign affairs on their behalf. They send no MPs to Westminster and so have no say at all on those matters. An arrangement which works for very small islands, however, is not so readily transferable to a nation of five million people. They would presumably be expected to contribute to the costs of defence (as they do within the UK) but how would they have any say over it? It is unlikely that the rUK would agree to give Scotland a veto over issues like military action or the position to take in international negotiations, though there could be some consultation rights over them.

At the very minimum, before any notion of 'independence-light' could be put to the voters in a referendum, it would be necessary to develop a completely new model of independence involving a quite different relationship with the rUK from simple independence. This could only be done with the full agreement and cooperation of the rUK. In that respect, 'independence-light' resembles arguments about further devolution: it is not a unilateral Scottish decision. What Scotland can decide for itself is whether or not to be independent, and then it can seek to negotiate the best way of living with its neighbours.

Independence: certainties and uncertainties

We began this chapter by saying that Scotland could become an independent country, separate from the rUK. This is certainly true, but there are significant uncertainties about what independence would mean in practice. Some things only an independent Scotland could decide for itself. So some unknowns are unavoidable, even if political leaders can make their aspirations clear. Additional uncertainties derive from agreements which will have to be reached with others once a decision about independence is taken, notably in negotiations with the rUK and the EU.

Scotland will always have to have a very close relationship with the other countries which form the UK. What that relationship will be, and whether it could continue to provide some of the aspects of the present union, is not possible to say: that can only be figured out after independence, if that is chosen. An independent Scotland might want to remain in a monetary union with the rest of Britain, but that looks highly uncertain and in any event constraints on Scotland's freedom of action would follow from it. An independent Scotland would probably be a member of the EU, though it is not clear precisely what the terms of membership would be or how long the process of getting there would take. As an independent country, Scotland could follow its own fiscal policy, subject to those constraints, but it would have to decide how to deal with the very significant fiscal effect of declining oil revenues. Whether in the long run Scotland would be richer or poorer as a result of becoming independent is simply not possible to determine: there are too many uncertainties about not just the terms of independence, but the approach of any future Scottish government, not to mention what happens to the UK, European and world economies. Voters will have to make their own judgments as to how these things might turn out, realising that any politicians who predict them with absolute certainty must surely know they will be wrong.

Notes

1. The sea boundaries are important, obviously, in relation to oil: see Chapter 7.
2. Northern Ireland has its own very particular position: both the UK and the Republic of Ireland recognise that it could choose to leave the UK and join the rest of Ireland.
3. Some lawyers argue that the idea that Scotland would leave the UK and become a new state, with the UK remaining as the 'successor state', is wrong and that both of the countries which resulted from the break-up of the UK would inherit all the rights and obligations of the UK. This, they say, is what happened when Czechoslovakia decided to split into two and become the Czech Republic and Slovakia. That however was the dissolution of a Federation, rather than a secession from an existing nation state, and the balance of legal opinion (and certainly the view of the UK government) is that the UK (no doubt renamed the United

Kingdom of England, Wales and Northern Ireland) would continue to exist, and inherit all the rights and obligations of the present UK. This is more like what happened when the USSR broke up and Russia as the largest part of it was recognised as the successor state.

4. Article 5 of the 1949 NATO treaty provides: 'An armed attack in Europe or North America against one or more of the (signatories) shall be considered as an attack against them all.' (NATO 2005)

5. For a well-informed set of guesses see Chalmers 2012.

6. Although formally amongst these, the Czech Republic is at best ambivalent about membership and may adopt a position similar to Sweden.

7. What the EU calls the 'Area of Freedom, Security and Justice', from whose European law-making powers Ireland, the UK and Denmark have some opt-outs.

8. Scotland Analysis: EU and international issues. Though it might also be that the UK rebate would be challenged by other member states during these negotiations.

9. Some commentators (e.g. Armstrong, K. 2014) have suggested that there might be an interim period during which Scotland was independent, but not a full EU member, perhaps while the other member states were going through the process of ratifying the accession treaty. Scotland might during that time be a member of the free trade European Economic Area only (like Norway) or perhaps the treaties could apply provisionally until ratified. It is not clear how this would work or what its effect on things like payments to farmers under the Common Agricultural Policy might be. This would all have to be dealt with in negotiation.

10. There is a purely statistical sense in which independence would make Scotland – apparently – richer. At present the economic activity from North Sea oil is not counted as part of Scotland's Gross Value Added (GVA), or Gross Domestic Product, but rather in a special offshore region of the UK. If Scotland were independent most of that would be counted as part of the Scottish economy, and the GVA number would be higher. But no one would be any better off.

11. Sales of pensions, for example, depend critically on how they are dealt with in the tax system.

12. At least initially: the advisers' report seems to suggest this might only be a temporary arrangement. For potential implications of that, see the discussion of the Czech–Slovak monetary union on pp. 37–8.

13. Aside from the obvious point that an independent Scotland would not be able to decide its own interest rates, which would take into account the interests of the rUK, as they do today.

14. According to the Office for National Statistics, Scotland has in every year from 2007 to 2010 had the third-highest GVA per head of any part of the UK, after London and the South East, but ahead of every other English region as well as Wales and Northern Ireland (ONS 2011a). By household disposable income, Scotland is the fourth-richest UK region (ONS 2011b).

3

The Calman Commission and the Scotland Act 2012

THIS CHAPTER LOOKS at the Scotland Act 2012, which makes important changes to the financial powers of the Scottish Parliament, set to come into effect over the next few years. It emerged from the work of the Commission on Scottish Devolution, the Calman Commission, set up to review the devolution settlement, and it will give the Scottish Parliament more tax and borrowing powers than it presently has. Whether the changes will be put into practice depends on the choice Scotland makes. If Scotland remains part of the United Kingdom then the additional powers will come into effect. They may be added to or extended at a later stage, especially if the option of more devolution is pursued. If however there is a vote to create an independent Scotland they will fall by the wayside.

The Calman Commission: background

The powers of the Scottish Parliament are set out in its founding legislation, the Scotland Act 1998. It defines the Parliament's legislative powers, and the Scottish Ministers' executive powers, which cover broadly the same areas. These in their turn were based on the previous administrative responsibilities of the Scottish Office, the pre-devolution department of the UK government. During the first two terms of the Scottish Parliament, from 1999 until 2007, a number of additions were made to these devolved responsibilities, using an Order in Council under the Scotland Act – a procedure which requires the consent of both the Scottish and UK Parliaments. For example, Ministerial responsibility for railways in Scotland was transferred to Edinburgh. But during this period there was no comprehensive review of devolved powers as a whole.

The Scottish Parliament election of 2007 however changed things.

The newly returned SNP minority government began to pursue their policy of seeking independence. They proposed an independence referendum and initiated a 'National Conversation' on Scotland's constitutional future. The majority in the Scottish Parliament however took a different approach. They proposed a review of devolved powers, focusing especially on financial accountability. This process was initiated in November 2007 in a speech at Edinburgh University by the then Labour leader in Holyrood, Wendy Alexander, and it was supported in the Scottish Parliament by the Liberal Democrat and Conservative leaders (Nicol Stephen MSP, now Lord Stephen, and Annabel Goldie MSP).

The Parliament resolved on 6 December 2007 to support 'the establishment of an independently chaired commission to review devolution in Scotland'. In March 2008, the UK government, under the leadership of Gordon Brown, announced that it too would support establishing a Commission. Its remit, agreed in the Scottish Parliament by a majority with SNP MSPs dissenting, and also by the UK government, was:

> To review the provisions of the Scotland Act 1998 in the light of experience and to recommend any changes to the present constitutional arrangements that would enable the Scottish Parliament to serve the people of Scotland better, improve the financial accountability of the Scottish Parliament, and continue to secure the position of Scotland within the United Kingdom. (Calman 2009: 3)

Its report was therefore to be submitted to both bodies. This unusual approach reflected the fact that the SNP government was in a minority at Holyrood and the parties which formed a majority, though unwilling to form a coalition administration, were prepared to work together on the constitutional question.

The Commission began work in April 2008. It was chaired by Sir Kenneth Calman, the Chancellor of Glasgow University. Its membership included nominees from the three major pro-union parties, six in total, though a majority of its fifteen members had no party affiliation and were drawn from business, trades unions and other aspects of Scottish life. Its work was supported by staff from the UK government (which provided much of its infrastructure) and the Scottish Parliament, but not from the Scottish government. Over a period of fourteen months the Commission took written and oral evidence, and undertook a programme of public engagement. It was advised by a group of academic experts on politics and economics led by the then Principal of Heriot Watt University, Professor Anton Muscatelli, who produced analytical papers and recommendations. The Commission itself produced two reports: the first preliminary and consultative in December 2008 (Calman 2008) and the second with a large number of recommendations in June 2009 (Calman 2009).

The Calman Commission: conclusions and recommendations

The Commission's First Report was largely consultative, but did conclude that devolution to Scotland was both highly successful and popular; it had clearly worked well in practice, and having a Scottish Parliament within the UK had 'consistently remained the preferred constitutional model of the significant majority of people in Scotland' (Calman 2008: para. 4.3). In line with their remit, the Commission took for granted that there would still be a political union between Scotland and the rUK. They considered the closely integrated UK economy, within which goods and services were constantly traded, as an economic union which it was to Scotland's advantage not to undermine. They were therefore opposed to devolving foreign affairs, defence and macroeconomic management. They saw the economic union as important for taxation because the scope to have different rates of tax inside a single economy without distortions arising was limited.

In the Commission's view there was also a social union, with common rights and responsibilities. They thought the Scottish and UK Parliaments should agree to the elements of these common social rights and responsibilities, but were clear that they included a common system of social security. The Commission saw their task as recommending how devolution might develop within this political, economic and social union, particularly to improve financial accountability, as their remit required.

The Commission's second report *Serving Scotland Better: Scotland and the United Kingdom in the 21st Century* was published in June 2009. Its recommendations form the basis of the Scotland Act 2012, and are therefore worth considering in some detail.

Reviewing the legislative powers of the Scottish Parliament, the report looked in detail at each of the reservations – those areas which remain the responsibility of the Westminster Parliament and UK government. Their main conclusion was that the most substantial reserved domestic policy, social security, should remain so.

Social security includes old-age pensions, and other contributory and non-contributory benefits such as Job Seeker's Allowance and Employment Support Allowance, Income Support and Pension Credit. Taken together, benefits account for nearly all of the 'identifiable' public expenditure in Scotland which is not already devolved to the Scottish Parliament and government, so this was a highly significant conclusion.

In the Commission's view financing this form of social protection from UK-wide resources, so that risks and the resources to deal with them were both shared, was a 'fundamental part of the Union' (Calman 2009: para. 2.4). (We discuss this more fully in Chapter 5.) They saw this explicitly expressed in national insurance (NI) where payments into a common National Insurance Fund entitled individuals to certain benefits, but linked it also to the pooling of tax income, such as VAT or oil revenues, across the whole UK. The Commission did however note that social security impacted on devolved policy areas, such as local taxation and housing, and proposed that there should be some flexibility in Housing Benefit and Council Tax Benefit to reflect this.

Social security is by far the most significant area of domestic policy not already devolved. If it is not to be changed, it is not surprising that the other recommendations which the Commission made for changes to the boundary between devolved and reserved matters were minor adjustments to deal with particular problems that had been identified rather than major shifts in responsibility.

Amongst these, the Commission proposed devolving some administrative responsibilities relating to elections; some adjustments to the methods of appointing the Scottish members of the BBC Trust and the Crown Estate Commissioner; devolving the regulation of airguns, and the prescription of controlled drugs such as heroin to addicts; and, on the roads, allowing the Scottish Ministers to set the national speed limit and drink driving limits. The Commission also recommended that two responsibilities be transferred from Edinburgh to Westminster: the regulation of all health professions, not just those which had existed at the time of the Scotland Act; and the rules to be applied by insolvency practitioners, so that they could be the same on both sides of the border.

Calman laid great emphasis on joint working and cooperation between the different levels of government. In their view inter-governmental relations had been good in some respects, such as reaching agreement prior to European Union discussions; cooperative working on those issues was a continuation of pre-devolution arrangements. There were also effective arrangements for considering Westminster legislation that affected devolved matters, so that the Scottish Parliament could be asked to consent to Westminster legislation affecting devolved law. Overall however the Commission concluded that intergovernmental and inter-parliamentary relationships were not well enough developed; considerably more emphasis should be placed upon them, and they should operate on the basis of mutual respect between the institutions. As they concluded that this did not require legislation but rather a change in working practices, this subject does not feature in the Scotland Act.

The Calman Commission: tax issues

The most important Calman recommendations, and so the major parts of the Scotland Act 2012, are about fiscal powers – taxation and borrowing. To understand their recommendations, it helps to know how devolved spending is presently funded.

Public spending can be divided into spending which is identifiably for the benefit of one of part of the country, such as health and education, and spending which cannot be geographically assigned in this way, such as spending on defence or foreign affairs, which is for the benefit of the whole country equally (HM Treasury 2012a). Most 'identifiable' spending in Scotland is the responsibility of the Scottish government and Parliament: expenditure on the NHS, schools, roads, law and order and so on. The main exception is spending on social security. It is the largest single spending programme and accounts for close to 40% of identifiable public spending in Scotland. The UK government is also responsible for 'non-identifiable' spending such as on defence or debt interest. All of this spending, devolved and reserved, is supported by taxes levied by the UK Parliament across the whole UK, including of course in Scotland. Westminster collects the taxes and sends a grant to Edinburgh to pay for devolved Scottish services.

Scottish devolved spending is therefore primarily paid for from grants from Westminster supported by the taxes it collects.[1] This grant is sometimes called a 'block grant' because it is not tied to particular spending requirements. It has for many years been calculated by the 'Barnett Formula' which determines changes in the grant to the Scottish government as a proportion of changes to the budgets of English government departments performing comparable functions. As the Calman Commission noted, this amongst other factors has led to levels of public spending in Scotland proportionately higher than in England (see Chapters 2 and 6 for more about relative spending levels).

The Scottish Parliament has complete control over how the budget is spent, but it does not have a great deal of influence over its total: it does not take the tax decisions. But it does have some tax powers. First of all, local authority spending is devolved. It represents about one third of devolved spending, and is partly supported by local taxes – council tax and business rates. The Scottish government has legislative and executive power over those taxes: Ministers decide the level of business rates, and exercise a very high degree of control over council tax (since 2007 the Scottish government has frozen council tax). As the Calman Commission noted, this gives the Scottish government a degree of tax freedom – they decide on taxes of about £4bn a year, compared to total spending of around £30bn.

The Scottish government has one additional degree of flexibility, the Scottish Variable Rate of income tax. The Parliament has the power to vary the basic rate of income tax applying in Scotland by up to plus or minus 3 pence in the pound. The resulting change in tax revenue is added to or subtracted from the Scottish budget. At the most, the difference could be something over £1bn a year. This applies only to the basic rate and not to the higher rates of taxation, nor to income such as bank interest. There is no obligation on the Parliament to use the power, and if it does nothing, income tax in Scotland remains unchanged, and so does the Scottish budget. No Scottish administration has ever proposed either to increase or decrease income tax.

The Calman Commission concluded that while this financial system had got devolution off to a good start, it needed amendment. Guided by the work of their Independent Expert Group, they concluded it had advantages of simplicity, stability, and predictability, but offered only limited fiscal autonomy and so accountability. They thought all funding systems should serve constitutional aims, and a funding system for devolution within a union had to balance three competing claims: equity – producing results which could be seen as fair across the UK; accountability – ensuring that taxpayers could hold the Parliament accountable for spending and taxing decisions; and efficiency – minimising economic distortion, and being simple to administer and explain. The present system, they concluded, fell short in providing accountability; nor did it allow the Scottish Parliament much scope to use taxation as a policy instrument by encouraging or discouraging different activities (for example they currently use their tax powers to give business rates relief to small businesses and rural petrol stations).

The Commission reviewed each of the taxes used in the UK to see which could be devolved to improve the fiscal accountability of the Scottish Parliament (we look at each of them in more detail in Chapter 4). The three largest taxes in the UK are VAT, national insurance contributions and income tax. Calman ruled out devolving VAT as European law does not permit different VAT rates within a single EU member state. They also ruled out devolving national insurance because of the close connection between contributions and welfare benefits such as old-age pensions. This was consistent with their view that preserving a single UK Benefits system was a key aspect of the union.

That left income tax, which they concluded offered the main way of enhancing fiscal accountability and increasing the taxation powers of the Scottish Parliament. It yielded significant revenues and had a direct connection with the electorate. It was a highly perceptible tax and although not all voters were taxpayers, almost all taxpayers were voters (in contrast to, say, corporation tax). The principle of having a different Scottish income tax rate already had a democratic mandate from the 1997 referendum. They were however against the total devolution of income tax as alone it would represent around 40% of the Scottish Parliament's revenues and they thought it unwise to depend so heavily on one tax. Additionally, setting income tax made the UK Parliament accountable too, so income tax should become a shared tax.

Two other significant sources of tax income are corporation tax and oil revenues. The Commission recommended against devolving either. For corporation tax, which is paid on business profits, they were principally concerned about the potential for harmful tax competition within the UK. If rates were lower in one part of the country companies would try to reduce their tax liabilities by declaring their profits there, so losing revenue to the UK as a whole without necessary promoting economic growth or even giving an incentive for economic activity and jobs to move to a low tax area. They were also worried about potential administrative costs for business. Oil taxation is a significant source of revenue, producing anything from £1bn to £12bn a year for the Exchequer. It is volatile as it is driven by the market price of a globally traded commodity. The Commission's Independent Expert Group advised that devolving these revenues would require a corresponding reduction in the block grant, which would expose a large proportion of the Scottish budget to very high levels of volatility that could not readily be absorbed. The Commission concluded that devolution of oil revenues would add risk to the Scottish budget without increasing the financial accountability of the Scottish Parliament (see Chapter 7.)

The Commission also reviewed other taxes. They did not recommend devolving excise duties because variable rates of duty could add to the avoidance problems already being experienced, notably in relation to alcohol and tobacco. Similar concerns about possible avoidance and administrative difficulty led them to recommend against devolving inheritance tax, capital gains tax and some other minor taxes. They did however recommend devolving four other relatively small taxes: Stamp Duty Land Tax, Aggregates Levy, Landfill Tax, and Air Passenger Duty. Of these Stamp Duty Land Tax is the most significant. It raises over £400m a year, and is paid on land and property transactions (they recommended against devolving the Stamp Duty which is levied on transactions of shares and securities). The Aggregates Levy is a tax on the commercial extraction of rock, sand and gravel. It raises about £50m a year. Landfill Tax is a tax on the disposal of waste and raises around £75m a year in Scotland. Air Passenger Duty is paid by the aircraft operators who carry passengers from a UK airport. It raises about £90m a year in Scotland.

Finally the Commission recommended that the Scottish Parliament should have the power to create new taxes, subject to UK agreement. It acknowledged that these might not be substantial revenue raisers, but rather like other small taxes, e.g. Landfill Tax or Aggregates Levy, could be designed to influence behaviour, and so be useful policy tools for governments. Examples that have been suggested include taxes on plastic bags, as in Ireland.

The Commission's proposals for a new financing system

The Calman Commission therefore proposed additional tax devolution, but not so much to allow the Scottish Parliament to raise all the money it spent. They considered two other methods of funding. Firstly, central grant (as at present), which they recommended should continue, with the amount reduced to take account of the new tax powers because grant is the most obvious way to allow central government to ensure that there is a degree of equity in the result of the funding system. They did not regard it as part of their job to undertake an assessment of relative spending need to determine what the amount of grant should be, but suggested that the Barnett Formula could continue to be used until such an assessment was made.

Apart from tax devolution and grant, the third way of allocating resources is 'assignment', that is to say allocating the whole or part of the yield of a particular tax to the Scottish budget, even though the Scottish government have no say in the tax rate. Assignment is not used in the UK (though it is possible to think of the television licence as an assigned tax, in this case assigned to the BBC, which gets licence fee income even though it does not set the fee). Assignment is however used in some federal countries, notably Germany, where the Länder are funded in large part through assigning a share of the yield of VAT, though the VAT rate is set nationally by the Federal government. In the Commission's view, assignment had the potential advantage that it would link the budget of the Scottish Parliament to the performance of the Scottish economy, as tax yield goes up or down as the economy grows or shrinks. But it would by the same token add uncertainty to the budget, and would not improve accountability to voters. They therefore did not recommend using assignment except to a small degree in relation to income tax (discussed below) and as a possibility in future to extend their recommendations further.

Devolving income tax

The Calman scheme for devolving a proportion of income tax was based on Canadian experience. Canadian Provinces are funded by a mix of transfers from the Federal government, devolved tax revenues and revenues from taxes shared with the Federal government. Grants are paid to provinces to achieve certain minimum standards, and to equalise fiscal capacity (that is, the capacity to raise income from taxation) rather than any assessment of spending need. Tax bases, that is to say the activity or asset on which a tax is levied, are shared between the Federal and Provincial governments, and have been since the 1950s. In particular, both the Provinces and the National government levy income tax, so that they share that tax base, and indeed the income tax collection system (apart from Quebec, which has its own collection agency).

The Scottish Variable Rate of income tax is an example of a shared tax base, and the Commission recommended that the idea should be extended. Rather than just having the power to alter a UK tax rate, the Scottish Parliament should levy an income tax of its own, sharing the tax base and collection system with the UK Parliament. In order to allow 'room' for it to do so, the UK income tax rate should be reduced in Scotland. The Commission proposed that UK tax rates should be cut by 10 pence (and the grant to the Scottish Parliament by an equivalent amount). The Scottish Parliament would have to set a rate of Scottish Income Tax, which would be added to the (reduced) UK rate to produce the total levy on the taxpayer. The revenue from the new Scottish Income Tax would be remitted by HM Revenue and Customs to the Scottish government. So, for example, if the UK rates of income tax were 20, 40 and 45 pence in the pound, these would be reduced in Scotland to 10, 30 and 35 pence. If the Scottish rate were then set at 11 pence, then the total rates applying to Scottish taxpayers would be 21, 41 and 46 pence; if the Scottish rate were set at 9 pence, the totals would be 19, 39 and 44 pence.

The Commission recommended a single Scottish rate applying across all tax bands, and rejected the idea of a different Scottish rate for each band. This was in part for reasons of simplicity, but also because of their view that redistributive decisions such as the progressiveness of the tax system were matters best decided at the UK level, consistent with their vision of the social union.

For similar reasons the Commission were against devolving the structure of the income tax system, such as setting the income tax bands, deciding on taxable allowances and so on. They saw two problems. First income tax was, as well as a revenue-raising device, also an instrument of redistribution. A progressive tax system has effects that are redistributive across different parts of the UK as well as between individuals. They thought that such decisions, and therefore the structure of the tax system, were properly taken at the UK level. Secondly, they saw possible problems of compliance and administrative cost for employers and the tax collection authorities.

Most income tax revenue is deducted at source from wages and salaries through Pay as You Earn (PAYE), and most taxpayers do not have to fill in an annual tax return. The administrative work is largely carried out by employers. One significant source of income tax revenue which is not dealt with in this way is the tax on income from savings and distributions, most commonly bank interest. This too is usually deducted at source by the banks and remitted to HM Revenue and Customs, at the basic rate of 20%. The taxpayer simply gets the interest paid net of tax, and basic rate taxpayers need do no more. Higher rate taxpayers who fill in an annual tax return declare the interest there; but for the most part tax on savings and distributions is received by HMRC without information about who the taxpayer is.

This creates a problem for devolving income tax on savings, as it would be a very major burden on banks and other financial institutions to identify which of their customers was a Scottish taxpayer, and so liable to pay the Scottish rate, and how much tax income therefore belonged to each government. The Calman Commission therefore recommended that this tax should not be devolved but that instead a share of this revenue, calculated on a formula basis, should be assigned to the Scottish budget, thus completing the sharing of income tax between two governments.

Overall effect of the Calman scheme

Taken together, the Calman Commission concluded their recommendations would increase the proportion of the Scottish government's current expenditure funded from tax decisions under their control to 35%. Using figures from 2006–7 (which were the latest at the time of writing – see Chapter 4 for more up-to-date figures) their arithmetic was as follows:

As it estimated that the total tax revenues in Scotland in that year were £39bn, or £46bn including a geographical share of oil taxes, the Commission therefore proposed devolving 23% of taxation, 19% including oil, compared to about 50% of spending. (The % varies in different years as tax yield, especially for oil, is volatile.)

Capital expenditure and borrowing

The information in Table 3.1 relates to current expenditure, such as wages and salaries. The Scottish Budget also contains capital expenditure, on buildings like schools and hospitals, roads, equipment and so on, amounting to between £2 and £3bn a year. Some of this is spent by local councils, mostly financed by their borrowing. That borrowing is virtually all from the Treasury, through a body called the Public Works Loan Board, because that is the cheapest way to do it; it is repaid from councils' current expenditure. Other public bodies such as the National Heath Service or the Scottish government itself spend capital too (for example, to build hospitals or prisons). This is simply financed from the block grant, just as it was when the Scottish Office was a government department. In effect the UK Treasury does the borrowing directly for

Table 3.1 Estimated current spending that would be supported by taxes decided in Scotland according to the Calman proposal

Estimated tax receipts 2006–7	£ million
Income tax basic rate	3,500
Income tax higher rate	650
Income tax on savings and distributions	500
Aggregates levy	50
Landfill tax	75
Stamp duty land tax	555
Air passenger duty	94
Non-domestic rates	1,884
Council tax	1,812
Total devolved tax revenues	9,120
Relevant budget (SE resource DEL plus NDR & Council Tax)[a]	26,049
% of relevant budget from own sources	35%

Source: Commission on Scottish Devolution Final Report, Table 3.4
[a] This is the Scottish Government current expenditure budgets in its Departmental Expenditure Limit (DEL) plus the expenditure which is financed from Council Tax and Business (non-domestic) rates (NDR)

this spending, and it is repaid from general taxation. The Commission estimated the Scottish share of this repayment for 2006–7 at £2.4bn, roughly comparable to the capital budget (Calman 2009: para. 3:188).

The Scottish government however has little control over how much this spending is in total in any one year (just as it has little control over total current spending). In the regular Spending Reviews held by the UK government, the Barnett Formula determines the block grant available for capital spending, just as it does the current budget. The Scottish government does not have to spend it all, but it can only add to it by transferring resources from current spending. It has no powers to borrow money to bring forward capital expenditure and repay the debt from tax or other current resources. The Calman Commission concluded that the Scottish government ought to be able to borrow to finance additional capital expenditure in any one year and so have a similar degree of flexibility over their capital budget as over their revenue spending. They said:

just as taxation powers give the Scottish Parliament responsibility for setting the total of the Scottish devolved budget or current spending, if it is to be fully accountable it should be able to borrow to determine the total of capital spending in any one year. It would be perverse if the Scottish Parliament could increase taxation above UK levels to finance additional current spending, but not use that resource to support additional borrowing. (Calman 2009: para. 3.197)

They therefore recommended that the Scottish government should be able to borrow for capital expenditure from HM Treasury, subject to set conditions and a cap on the amount of borrowing: the amount the Scottish government might borrow in any one year should be constrained by their overall indebtedness and their capacity to repay from tax and other receipts. The Commission said that they did not have enough information to specify what the limits should be.

Governments however do not borrow only to finance capital spending. They borrow short term to manage cash balances as income and expenditure often flow in and out at different times. Very significantly, they also borrow to finance polices that smooth the economic cycle, maintaining public service provision during a downturn, especially supporting spending on benefit payments. This is a key part of the macroeconomic responsibilities of a government – and is very much in the public eye at present given the high levels of borrowing that many countries have undertaken to deal with the recession.

The Commission were clear that the Scottish government would need borrowing powers to cope with fluctuations in revenue from their new taxes, which were unlikely to flow in at the same time as bills had to be paid: revenues from income tax are spread into the year after the tax year to which they relate and even after that. These powers were already available in the Scotland Act, though the Commission noted that the limit set there – borrowing of £500m – might need to be updated. They did not however think that the Scottish government should be able to borrow for the purposes of macroeconomic management. In an integrated UK economy, which they had described as an economic union, that was in their view the responsibility of the UK government. It was not possible to have two competing macroeconomic policies in the one economy.

Longer-term developments

The Commission concluded that their recommendations would:

give the Scottish Parliament real financial accountability, and will do so in a way which will neither disrupt the economic Union between

Scotland and the rest of the United Kingdom nor break the bonds of common social citizenship which we describe as the social Union. They set the right balance between accountability, equity and efficiency for Scotland in the United Kingdom. (Calman 2009: para. 3.207)

But the Commission did not see them as the end of the road. Indeed they went on to say that it might in future be desirable to increase the proportion of revenues from the Parliament's own sources further, though they maintained the view that a block grant should remain, to reflect the pooling of resources in the union with the rest of the United Kingdom. They suggested this might be done assigning revenue from taxes that it was not appropriate to devolve, such as Fuel Duty and Vehicle Excise Duty, or several percentage points of the Scottish yield of VAT.

How the Calman Report became the Scotland Act

The final Calman Report was published in June 2009, and was immediately given a broad welcome by the Labour UK government. The government announced it would take the Report forward in consensus with the other political parties who had been involved (Murphy [Secretary of State for Scotland] 2009). The Scottish government was less positive; although they were supportive of the non-financial recommendations, they expressed concern about the financial proposals. The majority in the Scottish Parliament however welcomed the report during a debate in June and agreed it should now be taken forward to implementation (Scottish Parliament 2009).

In November 2009 the UK government, after internal debate, produced its proposals for change in a White Paper entitled *Scotland's Future in the United Kingdom: Building on ten years of Scottish devolution* (HM Government 2009). This accepted the overwhelming majority of the Calman recommendations, in particular that better accountability should be achieved by a greater proportion of the Scottish Parliament's budget coming from its own tax decisions. The government accepted the Commission's analysis of Scotland as part of a political, economic and social union, and emphasised the social union as meaning that resources were:

pooled from taxation across the UK, so that wherever and whenever risks occur – risks like unemployment or the inability to work through ill health – help is there . . . (2009, para. 2.7)

Scotland's Choices

They undertook to implement the non-legislative recommendations (which were almost all accepted) and to introduce legislation on the rest as soon as possible in the next Parliament, as the General Election was no more that six months away. Describing the fiscal proposals the government said:

> Taken together, the proposals represent the most radical changes to the way in which Scotland is funded for a generation. (2009: para. 4.14)

The Labour government however rejected two fiscal proposals. They did not 'attach priority to' assigning half of the revenue raised by income tax on savings and distributions to the Scottish Parliament (on the grounds that it created difficult operational complications without genuinely improving financial accountability) nor to devolving Air Passenger Duty. According to the White Paper 'state aid rules, competition considerations and international aviation agreements restrict [the government's] ability to devolve Air Passenger Duty' (2009: para. 4.22). 'Competition considerations' may be a reference to fears that a tax-cutting Scottish administration could attract passenger traffic from north of England airports by reducing the duty. The new capital borrowing power was to be introduced alongside greater tax devolution. Most, but not all, of the Calman legislative recommendations on non-financial matters were also accepted.

In the UK General Election of 2010, the Labour, Liberal Democrat and Conservative Manifestos each committed, in slightly different terms, to taking forward the Calman plan. The Coalition agreement between the Conservatives and Liberal Democrats in May 2010 contained commitment to 'implement the proposals of the Calman Commission' (HM Government 2010a).

The Scotland Act: contents

Accordingly, the Scotland Bill was introduced into the House of Commons in November 2010. A further government White Paper, *Strengthening Scotland's Future*, accompanied it (HM Government 2010b). The White Paper emphasised that legislative change was part of a wider strategy including improved cooperation between governments, but laid great emphasis on the fiscal proposals, which were described as:

[t]he largest transfer of fiscal power from London since the creation of the United Kingdom. The Scottish Parliament will move from raising approximately 15% of its own budget to approximately 35%. (HM government 2010b: 11)

The 2010 White Paper ('the White Paper') gave a good deal of detail as to how the new fiscal regime would work. The main elements of the system (including some changes made during the Parliamentary process) are as follows:

- As recommended by Calman, all UK income tax rates in Scotland are to be reduced by 10 pence in the pound and the Scottish Parliament will have the power to levy a single Scottish Income Tax rate to replace it, at whatever level they choose;
- Stamp Duty Land Tax and Landfill Tax are to be devolved. Devolving the Aggregates Levy and Air Passenger Duty has not been ruled out. The Aggregates Levy is at present subject to a challenge in the European Court and the government say that they will consider devolving it once that case is decided. They also say that they are reviewing the future of Air Passenger Duty and will consider it for devolution at a later date;
- The Scottish government will be given new powers to borrow for capital expenditure, either from HM Treasury or from commercial institutions. (An amendment to the Bill during its progress also allowed for the possibility of the Scottish government issuing bonds to borrow from the market at a future date);
- The Scottish Parliament will have the power to create new taxes, subject to UK agreement; and the White Paper sets out what the UK would look for before agreeing;
- It is proposed that the tax powers should be available in 2016 to the next Scottish Parliament, but the borrowing powers are to be phased in earlier. It is proposed that the Scottish government should be able to borrow over £200m a year, subject to a total indebtedness of over £2bn;
- The White Paper contained detailed proposals for making the reduction in the grant to the Scottish government to take account of new access to tax revenue. The government enunciated a principle of 'no detriment' from having a shared income tax base, that is to say if changes to tax bands or allowances made by the UK government caused a loss or gain in tax revenues for the Scottish government a compensating adjustment would be made to their grant;

- The government set out detailed proposals for short term borrowing to manage cash flow, and in another addition to the Calman scheme, proposed a new Scottish cash reserve – essentially a savings account allowing the Scottish government to build up reserves for future use.

In a significant addition to the Calman scheme, the Scotland Act allows for additional taxes to be devolved by the UK to the Scottish government by means of an Order in Council, as well as for new taxes to be created.

Many of the non-financial recommendations of the Calman Commission are included in the Scotland Act. Among those excluded are the proposals to reserve the regulation of newer health professions and insolvency procedure to Westminster. These were unacceptable to the Scottish government. Also dropped was the idea of allowing Scottish variation in Council Tax Benefit or Housing Benefit: Council Tax Benefit is to be decentralised and Housing Benefit is to be absorbed (in a way that is not yet wholly clear) into the new Universal Credit, which will apply throughout the UK. The Act also deals with an issue which the Calman Commission did not – the procedure by which Human Rights issues in Scottish criminal cases come before the UK Supreme Court. This was a matter of considerable controversy in the legal world, but is not central to the scheme of devolution in the Scotland Act.

Parliamentary consideration of the Scotland Act in London and Edinburgh

The Scotland Bill was introduced into the House of Commons on 30 November 2010. The UK government made clear however that, because the Bill would affect devolved powers, they would seek the consent of the Scottish Parliament to it under what is known as the Sewel Convention (The Sewel Convention holds that, in general, the UK Parliament will not normally legislate on devolved matters without the consent of Holyrood; it has been extended to refer also to changes in devolved powers). As Table 3.2 shows, this drew out the legislative process from November 2010 until May 2012, so as to allow Westminster to consider and respond to points raised in the Scottish Parliament. The Bill was therefore subject to extensive scrutiny in two Parliaments, and many of the criticisms and concerns of the Scottish government were examined in great detail in two Scottish

Table 3.2 Legislative consideration of the Scotland Bill

30 November 2010	Bill Introduced in House of Commons	
1 December 2010	(First) Scotland Bill Committee set up in Scottish Parliament	To recommend whether the Scottish Parliament should consent
9 December 2010	Debate in Scottish Parliament	Scottish Parliament voted to support the 'General Principles' of the Bill; SNP members opposed
27 January 2011	Second Reading in House of Commons	SNP amendment defeated by 252 to 5.
3 March 2011	Scotland Bill Committee of Scottish Parliament reports	Recommends giving legislative consent, and some changes to Bill
7, 14 and 15 March 2011	Committee Stage in House of Commons	
10 March 2011	Debate in Scottish Parliament	Scottish Parliament votes to support Bill by 121 to 3 and for further debate to consider amendments to be made to Bill
9 June 2011	(Second) Scotland Bill Committee set up in Scottish Parliament	After the 2011 Scottish elections the SNP had a majority; this committee was set up to consider the Bill and possible amendments to it, as well as the responses to the previous committee report
21 June 2011	Report and Third Reading in Commons	Bill approved without a division
22 June 2011	Bill introduced into House of Lords	
6 September 2011	Second Reading in House of Lords	Agreed without division
15 December 2011	Report from (Second) Scotland Bill Committee of Scottish Parliament	'cannot recommend Bill' unless amendments in Committee's report made
26 January, 2, 28 February, 15, 21 March 2012	Committee Stage in House of Lords	
28 February 2012	Further Report from (Second) Scotland Bill Committee	Recommends legislative consent motion agreeing to Bill
21 March 2012	Written Ministerial statement in Westminster	Announcing various minor amendments to Bill
26, 28 March 2012	Report Stage in House of Lords	
18 April 2012	Debate in Scottish Parliament	Gave Scottish Parliament's Legislative consent with no opposition
24 April 2012	Third Reading in House of Lords	
26 April 2012	Commons Consideration of Lords Amendments	
1 May 2012	Royal Assent	

Parliamentary Committees. No Act of Parliament has been scrutinised in this way before.

Criticisms made of the Scotland Act

This extended Parliamentary process offered extensive opportunities for criticism of the provision of the Bill to be made, especially in the Scottish Parliament and by the Scottish government. These can be divided into two broad categories: criticisms of the scheme of the Bill or of individual provisions, and 'missed opportunities' – things which were not in the Bill but might have been added.

A major challenge to the Bill by the Scottish government before the 2010 election was that it would have a 'deflationary effect'. By this they mean that the Scottish budget under the Bill would not grow as quickly as it would have under the Barnett Formula; at one point the First Minister suggested that the effect might cost the Scottish budget £1bn a year. This was said to be because income tax grew more slowly than other taxes, and because the Scottish Income Tax was at a flat rate and so was a lower proportion of the higher income tax rates, revenue from which tended to grow more quickly.

This issue was examined in great detail by the first Scotland Bill Committee of the Scottish Parliament, who showed that the overall fiscal effect of the scheme depended crucially on the formula which was used to reduce the Westminster grant to the Scottish government to take account of the tax income they would now have. They recommended principles for calculating this (based on corresponding work done for Wales – Holtham 2010), which were intended to avoid this risk, and the opposite risk that Scotland might make a windfall gain from the change. These were accepted by the UK government. The Scottish government have now also accepted that these plans do not involve unacceptable risks to the Scottish budget.

There were a number of criticisms of the income tax powers. One was that it was unwise to rely so heavily on one tax; it would be better to have a basket of taxes, which might not all fluctuate in the same way. The Bill's proponents responded that in general all tax income moved with the economy, and the grant would remain markedly bigger than tax income, and it would be supported by UK borrowing as well as tax income so that it was a secure source of revenue. A second challenge was that having a single rate of income tax only, with no capacity to set different rates for higher rate taxpayers, tied the Scottish government's hands: it could not cut top tax rates to attract high earners to live in Scotland, nor increase them to bring in more revenue. The Bill's supporters were opposed to the idea that a devolved Scotland should try to become a tax haven where rich individuals (or companies) could try to shelter from UK taxes.

A number of points were raised by the Scottish government and others about the non-financial provisions of the Bill. Some of these resulted in changes which are reflected in the Scotland Act. For instance, there are no new reservations of power to Westminster (except to make clear that the Scottish Parliament cannot legislate for Antarctica) and proposed powers (which had not been recommended by Calman) to allow the UK to implement international obligations have also been dropped.

A major set of criticisms were related to the effect – or lack of effect – of the legislation on economic growth. Two arguments were made. The first that fiscal decentralisation itself would lead to economic growth: the First Minister at one point claimed that full fiscal autonomy would increase the Scottish growth rate by 1% per annum. Even more modest claims were highly controversial amongst economists. The first Scotland Bill Committee concluded – surely correctly – that what mattered for economic growth was not who had the various powers, but what use was made of them. A more focused version of this criticism however was that the Scotland Act did not contain any additional levers for the Scottish government to use to promote economic growth. This was highly topical at a time of economic recession and merits more careful consideration.

What the Scotland Act does not contain – and could not given it purpose and genesis – is power for a devolved Scottish government to run a separate Scottish macroeconomic policy, in particular to borrow to stimulate demand in the Scottish economy. A devolved Scotland is part of the wider UK economy and part of a fiscal (and currency) union. Those decisions are taken for Scotland by the UK government and Parliament. The extent to which it is possible even for an independent Scotland to run a macroeconomic policy separate from the rest of the UK is not wholly clear (and is discussed in Chapter 2). What is clear is that this is not an option which could have been made available under the Scotland Act.

Many of the levers which governments everywhere use to promote economic growth are in fact already devolved in Scotland. These include schooling, training, higher education, transport and other infrastructure, financial assistance to industry and many others. What is not devolved is taxation, notably corporation tax. There are however two main taxes which affect business directly. One is business rates, which raised about £2bn a year in Scotland in 2010–11; the other is corporation tax, which raised about £3bn. The Calman Commission and the UK government both rejected devolving corporation tax because of the risk of tax competition – business would recognise their profits in the low tax part of the UK and so reduce overall UK tax income even if this benefited Scotland. But the Scottish government argued strongly for it, so that they could use reduced rates to attract mobile investment into Scotland. (Whether there is indeed scope for devolving corporation tax in any wider system of devolution is considered in Chapter 4.)

A more general criticism of the Scotland Act is that it is 'not enough' devolution. Understandably, this comes from those whose aim is independence; understandably, because for them no amount of devolution will ever be 'enough'. There is little scope for discussion of that. But others also argue this, notably those favouring some form of so-called 'devolution-max'. It is not clear what 'devolution-max' is or whether there is scope for it within the UK (see Chapter 4) but the Scotland Act is not it. Its supporters certainly claim it is a major step – the first real tax decentralisation in the UK's history, markedly reducing the Scottish Parliament's fiscal dependence on Westminster. But it is avowedly a step – the Act itself envisages more tax devolution in future.

It is nevertheless reasonable to ask whether moving to a model in which about 30% of devolved spending is paid for out of devolved taxes will genuinely make the Scottish Parliament accountable, and give them scope to deliver polices that can be as different from the rest of the UK as the Scottish people might want. Such a system would move the UK from an unusually centralised system to being 'in the pack' of other countries who decentralise taxation (as we see in Chapters 4 and 6), but it will be by no means a leader. Only time may tell.

The Scotland Act: overall assessment

The process which led to the Scotland Act was an unusual one, but it has meant its provisions have been subject to an exceptional level of scrutiny. Remarkably, despite the initial and sustained opposition of the SNP, the Scotland Act now has the support of both the UK and Scottish governments. Unless there is a vote for Scotland to leave the UK, it is highly likely to come into effect in 2016.

The Act is intended to widen the tax and borrowing powers of the Scottish Parliament and government, but it does so in a way which is explicitly intended to secure Scotland's position inside the UK. Neither the UK government, nor the Scotland Act's supporters in Holyrood, see it as a step towards an independent Scotland. Those who seek that might therefore have been well advised to reject it. Those who see devolution to Scotland as a process leading to a rebalancing of power within a continuing UK on the other hand might well see it as a significant, if not a final, step in that direction.

Note

1. In the jargon, as we discuss in Chapter 6, this is a 'vertical fiscal transfer': a transfer of resources from one level of government to another. This is as it was before devolution, when the Scottish Office was simply a department of the UK government, and not a government in its own right.

4

The Possibilities for More Devolution

THE IMMEDIATE CHOICE the Scottish electorate will now face in the referendum is between independence and the proposals for devolution under the Scotland Act 2012 described in the previous chapter. But there is a wider range of possibilities for change which might, perhaps later, be considered.

Certainly most political parties appear in principle to favour greater devolution if Scotland remains within the UK. The SNP is for independence, but might see greater devolved powers as a step in that direction or even as an acceptable compromise. From 2007 to 2009, the SNP Scottish government conducted a 'national conversation', which looked at the scope for further devolution as well as independence. Many of same issues were looked at by the Calman Commission. Both the Liberal Democrat[1] and Labour[2] parties in Scotland have now published blueprints for enhanced devolution that go beyond the provisions of the Scotland Act 2012 and which are intended to provide an alternative to independence. These are discussed below. The Conservative Party, in the form of both the Prime Minister and its Scottish leader, Ruth Davidson, is also willing to consider further devolution within a UK-wide framework should Scotland vote to remain within the UK (see Johnson 2012 and Black 2013). In March 2013 Davidson set up a commission, chaired by Lord Strathclyde, to consider options for strengthening the powers of the Scottish Parliament. Press reports suggest that it may come out in favour of beefing up Holyrood's taxation powers (Johnson 2014).

Alongside the political parties a number of think tanks have been looking at proposals for further devolution schemes. The two most substantial are the Devo Plus group run by Reform Scotland (see for example, Reform Scotland 2012) and IPPR's 'Devo More' programme (see Trench 2013 and Lodge and Trench 2014).

Significantly, none of the proposals from the unionist parties or the think tanks support the proposition known as 'devolution-max' – the most radical form of devolution, which would see the Scottish

Parliament responsible for all domestic policy and for raising the revenue to fund it. Each argues that such a model is impossible to make to work within the UK state. However, while there are some clear overlaps between these proposals it looks unlikely that the pro-Union parties will present a detailed cross-party agreement on a package of new powers before the independence vote in September 2014. Instead versions of these proposals will likely be put to voters in party manifestos for the general elections for the Scottish and UK Parliaments and implemented thereafter. Chapter 9 discusses how change might be implemented, depending on how it is put forward. The important point for present purposes is that schemes of devolution within the UK require the agreement of the whole country, which means in practice the agreement of the UK government and Parliament, with the legislation passed at Westminster, with the consent of the Scottish Parliament, as for the Scotland Act 2012.

It is certainly clear that Scottish public opinion is predisposed towards more powers for the Scottish Parliament. Survey evidence regularly suggests that a majority of the Scottish public would favour devolving more domestic policy, over a wide range of subjects, including taxation and social security (for which see Chapter 5). The evidence also suggests that Scotland has, by international standards, a strong appetite for decentralisation. Evidence from an international comparative study[3] is given in Table 4.1. In many countries the population tends to think that

Table 4.1 'Which level of government does/should have the most influence?'

	a) Regional should (%)	b) Regional does (%)	a) – b)
Scotland	73	38	35
Wales	70	40	30
Catalonia	79	58	21
Brittany	76	58	18
Salzburg	89	73	16
Upper Austria	82	67	15
Vienna	79	65	14
Alsace	75	61	14
Thuringia	76	63	13
Lower Saxony	73	60	13
Galicia	65	54	11
Ile de France	66	53	9
Bavaria	75	67	8
Castilla la Mancha	55	58	−3

Source: CANS

regional administrations should have more power than they currently do. Scots (like the Welsh and Northern Irish) are most strongly of this view in the countries surveyed: they tend to think the UK government *does* have most influence over the way their territory is run, but that the devolved administrations *should* have the most influence, showing the biggest gap between those who think the devolved administrations should have most influence and those who think it does. It remains to be seen whether Scots will take the view that the proposals for additional powers so far offered by the main unionist parties prove strong enough to maintain their support for the Union, or whether they might be tempted by independence (Curtice 2014).

The scope for devolving more powers

Accordingly, this chapter looks at the range of possible changes short of independence, mainly concerning taxation and social security. It examines the potential advantages and disadvantages of each, both to Scotland and the rest of the UK, and whether they might offer coherent schemes of further devolution.

Defence, foreign affairs and citizenship

Responsibility for defence and foreign affairs is the hallmark of an independent state. How they might look in an independent Scotland is discussed in Chapter 2. A devolved Scotland will not have a defence policy or a separate international legal status, but it might seek some extension of its role in international affairs. The Scottish government's national conversation document on Foreign Affairs and Europe for example says 'it would be possible for the FCO to set aside a part of its current budget to allow Scotland, Wales and Northern Ireland to appoint specialist diplomats whose job it would be to pursue points of particular interest to the devolved administrations' (Scottish Government 2009a, para. 4.5).

The most significant area however relates to the EU. Most of the domestic policy issues in which the EU has a strong interest, such as agriculture and fisheries, are already devolved. Over recent years, the European Union has become involved in more policy areas – such as justice and home affairs, or the environment – so that most issues with which the EU is concerned will have some devolved dimension. The devolved administrations already play an important role in EU discussions, and have pressed for their influence to be strengthened: the Scottish government has argued that there should be a legal obligation for them to be represented in EU discussions which affect them.

An independent Scotland would decide issues of citizenship, or nationality, and immigration and border control. Short of independence, these will remain the responsibility of the nation state to which Scotland belongs. In a national conversation document on business and enterprise, the Scottish government suggested devolving more immigration powers, but made no detailed proposals for what these should be. The Calman Commission too suggested some flexibility in immigration rules, to allow more migrants to enter Scotland to fill gaps in the labour market. This plan was not, however, taken forward; the difficulty the UK government may see is ensuring migrants are obliged to settle in Scotland only.

The UK enters into international obligations which bind Scotland. The most significant of these is adherence to the European Convention on Human Rights, which is already built into the constitutional framework of the Scottish Parliament, so that all its laws, and the actions of Scottish Ministers, must be consistent with the Convention rights. This will continue under any further devolution for as long as the UK remains a signatory to the Convention. The Scottish Parliament might seek a bigger say in some of these decisions. At the moment, the Scottish government will be consulted about international obligations which affect them, but the decision is a UK one. Holyrood might press for more influence: in some federal countries, some international agreements have to be ratified by state as well as national governments.

Economic and monetary policy

The first major area of domestic policy not devolved to the Scottish Parliament relates to the economy. This includes monetary and fiscal policy, but also economic regulation more generally. The UK operates as a large, single domestic market, with common legislation relating to trade, company formation, the sale of goods and services and so on. It also has UK-wide regulation, under European law, of certain specific business sectors, such as banking and financial services, telecommunications and the energy sector. It has a single labour market policy, with uniform workers' rights, employment law and common pension legislation.

Running its own monetary policy is another hallmark of an independent state. The SNP however now favours a UK monetary union even after independence, and so devolution of monetary policy can be ruled out. Monetary policy is closely connected to the regulation of banking and financial services, and if the central bank acts as lender of last resort it has a strong incentive to ensure proper regulation of the finance sector. An argument might be made for devolving financial regulation so that Scotland could, like the Isle of Man or the Channel Islands, operate its own system of financial regulation. This might be 'light touch' so that, alongside a low tax regime, banks and other financial services companies could be encouraged to set up in Scotland to reduce their regulatory and tax burdens,[4] and Scotland could be more like an offshore tax haven. Since the financial crisis, however, the pressure for equally stringent regulation in all jurisdictions is now much greater; and the UK is unlikely to wish to increase risks to the stability of its own financial system by allowing a laxer regulatory framework inside a single monetary area. The Scottish government in the national conversation appeared to accept this argument, saying 'For example, financial regulation, employment and competition law would be likely to remain centralised at the UK level' (Scottish Government 2009b, para. 4.25).

The UK also operates as a single market for energy and telecommunications. The regulatory systems are intended to allow competition in what might otherwise become monopolies. EU member states operate within a common regulatory framework, which is intended to ensure that former monopolies do not squeeze out new entrants and so reduce competition: the objective is to secure continuity of supply and benefit consumers. Decisions on individual power station licences are already devolved (they are like planning decisions) and the Scottish government have argued for the option of a separate Scottish energy regulation within the EU framework (Scottish Government 2009d para. 4.25); but the White Paper says that an independent Scotland would remain within a GB energy market.[5] The Calman Commission saw advantages in a single UK market for Scottish suppliers and consumers. No proposals have been made to devolve telecommunications policy.

Perhaps surprisingly, no argument has been made by the Scottish government for devolving labour market law, such as workers' rights, unfair dismissal, maternity leave and so on. It could be argued that the contractual questions are part of Scots private law, which is already devolved, and could be linked to supply-side issues in the labour market, alongside policy on training and education. They could in principle form part of a different Scottish social model. (Scotland might choose to have more flexible labour laws to encourage businesses to employ people, or to have stronger safeguards for individual workers' positions.) The Scottish Labour party has proposed devolving employment tribunals, though not employment law. Policy on occupational pensions (such as tax relief and pension regulation) is linked to state old-age pensions, and an argument could be made to devolve it if social security were devolved. The contrary arguments are, of course, that divergent labour laws would reduce the mobility of labour, and hence the opportunity for Scots to seek employment elsewhere in the UK, as well as the 'social union' arguments about maintaining a common benefit and pension system.

Fiscal issues: the case for tax devolution

The main area for debate, however, relates to fiscal issues – the devolution of tax and borrowing alongside spending powers. Chapter 6 discusses the theoretical background to these issues ('fiscal federalism') more fully. As we explain there, all countries find it easier to decentralise spending rather than tax. It is relatively easy to make different spending decisions in different parts of the country. Tax is more slippery, as different tax rates allow increased opportunities for evasion or avoidance, and can create economic distortions. The consequence is what is called in economics jargon 'a vertical fiscal gap', as central governments tend to control more of the tax resources, and subnational governments have more of the spending responsibilities. Some money has to be transferred from central to local governments. This is true in virtually all countries, but in Scotland's case, the gap is large. (Though it is striking that UK central government transfers are made with no strings attached: in many other countries the federal government will attach conditions to grants saying what spending policies must be followed.)

The UK has a highly centralised tax system. Almost all taxes are collected centrally by the Treasury. The main exception is local taxes – council tax and non-domestic rates. This will change once the Calman scheme comes into force. As we saw in Chapter 3, their recommendations were to devolve nearly 20% of taxes. Other countries set different balances of decentralised spending and taxation.

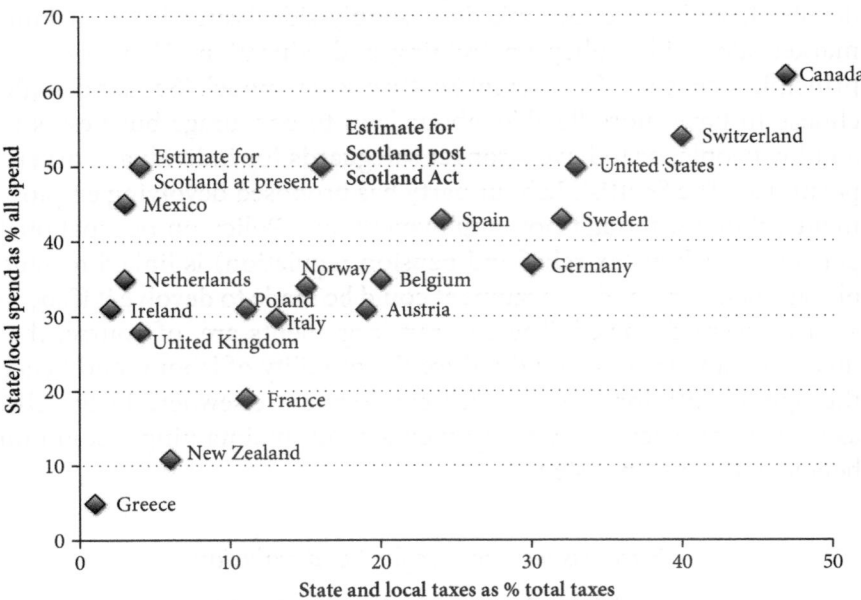

Figure 4.1 Subnational taxing and spending, selected OECD countries

Source: OECD databases, authors' estimates

As Figure 4.1 shows, Scotland is unusual in two respects. First, the proportion of *spending* which is decentralised is unusually high – the Scottish Parliament is responsible for nearly half of the total public expenditure spent for Scotland; but the proportion of *taxation* which is decentralised is at present very low, though it will reach a more typical, though not especially high, level once the Scotland Act comes into force. It is these two factors together which make the gap so wide.

When the Scottish Parliament was set up in 1999, it was given wide spending powers, but limited tax powers. The Calman Commission argued that this provided only weak fiscal accountability for the Scottish Parliament – it does not have to take responsibility for raising taxes, even while it can claim credit for spending. Nor is the budget of the Scottish Parliament linked to how well the Scottish economy performs. Proponents of further devolution also argue that greater tax powers would give the Scottish Parliament the tools it needs to promote economic growth in Scotland. The Scottish government argued in the national conversation papers that greater fiscal autonomy would 'generate a more efficient allocation of spending and taxation and hence lead to an improvement in welfare' (Scottish Government 2009b para.

5.9) – though not all economists agree that there is a direct and simple link between tax decentralisation and growth.

The main function of taxation is to raise the money to pay for public services. But that is not all it does. Tax policy affects economic growth, and is an important instrument of redistributive policies, alongside welfare payments. The level of taxes, and how progressive they are (that is, the extent to which they take a greater proportion of higher incomes) are critical tools for governments if they wish to change the distribution of wealth in society. Scandinavian countries, for example, support high levels of public spending by high and progressive taxation, and tend to have more equal societies. The US, by contrast, aims to promote economic growth through low taxation and low levels of public spending, and has greater wealth inequalities. The UK, and Scotland within it, is betwixt and between. Taxes are also used to support other policy aims – discouraging behaviours like smoking or drinking, or promoting desired activities – for example tax on burying rubbish in landfill is an incentive for recycling.

There are, however, conflicting considerations here. Greater tax powers would increase the autonomy and accountability of the Scottish Parliament, and could give it useful policy levers. But the amount it spent would then be more dependent on the amount of tax revenue arising in Scotland, and less on any assessment of Scotland's spending needs. Obviously, if Scotland were an independent country, then comparing its needs for public spending with other parts of the UK would not be a relevant consideration. But if Scotland remains within the UK, some degree of sharing of tax revenues is likely, and the principles on which they are allocated must be seen as fair by those affected, both in Scotland and the rest of the UK. Of course whether the present system is at all equitable is often hotly disputed. Although the largest element of spending – social security – is determined by individual needs, devolved spending is not based on any measurement of need. Budgets have been inherited and adjusted by the Barnett Formula. Many in England would claim that Scotland's relatively high levels of public spending are unfair. The proportion of people in England who think that Scotland gets more than its fair share of public spending has increased from 25% to 45% over the last decade (Wyn Jones et al. 2012).

The economic effects of tax decentralisation also need to be considered. Proponents argue it should promote economic growth, by allowing taxation as well as spending decisions to match more accurately the preferences of the devolved nation. 'Tax devolution promotes investment, cuts government spending and to some degree raises the rates of economic growth' (Hallwood and MacDonald 2009: 15). Others would argue that the evidence about growth is much less clear, and draw attention to 'spillover' effects: that is to say the effects of decisions on other parts of the country, especially through tax competition. If one part of the country has lower tax rates, there will be an incentive for taxpayers to pay their taxes there. This might be an incentive for a real economic change – the relocation of business or employment, or of higher rate taxpayers coming to live in a low-tax area. Alternatively it might be nothing but a paper transaction and so distort the economy and reduce tax take overall. This depends very much on the nature of individual taxes. Broadly speaking, taxes on things that do not readily move about are highly suitable for devolution; taxes on more intangible bases are harder to pin down.

The scope for tax devolution

Although taxes are collected centrally by HMRC, estimates have been made of the yield of taxes in Scotland since 1991 (see Scottish government *GERS*). Table 4.2 shows the sources of revenue; the scope for devolving them is discussed below.

Three main taxes – income tax, VAT and national insurance – represent two thirds of domestic tax revenue. The remainder comes from a long list of smaller taxes, a few of which are already devolved. Only these large taxes could make an impact on the 'vertical fiscal gap' to a substantial degree. VAT, however, cannot be devolved under EU rules (it must be uniform across a member state).

Income tax is the most obvious candidate for devolution. Individuals will be domiciled in one part of the country, and it is administratively possible to levy different tax rates on them. Doing so gives a very direct fiscal accountability for the devolved Parliament. It already has had the power to vary the basic rate of income tax and the Scotland Act 2012 will take this further from 2016. Although these schemes allow the Scottish Parliament to levy a different rate of tax, it cannot alter the structure of the tax system: the definitions of taxable income, allowances, and tax bands remain reserved to the UK. So it is not possible for the Scottish Parliament to change the thresholds at which income tax becomes payable, or the higher rates are effective; nor can it alter tax allowances or reliefs – such as the tax relief for pensions, or allowances for age, expenses for the self employed and so on.

The Possibilities for More Devolution

Table 4.2 Revenue sources in Scotland

Taxes collected in Scotland	£ million revenues in 2012–13	% of total non-North Sea revenue	Scope for devolution? See following paragraphs
Income tax	10,865	22.8%	Already partly devolved; more possible
VAT	9,347	19.7%	Not possible under EU rules
National insurance contributions	8,521	17.9%	Possible but linked to benefits
Corporation tax (excl. North Sea revenue)	2,872	6.0%	Possible but tax competition issues
Fuel duties	2,258	4.7%	Possible with administrative changes, subject to EU law
Tobacco duties	1,125	2.4%	Concerns about avoidance and subject to EU law
Alcohol duties	980	2.1%	Concerns about avoidance and subject to EU law
Stamp duties	472	1.0%	SDLT already devolved
Capital gains tax	292	0.6%	Possible in principle
Other taxes on income and wealth	271	0.6%	Concerns about avoidance
Insurance premium tax	207	0.4%	Concerns about avoidance
Betting and gaming and duties	120	0.3%	Concerns about avoidance
Air passenger duty	234	0.5%	Under review and to be considered for devolution
Landfill tax	100	0.2%	To be devolved
Climate change levy	62	0.1%	
Aggregates levy	45	0.1%	To be devolved
Inheritance tax	243	0.5%	Possible in principle
Vehicle excise duty	481	1.0%	Possible in principle
Non-domestic rates	1,981	4.2%	Already devolved
Council tax	2,006	4.2%	Already devolved
Other revenues (public sector trading surpluses, rents, TV licences, National Lottery distribution, etc.)	5,060	10.6%	Not relevant
Total current revenue (excluding North Sea revenue)	47,556	100.0%	
North Sea revenue: Geographical share	5,581		Discussed in Chapter 7

93

Table 4.2 *(cont.)*

Total public spending for benefit of Scotland	65,205	For comparison
Within which, total spending by Scottish government and local authorities	38,546	For comparison
Within which, social protection expenditure	22,458	For comparison

Note: The data in this table are taken from *Government Expenditure and Revenues in Scotland 2012–13*. During this year, the UK ran a very substantial deficit, and tax revenues overall were markedly less than spending and a deficit of 7.3% of GDP. (With a geographical share of North Sea oil revenues in that year, Scotland's deficit was proportionately slightly higher.) It is important to realise that these are estimates, as taxes are not collected on a geographical basis, and the yield of a devolved tax might not be as estimated here.

It would be possible to widen the Scottish Parliament's powers. It could have more 'tax points', say 20 pence in the pound rather than 10; or could determine each rate; or it could be given responsibility for the whole income tax system, including thresholds and allowances.

The Scottish Liberal Democrats, IPPR and Reform Scotland all support the full devolution of income tax. Scottish Labour's Devolution Commission toyed with full devolution in its interim report but ultimately opted for a more modest policy in its final report: under Labour's plans the Scottish Parliament would increase its control over 'tax points', rising from the 10 pence recommended by Calman to 15 pence. This would see the Scottish Parliament responsible for raising about 40% of its present devolved spending (up from roughly one third, provided by the Scotland Act 2012).

Three issues arise as a result of more ambitious change. The first is purely administrative. The UK operates an integrated income tax system at present, and while arrangements are being made to levy a separate Scottish tax rate (and might be for different rates), it would be more challenging for HMRC to operate a system with wholly different allowances, reliefs and thresholds for Scotland.[6] This could increase the cost of collecting income tax, including for employers who do most of the work. Most income tax is collected through PAYE and many companies will have employees in Scotland and elsewhere in the UK. So there would be an administrative burden and cost. The second is a question of principle. One of the arguments for retaining a UK income tax framework was that it is used to affect the distribution of wealth.

Alongside the social security system, income tax is the main way in which resources are transferred from better off to poorer people. So if benefits were to be devolved then the wholesale devolution of income tax would certainly be appropriate as well.

The third relates to the issue of tax competition: the Labour party in particular has expressed concern that if income tax is to be devolved in full then it would open the way to a potential 'race to the bottom' with Scotland and the UK government competing to offer the most competitive environment for higher or top rate taxpayers. For this reason the Scottish Labour Devolution Commission backed away from full income tax devolution and instead proposed that the Scottish Parliament should be given the power to raise the higher and top rates, but not to cut them unless it cut the basic rate too. It is difficult to say how well-founded Labour's concerns about tax competition are. The international experience suggests that tax competition is much stronger when it comes to taxes on capital than on labour – businesses are much more mobile than individuals. Moreover, the international evidence also suggests that tax is just one variable among several individuals and businesses consider when deciding where to locate, though some of the very rich do head to tax havens (see Schmuecker, Lodge and Goodall 2012).

National insurance (NI) is in many respects similar to income tax. For most people NI is collected at source like income tax, directly from wages or salaries. Many employees will not distinguish it from income tax, but there are important differences. Employers pay NI contributions too, directly to HMRC, based on employees' wages or salaries. It is, for employers, a payroll tax. The structure of NI is also different from income tax. It is not progressive. For the individual, NI is paid at a rate of 12% on income between £146 and £817 a week, and at a rate of 2% on income above that. The structure of employers' contributions is similar, though more complex, as it depends on the pension arrangements made by individual employees. NI is like this because it is a contribution to an insurance scheme. Although there has never been a real insurance fund, being a paid-up member of the scheme entitles individuals to certain benefits: old-age pensions, some forms of jobseekers allowance, employment and support allowance and others. These so-called 'contributory' benefits are paid out of the National Insurance Fund, a notional fund into which all contributions are paid. These are not the only social security benefits available, but are important parts of the system.

Administratively, devolving national insurance would be similar to devolving income tax. Scottish taxpayers can be separately identified and different rates of NI contributions levied on them. Changing the thresholds and other rules would be more difficult, especially for employers, but could be done at an administrative cost. It might even in principle be possible to split employers' and employees' NI contributions, devolving one and not the other, though that would add considerable complexity to the system. The policy question is whether devolving national insurance would have to be matched by devolving some or all aspects of social security. The Calman Commission took the view that social security should remain a UK service, and NI should stay part of it.[7] The national conversation papers made no specific reference to NI, but implicitly assumed that in a system of 'devolution-max' it would be the responsibility of the Scottish Parliament alongside social security. The Scottish Labour Devolution Commission emphasised its role as part of the pooling of resources in a UK social union.

Corporation tax has been the subject of extensive debate. It produces about 6% of Scottish tax revenue, but the debate has been principally about using it to promote economic growth. The comparison is made with Ireland, which has for many years had low corporation tax, to attract international companies. Much of the tax revenue which accrues to Ireland might otherwise have been collected in other countries. Companies will register their businesses in Ireland, and book profits there, even if the associated economic activity is elsewhere. The Microsoft Corporation operates its worldwide business from centres in three low tax jurisdictions – Ireland, Puerto Rico and Singapore. These reduce its effective tax rate to 17.5%. If all its profits had been taxed at the Federal US rate (35%), Microsoft would have paid around $5000m more in tax (Microsoft 2011). This tax reduction was entirely legal, and was facilitated by having different corporate tax rates in different countries.

A low rate of corporation tax can encourage companies to set up or relocate and, together with other policies, be used to try to promote economic growth.[8] To take advantage of it however, all that the company actually has to relocate is its taxable profit. This is relatively easy to do through accounting devices, so that profit is recognised in the lowest tax jurisdiction in which the company operates. If Scotland were able to set a lower corporation tax rate than the rest of the UK, companies might be attracted to set up businesses in Scotland. There would also however be a strong incentive for them simply to recognise their profits in a company registered there, even if no economic activity were relocated to Scotland. The net result might be extra tax revenue in Scotland, but not as much as had been lost to the rest of the UK. It was this risk which led to the Calman Commission to recommend against devolving corporation tax. A similar argument was made by the Scottish Labour Commission and IPPR, which also ruled out devolving corporation tax.

An ingenious scheme was, however, suggested by the Holtham Commission, which looked at fiscal issues in Welsh devolution. They suggested devolving corporation tax to act as a stimulus for the Welsh economy and a Welsh rate of corporation tax. Companies which employed people in Wales would be able to apply to pay the Welsh rate. It would apply to the same proportion of their profits as the proportion of their payroll located in Wales (Holtham 2010: para. 7.9). This scheme appears to avoid the risk that profits will be relocated on paper only, and could give companies a real incentive to relocate employment to Wales.[9] The same issue has arisen in Northern Ireland, which faces particular pressures because it shares a land border with the Republic of Ireland, where the corporation tax rate is 12.5%. (The UK rate, which applies in Northern Ireland, is currently 23%, due to come down to 22%.) Northern Irish politicians have pressed for a reduced rate to apply there, but despite extensive discussions the UK government has not yet agreed to this.

All schemes of taxation must comply with EU law. Particularly relevant are the 'state aids' rules, which are intended to prevent member states distorting competition by giving state support to industry or commerce. There is a risk that reduced tax rates within a member state might break these rules (being deemed equivalent to a subsidy to firms in one part of the country). Recent judgments of the European Court of Justice, however, suggest that, so long as the central government does not make up the loss of tax revenue to the devolved administration, then devolving corporation tax rates should not fall foul of these rules.[10]

EU law is also relevant to the next major set of taxes, excise duties. These are paid on tobacco, alcohol, and fuel. Although rates are decided nationally, they operate under an EU framework. Tax is typically imposed at the point of production or import, rather than sale, though of course the cost is paid by the ultimate consumer. Taken together, these duties yield nearly £4bn a year in Scotland, almost 10% of the total tax take. They are significant and perceptible taxes. The duties on tobacco and alcohol in particular are used to meet public policy aims, discouraging smoking and excessive drinking. The Scottish Parliament has enacted the Alcohol (Minimum Pricing) (Scotland) Act 2012 to impose a minimum price on alcohol for similar reasons. It is not however clear that EU law allows for different rates of excise duty within a member state, because of the potential effect on trade. The 2012 Scottish Act is being challenged in the European Court.

Legal problems aside, the difficulties in devolving excise duties relate primarily to the risk of avoidance or tax evasion, especially for tobacco and alcohol. Excise duty rates already vary between different EU countries, and there is a significant movement of tobacco and alcohol into the UK to take advantage of lower rates in other EU states. Differing excise rates on tobacco and alcohol across the border between Scotland and England would be likely to create similar but proportionately larger problems. Just how big the problem would be is hard to estimate, though some evidence can be gleaned from Irish experience: in his 2009 budget the Irish Finance Minister announced big reductions in alcohol duty because of the ease with which it could be bought more cheaply in Northern Ireland (and potentially re-sold illegally). He estimated that 44% of cross-border shoppers were purchasing alcohol (Lenihan 2009). Ironically, at the same time the UK government was making estimates of the amount of revenue it lost in Northern Ireland by having higher fuel duty than the Republic (HM Treasury 2011b). It was the potential of problems like this which caused the Calman Commission to recommend against devolving tobacco and alcohol duties. The Scottish government appeared to accept this argument: in the submissions to the committee of the Scottish Parliament considering the Scotland Bill in 2011, they proposed that instead of devolving the capacity to set excise duty rates, the UK government should simply pay over to them the yield of excise duty in Scotland.[11] The problems from devolving fuel duty might not be so acute, though there would be administrative difficulties as the duty is levied at the point of production or import. If these could be overcome, perhaps by a supplement to duty for fuel sold in Scotland, along the Spanish model, then fuel duty would be a candidate for devolution (again provided any EU legal issues were resolved).

Amongst the other minor taxes, the most promising candidate for devolution is vehicle excise duty. It too might be subject to some risks of tax avoidance – as the sellers of vehicles, or owners of fleets, such as hire car companies, will have an incentive to register them wherever the rate of duty is lowest. Most ordinary users, however, will be the registered keepers of vehicles, and have a clear geographical location for tax purposes. As it yields around £400m per year, devolution may be worthwhile.

There is, therefore, clearly some scope for further tax devolution, but devolving taxes has to be seen in the context of the full range of devolved powers, and the relationship between Scotland and the United Kingdom – most notably how transfers from the UK government also support devolved services. Before looking at this possibility, it will be helpful to consider borrowing powers, and social security.

Fiscal issues: borrowing

Governments get money by borrowing as well as taxing. Borrowing and taxation are closely linked: because governments can raise money through taxation, which they can compel people to pay, they are attractive to lenders, as the risk of default is low. Hence the rate of interest on government bonds is called the 'risk free' rate. Borrowing performs a number of functions. First, it smooths cash flow: bills or salaries have to be paid regularly, but tax income may flow in irregularly. Second, it allows governments to bring forward capital spending: borrowed money can finance the creation of assets, and the loans can be repaid over their lifetime. Third, borrowing is used to manage the economy as a whole: if private sector economic activity slows down, public borrowing can be used to stimulate demand, either through the consequent increases in social security benefits paid (a so-called 'automatic stabiliser') or by additional spending. Recent heavy borrowing by national governments across the developed world has largely been for this purpose. Subnational governments however often borrow as well, either directly from the markets or from national governments.

If the Scottish government is to have tax powers, it will certainly need borrowing powers to manage its cash flow. The Scottish administration has always had some formal borrowing powers, but they have never been used; the scheme under the Scotland Act 2012 has extended them. Until this change, the Scottish government has had no borrowing powers for capital expenditure: instead, part of its budget is earmarked for capital spending by the UK, which does the necessary borrowing. There are some advantages to this, as the UK borrows at attractive rates, and the Scottish government is not charged directly for the interest. Local authorities, by contrast, borrow for capital spending, though almost always from central government. The Scotland Act 2012 gives the Scottish government new borrowing powers for capital spending, either from central government or from the markets.

Further borrowing powers could be devolved. For example the capital spending regime could be changed so that all capital spending was financed by borrowing, thus perhaps giving more flexibility over the scheduling of capital expenditure. (Borrowing of course creates no new resources, and merely brings spending forward in time. It has to be paid off later.) Arguably, this would make clearer to the Scottish government and Parliament the full economic impact of their choices.

Borrowing, however, is where fiscal policy and monetary policy interact very closely. Governments cannot borrow without limit without serious effects on the currency and monetary system (as many are finding at present). For that reason, a devolved Scotland, like an independent Scotland within a UK monetary union, would find its capacity to borrow constrained by the UK government for reasons of prudence. Although in principle it might be possible for the UK to allow the devolved government to default on its debts because it had borrowed too much, this is unlikely to be possible in practice, especially if UK taxation continues to support devolved spending. In Spain at present, for example, Autonomous Communities have borrowing powers but some have been seeking central government support because the markets will not lend any more money to them.

Certainly the risk that markets would assume that the UK would have to stand behind Scottish debt means that any prudent UK Treasury will take an interest in devolved borrowing. Similarly, in a single economy and monetary union, it is not possible for a devolved Scotland to run a separate macro-economic policy and borrow to manage demand: that can only be done at the national level. This tension is seen in Euro area countries, especially Spain, at present, where national government is cutting public spending for macroeconomic reasons, leading to disputes with Autonomous Communities over their budgets and borrowing.

Social security

The other very large area of domestic policy not devolved is social security. It is the largest domestic spending programme in the UK and in Scotland, where it accounts for about 40% of the 'identifiable' public expenditure. So if it were devolved, almost all Scottish domestic spend-ing would be the responsibility of the Scottish Parliament, increasing its budget from around £35 billion to over £50 billion. This would be 90% of the public expenditure for Scotland; the remainder is largely non-identifiable expenditure such as defence and foreign affairs. Social security spending in Scotland is high, about 2% per head higher than the UK average. This is despite the fact that Scottish economic activ-ity and incomes are close to the UK average. Entitlement to benefits depends on personal circumstances, and the distribution, not just the average, of income.

Social security covers a wide range of benefits: old-age pensions, jobseekers allowance ('unemployment benefit'), disability benefits, attendance allowance, supplementary benefit and many others. Some benefit payments are linked to national insurance contributions, but others are paid on the basis of need. Benefit policy and payments are managed at UK level by the Department of Work and Pensions, who have a network of local offices and a number of large national computer systems to administer it.

Chapter 5 on social citizenship discusses the origins and nature of the UK welfare state, and what sort of union it makes the UK. In this chapter, however, we look at the scope to devolve social security, and what that might mean in practice. Survey evidence certainly suggests that Scottish voters favour devolving decisions about benefits, though paradoxically they also favour keeping them at the same level through-out the UK. There are arguments for devolution. At present benefits are the same across the UK and neither the amounts paid nor the structure of the benefits take any account of local conditions, such as the cost of living.[12] Nor does the uniform structure allow for political decisions to take a different approach to benefits – whether more or less generous – in different parts of the country. So it is not possible for the Scottish Parliament to provide more generous old-age pensions in Scotland; nor to alter in-work benefits to increase the incentive to work.

Some benefits are especially closely related to devolved responsibili-ties. Elderly people, for example, are entitled to attendance allowance if they need assistance at home; but at the same time (devolved) health and social work bodies provide just that assistance. Similarly, disabled people receive devolved services directly, as well as receiving cash ben-efits. The state supports all children through national child benefit, but through devolved services focuses education or social work support on children in need of special help. Housing benefit is used to subsidise the rents of low income groups and is set by the UK government, but all other aspects of housing policy are the responsibility of the Scottish Parliament. In such policy areas, an argument can be made that devolution would allow better integration of provision to improve services overall, and perhaps contain their costs.

There are of course contrary arguments: leaving aside questions of citizenship or fairness, having a uniform pension and benefit system across the country makes it easier for people to move across the UK to work or live. Old-age pensions in particular are closely linked to occupational pensions; regulating those too might have to be devolved if a coherent pension system were to be maintained. If there were different benefit rules for people in Scotland, arrangements would have to be made for those who have moved around or whose contribution records were only partly in Scotland, there would be administrative challenges in operating different benefit levels.[13] Additionally, benefit spending is one of the automatic economic stabilisers discussed above. If it were devolved, the Scottish government would have to have substantial borrowing powers to cope with cyclical demand for expenditure. (At the moment, devolved services are for the most part not driven by cyclical demands, and so can be budgeted on a relatively stable basis. Benefits expenditure is demand driven, and has to be managed annually.) Arrangements would have to be made for this borrowing to be managed in a way agreed with the rest of the UK.

Other issues presently reserved to Westminster

Social security, macroeconomic and taxation polices are the main domestic policy areas presently reserved to the Westminster Parliament, but there is a list of other issues which are not devolved to Holyrood. These include road traffic law; some other transport issues, including aviation and the legislative responsibility for the structure of the railway industry; the funding of university research through the research councils; the law on abortion; broadcasting; the Crown Estate; and a number of other areas. The most comprehensive review of whether any of these subjects was suitable for devolution was by the Calman Commission. It recommended only relatively small changes (for example some flexibility over speed limits on roads, and greater devolved involvement in appointments to bodies like the BBC Trust and the Crown Estate Commission). The Scottish government's national conversation dealt with a few of them, and did make a case for greater devolution of powers in relation to broadcasting, including perhaps allowing the Scottish government to set up public service broadcasters of its own.

Different potential models of devolution

Can a coherent scheme or schemes of devolution be developed from this long list of possibilities? To some extent, any scheme of devolution will be a compromise between those looking for autonomy, or even independence, and those who see strength in staying in the United Kingdom. But to work well, a scheme of devolution ought to add up to an internally consistent whole, with a coherent purpose, and a clear articulation of the expected relationship between Scotland and the rest of the UK. The 1999 devolution settlement, with wide legislative and spending powers but narrow taxation powers, allowed the Scottish Parliament to fit quite neatly into the role previously filled by the Scottish Office under administrative devolution, and operated with a budgetary system that was virtually identical. It is striking how little change was made to the rest of the UK to accommodate Scottish (or indeed Welsh or Northern Irish) devolution. The scheme proposed by the Calman Commission can be accommodated within this framework, but more radical schemes are likely to need more change to the UK relationship. We look now at three broad possible conceptions for further devolution.

Closing the fiscal gap: 'devolution plus'

The first approach is to see the problem to be solved as closing the gap between the Scottish Parliament's spending and its tax-raising capacity. Ideally, the argument runs, each level of government should raise the taxes it needs to finance its expenditure. Matching tax and spending responsibilities, it is argued, leads to fiscal responsibility: the choice at the margin will always be between raising or lowering taxes and increasing or decreasing expenditure. If that choice is clear and simple, so that one pound of extra taxation leads to one pound of extra expenditure, then governments will have the incentive to make the right choices. This will promote economically efficient decisions, and in the long run economic growth. Wholly dependent on tax revenues in Scotland, the devolved government will have strong incentives to promote economic growth. Economic theory certainly suggests that fiscal autonomy ought to promote economic growth, and many countries with decentralised fiscal systems are economically very successful (Switzerland, say). But it is hard to find compelling evidence that decentralising taxes is what makes countries richer: in the end, economic success is likely to be linked to the use made of tax and other powers, rather than who exercises them (Hallwood and MacDonald 2009; Hughes Hallett and Scott 2010; Scottish Parliament 2011a, b).

There are, however, as we explained above, trade-offs here. Fiscal responsibility might promote economic growth, but links the amount of expenditure to the tax yield. If the Scottish Parliament were wholly financed by taxes raised in Scotland, then no account would be taken of spending need relative to the rest of the United Kingdom. Similar issues arise in the other devolved parts of the UK: while Scotland's tax base is relatively strong, especially if oil is taken into account, tax revenues in Wales and Northern Ireland are estimated to be much lower. If such a system applied there, very large reductions in public expenditure would follow. Within the UK, the principle of distributing spending according to need, rather than where the tax revenues arise, has always been a strong one, though never successfully put into operation.

Fiscal responsibility has been championed by a number of actors. The cross-party 'Devo Plus' group promotes 'the idea of the Scottish Parliament, as far as possible, raising the money it spends' (Devo Plus 2012). The Steel Commission set up by the Liberal Democrats put it this way: 'no self-respecting Parliament should exist permanently on a grant from another Parliament' (Scottish Liberal Democrats 2006). IPPR's Devo More programme recommended devolving a suite of tax powers that would see the Scottish Parliament become responsible for raising its own revenue to cover between 50 and 60% of devolved spending (Trench 2013).

Since it is unlikely that it would be acceptable in Scotland to narrow the gap by reducing the spending power of the Scottish Parliament, discussion focuses on what taxes are suitable for devolution. As we discussed above, it is clear that a greater proportion, indeed all, income tax could be devolved. If the aim was not for Scotland to have a wholly separate redistributive policy, then the simplest system would probably be for the Scottish Parliament to set the different tax rates across all bands, and receive all income tax revenue, rather than also set thresholds and allowances. This would clearly be administratively easier, and would give the Scottish Parliament some scope to alter the balance of the rates.[14] Given the objective of promoting growth, there would also be a strong argument for devolving corporation tax, with safeguards to prevent unhealthy tax competition, perhaps along the model proposed by the Holtham Commission for Wales. This would give the Scottish government the choice between cutting business tax to promote employment in Scotland and providing additional public services. In the long run, it might hope that the stimulus to business will produce more tax revenue, in a virtuous circle. (As the same corporation tax rates would have to apply to existing businesses some loss of revenue is inevitable. This effect might be reduced by announcing plans to make cuts in the future.)

Some other smaller taxes might also be devolved, but together they could only amount to a trivial proportion of Scottish government spending. It is unrealistic to expect that domestic tax revenue devolved will equate to devolved spending. The fiscal gap will remain.[15] It could continue to be filled by a grant from the UK government, as at present. The challenge is then to decide how to calculate the amount of this transfer. Should it bear any relation to spending need, or should it be done on some other basis? If the transfer were calculated according to need, Scotland might well lose out. There is no agreed basis of needs assessment – and it is a highly political process. The last needs assessment conducted across the UK was done by the Treasury in 1978, but it is hopelessly out of date. Recent estimates by the Holtham Commission for Wales concluded that Wales was under-resourced (Holtham 2009) but also suggested that Scottish need for devolved services was about 5% per head higher than the UK average, compared to expenditure which is roughly 18% higher at present. The House of Lords Select Committee on the Barnett Formula did not make an overall estimate, but pointed out that on most of the indicators which they thought relevant Scotland's needs were less than those of Wales or Northern Ireland (House of Lords 2009). Certainly, Scotland is wealthier than both of them, and if poverty is a needs indicator, Scotland should spend less than both. It presently spends markedly more than Wales, and slightly less than Northern Ireland (see Chapter 6 for a fuller discussion).

Alternatively, the gap might be reduced by assigning the proceeds of particular taxes to the Scottish government. Trench (2013) proposes assigning a share of VAT. Assigning a tax means that although the Scottish government would have no control over the nature or rate of the tax, some or all of the revenue would automatically pass to them (see Chapter 6). This too is done in a number of countries. For example in Germany, a share of the yield of VAT goes to the Land governments.

Similarly, the 'fiscal autonomy' of the Basque country in Spain includes keeping the proceeds of some indirect taxes, even though they cannot alter the rates. Assignment has both advantages and disadvantages. Grants, as the name implies, are given, and might be withheld, by central government. Assigned revenues may pass as of right. Assigned revenues also give the devolved government a very keen incentive to promote economic growth, and so tax revenues, in their area. On the other hand, assigning revenues imports risk without controls to mitigate its effects: income will fluctuate, and could fall unpredictably. Assigning oil revenues, for example, would import a great deal of volatility, as well as the long-term downward trend in budget.

Assignment is an alternative to grant, but what and how much to assign is a political decision, just like grant. Exactly what revenues were assigned, and in what proportion, would heavily influence the spending power of the Scottish Parliament and that decision would in many respects be no different to the present debates about how grant is determined. It might be possible to assign a share of revenues so that the overall spending power of the Scottish Parliament was at least initially unchanged, but any formula for assignment inevitably leads to questions about whether need should be taken into account. To put it another way, what contribution would Scotland make to common UK services, and to supporting less well off parts of the UK, and why?

Whether increasing the tax powers of the Scottish Parliament has any implications for Scottish representation at Westminster is discussed below.

Welfare nationalism

Another potential approach is to consider whether there is a bundle of devolved powers which would enable Scotland to have a different social model from the UK in relation to welfare. All developed countries have to decide where to place themselves on the spectrum related to taxation and spending. Are they to be high tax-and-spend countries, with high levels of social welfare, or low tax countries which promote enterprise and self-reliance? Scandinavian countries are the archetype of the first, and the US of the second. Small countries too have to decide what strategy to follow. A country like Denmark very definitely takes the Scandinavian model, while some of the new Eastern European democracies opt for a low tax path. The UK is awkwardly in the middle:

it aspires to high levels of welfare, but is attracted by US levels of taxation. Could devolution enable Scotland to make its own choice while still in the UK?

This might respond to views in Scotland that decisions about benefits should be taken locally, and to the perception that Scotland is more inclined to support higher tax-and-spend policies than the rest of the UK. Survey data suggest that over 60% of Scots think that the Scottish Parliament should decide the level of benefits and old-age pensions (Scottish Social Attitudes [SSA] 2010, 2011). However over 60% also think that old-age pensions should be the same across the UK, so care should be taken in drawing conclusions from the data. In Scotland 40% of voters favour increasing taxation and government spending, compared to 30% in England (SSA 2010).[16]

Directly provided welfare services (health, education, social work, housing) are already devolved, even though redistributive welfare (in the form of benefit payments) is not. The Scottish Parliament has taken a different line on some of these issues from the rest of the UK: free prescriptions, free personal care for the elderly and free university tuition are the most obvious examples. But it cannot change cash benefit payments. One limited form of welfare nationalism would be for the Scottish Parliament to have scope to alter some of the benefits system to meet Scottish demands. On this model, the main contributory and non-contributory benefits – old-age pensions, jobseekers allowance, and tax credits – would remain reserved. However, those benefits which have strong overlaps with existing devolved responsibilities could be devolved so that it would be possible to adjust them to fit better alongside devolved services. The IPPR and the Scottish Labour Devolution Commission both agreed that the best candidates for devolution on these grounds are housing benefit and attendance allowance (Lodge and Trench 2014; Scottish Labour 2014). The Scottish Parliament is already responsible for key aspects of the housing market – they control not just housing policy and investment, but also planning policy. As a result of the Scotland Act 2012, the Scottish government will also have responsibility for all property taxes. Devolving housing benefit – a major policy level – would enable the Scottish government to make policy for housing in a more holistic way, taking into account the preferences of their voters and their local needs and circumstances. Given its close overlaps with devolved policy in the health and social services a similar logic applies to attendance allowance. In addition to devolving these individual benefits IPPR also proposed devolving

responsibility for welfare-to-work programmes to the Scottish government, enabling it to better coordinate policy for getting the long-term
unemployed back to work with other relevant devolved services.
(The Scottish Labour Devolution Commission proposed devolving the
Work Programme – the main welfare-to-work initiative for the long-
term unemployed – to Scottish local authorities.) Alternatively it might
be possible to devise a scheme which allowed the Scottish Parliament to
supplement benefits as proposed by IPPR in its Devo More programme
(Lodge and Trench 2014). Under this model, the level of benefits set
by the UK government would serve as a floor, but not a ceiling, for
devolved welfare payments. Any increase in a particular benefit would
have to be funded exclusively from devolved budgets.

There is potentially a more radical version of welfare nationalism,
in which the whole of social security would be devolved, and the
redistributive and insurance functions of the state would be exercised
from Edinburgh rather than London. Risks would be pooled across
Scotland, rather than in the wider UK, and income would be redistrib-
uted amongst Scottish residents rather than across the whole UK. So if
Scotland were prospering economically, there would be scope to pay
more generous benefits; conversely if the Scottish economy suffered an
adverse shock, Scotland could not look to the rest of the UK to support
benefit payments.

To achieve this both income tax and national insurance would have
to be devolved. Those personal taxes – rather than VAT – would then
bear the burden of any more generous social provision. Since they
amount to about 40% of domestic tax revenue, this should be possible,
though the scope to do so will be constrained by public willingness to
pay tax, and the risks of tax competition with the rest of the UK (higher
rate taxpayers, for example, might relocate). On this basis, the expenditure responsibilities of the Scottish Parliament would be very wide
indeed, but its tax powers less so. Its spending responsibilities would
have been hugely extended, but there is not the same scope to increase
its tax powers: so the fiscal gap would remain and indeed probably
grow. On this model, as Scotland had full discretion over almost all
domestic expenditure, it is hard to see how a needs-based grant could
make up the gap. There would have to be a basis, agreed with the UK,
for sharing out the common UK taxes, perhaps on a formula or per
capita basis. The Scottish Parliament also have to be able to borrow for
cyclical fluctuations in spending, also on a basis to be agreed with the
UK, for macroeconomic management reasons.

To permit present levels of provision to remain with present levels of taxation, at a minimum the geographical share of oil revenue would have to be assigned to support domestic Scottish spending. As we have seen, Scotland at present enjoys higher levels of public spending than the rest of the UK. Domestic Scottish tax revenues are roughly, per capita, the same as the UK average. Much of the difference could be made up by oil revenues. During the 1980s, oil revenues supported the UK economy as a whole, but now the net effect is, very roughly, closer to the higher levels of public spending in Scotland. If Scotland seeks to support a different social model from the rest of the UK, it can only do so by relying on oil to pay for present levels of spending or by increasing other taxes. Should oil run out without an alternative source of revenue being developed, then it will be difficult for Scotland to maintain present levels of public spending.

Given the very substantial tax powers to be devolved, this model could well have implications for Scottish representation at Westminster.

'Devolution-max' or full fiscal autonomy

The term 'devolution-max' has been much bandied around, but is seldom defined. The most sweeping conception of further devolution which might merit this label is one in which Scotland's relationship to the rest of the UK is more like that of the Channel Islands or the Isle of Man. A proposition like this has been called 'full devolution' or 'full fiscal autonomy' by the Scottish government. The national conversation document on fiscal autonomy describes it as follows:

> Devolution max – full fiscal autonomy within the UK – would make the Scottish Parliament and Scottish government responsible for raising, collecting and administering all (or the vast majority of) revenues in Scotland and the vast majority of spending for Scotland.
>
> By collecting all tax revenues in Scotland, a payment from Edinburgh to London would be required to cover common UK public goods and services (that is, 'shared services'). The range of services included in this basket of 'shared services', how they would be paid for, and the authority the Scottish Parliament would have over such policies, would be subject to negotiation at the time of any revised settlement. In essence, this framework is the maximum form of tax and policy devolution short of independence. (Scottish Government 2009b: para. 4.22–4.23)

It goes on to describe this as similar to the arrangements in the Basque country and Navarre in Spain, where the Autonomous Communities collect taxes and make a payment to the central excequer. On this basis, the UK Parliament would deal with defence and foreign affairs, and macroeconomic and monetary policy, including financial regulation. The Scottish Parliament would be responsible for all domestic policy (including many presently reserved areas) and nearly 90% of public spending, including social security.

Conceptually, it is very hard to distinguish 'devolution-max' from an independent country which has entered into a confederation with a larger neighbour of the sort discussed in Chapter 2. If the Scottish Parliament determined all the taxes and negotiated some authority over the 'shared services' with the rest of the UK, it is hard to imagine that the rest of the UK would agree to have Scottish MPs at Westminster as well. They would have no responsibility for any domestic policy or taxation. Having no Scottish MPs at Westminster is the one characteristic of independence about which there is no doubt, so it would not be unfair to describe this model as 'independence-light'. Indeed, as proposals for independence already include continued monetary and economic union and might even include continued defence cooperation, 'devolution-max' looks very close to that.

Compared to full independence, however, 'devolution-max' has one potential advantage from a UK perspective: it might not disrupt existing UK defence policy. In that sense it would be a very 'light' version of independence indeed. Fiscally, the rUK would lose access to most Scottish tax revenues, including perhaps some or all oil revenues, but would have no obligation to fund most Scottish public services. In the short run, this might be broadly fiscally neutral for the UK (indeed it would have to be to avoid disruption to public services in Scotland) but in the long run, as oil revenues run out, it might be marginally advantageous for the UK, as well as difficult for Scotland. There would however be more immediate concerns, especially based on Channel Islands experience, about tax competition. Small offshore tax havens have a real but limited effect on UK tax revenue. A tax haven of five million people with a land border and excellent communications with the rUK would be a greater challenge. Conversely, if Scotland chose to become a high tax economy, it could easily lose tax revenue in the same way. Given that Scotland would have to use cyclical borrowing to support social security payments during a recession, there would have to be a borrowing agreement with the UK which allowed this, but which did not carry unacceptable risks for UK macro economic policy.

Could 'devolution-max' be made to work in practice as a form of devolution rather than independence? The resemblance to the Channel Islands is instructive here. They are not part of the United Kingdom and, even though they share its monarchy, they are separate realms. They send no MPs to Westminster. The UK however provides defence and foreign affairs services for the islands. Nor are they part of the EU, so EU law does not apply there. Residents do not pay UK taxes, and the different islands are tax havens: their low rates of income tax attract small numbers of very rich individuals: in Jersey, for example, a special tax scheme allows 'high-net-worth' individuals to settle there, and their income over £625,000 per annum is taxed at 1%. The Islands share a Common Travel Area with Britain and Ireland. Residents can therefore move in and out of the EU freely; the free movement of goods is permitted as well. Businesses, especially financial companies, also set up offices there to reduce their tax bills.

Operating a Channel Islands style system inside the EU is not so easy, as the example of the Basque country shows. Although it is described as having 'full fiscal autonomy' in fact its autonomy is considerably more limited. It collects many taxes as a tax collection authority,[17] and controls personal income tax and corporate taxation, but it does not decide on VAT, social security taxes or excise duties. In Scottish terms this is equivalent to devolving income tax and corporation tax, but not VAT, NI, or excise duties. On this basis, at most 50% of domestic taxation would be devolved, but over 90% of the expenditure. If, contrary to the Basque example, NI were to be devolved alongside social security, up to about 70% of domestic taxation might be devolved. Fiscal transfers from Westminster, financed by taxes decided by the UK, would therefore be inevitable.[18] The scale of transfers would depend on how oil revenues were treated. They might be wholly devolved, or the revenues assigned to Scotland to support domestic public services only. Alternatively, the UK might take the view that a proportion of those resources should be used to support shared services, such as defence and foreign affairs or debt repayment. In either case, given that Scotland would have full discretion over domestic policies, sharing out the proceeds of VAT and other UK taxes would have to be done on a formula basis, such as an estimate of the proportion arising in Scotland ('assignment', discussed above), or simply a population share, rather than taking account of spending need.[19]

'Devolution-max' – in the sense that the Scottish Parliament runs all domestic programs, decides on all the taxes and pays for UK 'shared services' – is not deliverable as a form of devolution. Not all taxes can be devolved, so there would never be enough devolved revenues to cover the cost of all services other than defence and foreign affairs. So some transfer from, rather than to, Westminster is inevitable. That transfer might be by grant, or tax assignment, but the UK would first be able to decide what proportion of the taxes it collected were spent on matters such as defence or foreign affairs, as it does now. Even if Scotland were simply assigned an estimate of all the taxes arising in Scotland, the issue about how to decide the size of the fiscal transfer inevitably arises: what share of UK services should Scotland pay, and why? And then the question of Scottish representation at Westminster becomes much more pressing.

The choice among these models

The proposals that have emerged from the political parties and think tanks contain some elements of each of these models. IPPR's Devo More programme and Reform Scotland's proposals combine aspects of what we have called 'devo-plus' as well as limited versions of welfare nationalism. The recommendations of the Liberal Democrat Campbell Commission are a 'devo-plus' solution albeit set in what they see as a federal framework. Scottish Labour's proposals provide for a modest form of fiscal devolution alongside proposals to devolve some discrete welfare benefits. They (like IPPR) emphatically reject the more radical form of welfare nationalism: their core argument is that the UK is a union that is based on sharing resources to guarantee the same levels of welfare throughout the country. So the substance of the benefits system should remain reserved, and tax devolution should be limited by the need to guarantee that resources for key elements of the welfare state can be guaranteed by UK funding. It seems likely that the Scottish Conservatives will major on proposals for strengthening the tax powers of the Scottish Parliament, in particular over income tax. Any plan which is to be put forward will however have to make a choice between the conflicting considerations of greater autonomy versus sharing with the UK, or more tax powers versus economic spillovers. Choices have to be made. 'Devolution-max' is essentially a variant of independence, which its leaders might seek to negotiate if Scotland had voted only very narrowly to leave the UK. For more devolution within the UK, the most important choice is whether Scotland wants to be able to run a wholly or partly different social model, potentially with significantly higher taxes and more generous welfare provision. Alternatively, should the constitutional framework be designed primarily to promote economic growth? In each case, the effects on Scotland's UK representation would also have to be considered.

Scotland and the UK

Devolution to Scotland, Wales and Northern Ireland has had surprisingly little effect on the governance of the UK as a whole. Parliament at Westminster remains substantially unchanged. Scotland used to have more MPs than its population share, but the number was reduced to a roughly proportionate level after devolution. (Wales still has more MPs than its population share, but this will change if the Parliamentary Representation and Voting Systems Act 2011 comes into effect.) The UK Parliament even still legislates on devolved matters, but now with the agreement of the Scottish Parliament, when it makes practical sense. The UK government also looks very similar: some issues affecting Scotland that were previously discussed in Cabinet committees are covered in intergovernmental meetings, so that instead of a dry civil service minute there may be a couple of florid press releases. These changes aside, it would be hard to say in 2012 that devolution in 1999 has changed British national government very much.

Independence would change that. Scotland would no longer send MPs to Westminster, and the (new) UK would have a new land border and a separate country on it to deal with. British politics would be changed irrevocably. But further devolution is also likely to change the UK's territorial constitution. Both the Labour and the Liberal Democrat parties argue that the Scottish Parliament should be 'entrenched' in the UK constitution, so that the UK Parliament could not unilaterally abolish the Scottish Parliament or cut its powers. This is of course the political reality, but there is no legislative provision to this effect at present.

Devolution in the UK is not just about Scotland and is profoundly asymmetric. It affects only 15% of the population, and there is no real prospect of the same sort of devolution for England. Parliament at Westminster, therefore, will remain the legislature for England and for the UK. This gives rise to the 'West Lothian question'. Scottish MPs at Westminster cannot vote on devolved Scottish matters, but they can vote on the same issues for England. The issue arises for Wales too, now the Assembly has fuller legislative powers. (For most of the time since 1923, it has also arisen for Northern Ireland.) So laws passed at Westminster affecting only England may not reflect the balance of English opinion. Moreover the UK government is also the government of England: it might not enjoy the confidence of a majority of English MPs because it is sustained by an overall UK majority (for a full explanation see Gallagher 2012). There is no obvious, simple solution to this problem. An English Parliament would turn the UK into a fully and formally federal state. The Liberal Democrat party has always argued that the UK should be a federal state, though they do not support having an English Parliament: certainly it is very hard to envisage that a federal state in which one unit of the federation contained 85% of the population would be stable.

It has been possible to argue that the West Lothian question is a largely theoretical anomaly, with no real impact in practice. Scottish MPs make up only a small proportion of the total, and their votes are seldom critical to issues affecting England only. There were occasions (in 1964 and 1974) when UK Labour governments depended on Scottish MPs for an overall majority, but this happened when the English opinion was split down the middle, and the result was an unstable government. The February 1974 government, for example, lasted only six months. Now that the number of Scottish MPs has been reduced, the risk is even more theoretical.

It is not clear however that this argument can be sustained, especially if there is greater devolution. Two possible solutions have been offered. The first is a legislative procedure at Westminster which gives a greater say to English members over English legislation. This was canvassed under the slogan 'English votes for English laws'. The Conservative manifesto for the 2010 General Election stated:

> Labour have refused to address the so-called 'West Lothian Question': the unfair situation of Scottish MPs voting on matters which are devolved. A Conservative government will introduce new rules so that legislation referring specifically to England, or to England and Wales, cannot be enacted without the consent of MPs representing constituencies of those countries. (Conservative Party 2010: 84)

The McKay Commission set up by the UK government recommended changes to legislative procedures but even they do not get round the difficulty that Scottish MPs might still be critical to the formation of a UK government. A pragmatic alternative which has

Table 4.3 Devolution options for Scotland

Devolution model	Parliamentary process for English legislation	Scottish representation at Westminster	Comment
Status quo	No English process	Number of Scottish MPs proportional to population	The West Lothian question seen as a theoretical, rather than as a real problem
Scotland Act 2012	Case can be made for English legislative process	Unchanged	Scottish MPs still vote on UK income tax affecting Scotland
'Devolution-max'	English process not needed	None or only token Scottish representation at Westminster	Leaves Scotland with only indirect influence over remaining UK issues
'Welfare nationalism'	More English process necessary, as more issues have become purely English	Devolution discount, certainly if all welfare devolved	Less radical version might involve no or smaller discount
'Closing the fiscal gap: devo-more'	Case can be made for English legislative process	Devolution discount	Size of discount may depend on extent of tax devolution. English legislative process needed no more than at present, and may be unnecessary given reduced number of Scottish MPs

also been advocated is simply to reduce the numbers of MPs to below a proportionate level – a 'devolution discount'. This was the practice for Northern Ireland from 1923 until 1972, when the Stormont Parliament had very wide responsibilities. This would obviously reduce Scottish influence over English domestic matters, but at the price of reducing Scottish influence over UK issues which still affected Scotland directly.

Tax devolution might well make some change inevitable. At the extreme end of 'devolution-max', with all taxes being decided in Scotland, it could be very hard to justify any Scottish MPs at all. They would be voting on taxes which had no effect on their constituents, and not on those that did. On the other hand, defence and foreign affairs decisions would still affect Scotland. Even with less tax decentralisation, the case for a 'devolution discount' can still be made. There is no obvious formula for deciding on this, but Table 4.3 gives the range of possible responses at a UK level to each variant of potential Scottish devolution. The consequences at Westminster are a key part of any devolution package to be offered to the Scottish people; but they can only be decided along with the rest of the UK.

Conclusion

It is certainly possible, as we have seen, to devise more wide-ranging schemes of devolution. 'Devolution-max', at least as described by the Scottish government, is in effect a variant of independence, and it is unlikely to be deliverable as a scheme of devolution. With other schemes, such as those based on welfare nationalism, there are choices and trade-offs. The most important trade-offs relate to Scotland's relationship with the rest of the UK. Does it want to be part of a common welfare system, pooling risks and resources, or take responsibility for managing these risks, and the resultant opportunities, within its own resources? More tax decentralisation leads to questions about how UK tax revenues are used to support Scottish domestic spending, and how much influence Scotland can have by sending MPs to Westminster. If Scotland rejects independence in 2014 then these issues will rise to the top of the political agenda and will be tested out in the general election campaign and dealt with thereafter.

Notes

1. On 1 November 2011 the Scottish Liberal Democrats announced a 'Home Rule Commission' to be chaired by Sir Menzies Campbell: its report was published in November 2012 (Campbell 2012). A short follow-up report – 'Campbell II' – was published in March 2014 (Campbell 2014).
2. Labour's Commission, chaired by its Scottish Leader Johann Lamont, began work in October 2012. An interim report was published in April 2013 (Scottish Labour 2013), with the final report appearing in March 2014 (Scottish Labour 2014).
3. The authors are grateful to the Citizenship-after-the-nation-state (CANS) research team for providing us with these data.
4. In principle it could also be a more rigorous regime, but that would be unlikely to attract inward investment.
5. 'The Scottish Government strongly believes that it is in the shared interests of Scotland and the rest of the UK to continue a GB-wide approach to the operation of energy infrastructure and markets after Scottish independence, in line with the drive towards more integrated energy markets across the EU.' (Ewing 2012)
6. This is a question of degree. Some countries, such as Canada, allow scope for different Provincial allowances to be added to national income tax systems.
7. Social security is in fact formally speaking devolved in Northern Ireland, but the

arrangements for consultation, and the fact that the Treasury funds NI welfare spending, mean that it is the same as elsewhere in the UK. National Insurance is not devolved there.

8. Just how significant this effect is, compared with other issues that affect companies' location decisions, is unclear.

9. Holtham recognised that the scheme effectively allowed a lower but not a higher rate of corporation tax in Wales.

10. Região autónoma dos Açores v Council (T-37/04) [2008] E.C.R. II-103; [2008] 3 C.M.L.R. 30, at [54]-[56] (appeal dismissed by Região autónoma dos Açores v Council (C-444/08) November 26, 2009); Unio´n General de Trabajadores de La Rioja (UGT Rioja) v Juntas Generales del Territorio Histo´rico de Vizcaya, [2008] 3 C.M.L.R. 46.

11. They also suggested reducing the grant paid by a smaller amount, so as to increase the Scottish budget overall; the UK government, unsurprisingly, did not agree to this.

12. Two benefits are exceptions: Council tax benefit depends on the rates of council tax locally, and housing benefit takes account of local housing markets. Council tax benefit is to be decentralised by the present government. Housing benefit is to be absorbed into the proposed new universal credit, and it is not at present clear what account is to be taken of local housing conditions in that.

13. Of course this already applies to people moving inside the European Union, and these challenges can be overcome, but they would be more numerous inside the UK.

14. Arrangements would be needed, as under the Scotland Act 2012, for the UK government to take responsibility for the fiscal effect of any changes it made to the tax base.

15. For example, as can be seen from Table 4.1, if it were possible to devolve all income tax, vehicle excise and fuel duties and some of the other small taxes, tax revenue might be about 60% of the devolved budget.

16. Of course the data imply that the majority *do not* favour doing so. Review of these data led John Curtice and Rachel Ormston to conclude 'Scotland is somewhat – but only somewhat – more social democratic than England; Scotland has become somewhat less social democratic during the last decade.' (Curtice and Ormston 2011)

17. Strictly speaking there are three separate tax collection authorities in the Basque country.

18. It is possible in principle to have an arrangement under which Scotland would set up its own tax collection authority to collect all the taxes that were decided on by Westminster, as well as its own. From the point of view of taxpayers, and cost of collection, however, this is an additional burden, and there is no obvious reason why the UK should agree to it.

19. One attempt to design a system of full fiscal autonomy, recognising the problem created by retaining VAT at a UK level, is Hughes Hallett and Scott (2010). This suggested that as well as VAT, the UK should retain responsibility for paying old-age pensions. This however ignores the connection between national insurance contributions and old-age pensions, and still leaves the question of a balancing item, as the bundle of the devolved taxes would not yield revenue equal to the cost of devolved services.

5

A Social Union?
Welfare and Citizenship in the UK

BRITAIN IS OFTEN described as a 'welfare state', and so it is. State provision for many aspects of life is indeed available 'from the cradle to the grave'. Schools and hospitals are probably the welfare state's most visible manifestation, but the largest expenditure by some way is on benefits – old-age pensions, child benefit, income support, disability benefits and so on. Social security is the biggest spending programme that the UK government has (HM Treasury 2012b, Table 1.1) and as we have seen accounts for nearly 40% of the identifiable public spending in Scotland. The UK provides higher levels of state welfare, and so taxation, than countries like the US, but not as high as some Scandinavian countries. It is about just over half way up the league table of OECD countries for social spending: 21% of GDP, compared with Sweden at 29% or Canada and the US at 16% (OECD 2009). What significance does this have for the choices Scotland now faces?

The welfare state is a creation of the twentieth century. It grew out of the minimal Victorian poor law provision, and friendly societies and similar bodies with their systems of mutual insurance, offering their members protection against the problems of old age, illness, and unemployment. When the Liberal government of 1906 introduced welfare benefits (e.g. pensions for the over 70s, when life expectancy was under 50) they mostly stuck to the insurance principle: benefits were an entitlement gained by paying contributions, rather than something paid out of general taxation. Even though the fund into which contributions were paid never really became effective (see Chapter 6 for how the wily Lloyd George ignored the advice he was given about this) the insurance principle is still around today. It is important for two reasons. First, (national insurance) contributions still determine some benefits entitlements – such as old-age pensions. Secondly, welfare systems are in substance (even if not in strict form) still systems of mutual insurance. Everyone faces risks like old age, illness, and unemployment: rather than carrying these risks individually they are pooled – not in an insurance company, a pension fund, or a friendly society, but across an entire country or society, to become not private but 'social' insurance. Individuals pay in, via contributions or increasingly via general taxation (which is related to ability to pay rather than being a strict insurance premium) and take the benefits when their circumstances mean they require them. Obviously the larger the pool, the more the risks are likely to average out, and the easier an insurance scheme is to manage; social insurance provides the largest pool of all.

This approach remained an important part of the critical development of the welfare state, which took place after World War II and was based on the Beveridge Report of 1942, *Social Insurance and Allied Services* (Beveridge 1942). Beveridge regarded social insurance as an 'attack on want', but it had to be supplemented both by other forms of income support ('means tested' and paid from general taxation), family allowances and direct provision of services. The wartime and immediately post-war governments put these recommendations into effect in landmark legislation: the ('Butler') Education Act of 1944; the National Health Act 1948; the Family Allowance Act 1945; and the National Insurance Act 1946. Significantly, for our purposes, the first two of these were matched by parallel Scottish legislation, but the latter were not. From the 1950s to the 1970s there was a broad political consensus on the development of welfare provision, though the strict social insurance principle became less dominant. By the 1980s pensions were increasingly provided by employer and private schemes, additional to state old-age pensions, and an increasing proportion of benefits paid had become means-tested rather than contribution based. The system was no longer in form predominantly a strict insurance based one: it was pay-as-you-go and supported substantially from general taxation, with risks pooled across the whole community.[1]

Scotland has been an integral part of the UK welfare state since it was founded. Scots have paid into the National Insurance Fund, and into general taxation, and taken pensions and benefits as they became entitled to them. 'Social protection' is the largest item of Scottish public spending, and is at a higher level than in the rest of the UK. Table 5.1 and Table 5.2 give an indication of the level of spending and the main benefits it supports.

Scotland's relatively high level of benefit spending is driven by the individual circumstances of claimants, and these are in their turn

Table 5.1 Social protection spending in Scotland 2006–7 to 2010–11

	2006–7	2007–8	2008–9	2009–10	2010–11
Social protection spending (£m)	15,955	16,956	18,317	19,903	20,741
Of which social services (£m)	2,420	2,834	3,051	3,180	3,265
Per head (£)	3,130	3,310	3,546	3,835	3,972
Per head indexed to UK = 100	110	108	109	108	109

Source: HM Treasury 2012b

Table 5.2 Main components of social protection spending in Scotland per head 2010–11 (with England for comparison)

Main benefits (£)	Spending per head Scotland (£)	(Comparable English figure)
Old age pensions	1,413	(1,329)
Incapacity, disability, etc.	579	(449)
Family benefits, tax credits, income support	757	(752)
Unemployment benefits	93	(82)

Source: HM Treasury 2012b [PESA] Tables 10.5, 10.6

driven by significant social trends, most notably the age structure of the population, and changing patterns of economic activity. Scotland is now economically typical of the UK in terms of income and unemployment, and some continuing high levels of benefit spend may still be linked to the de-industrialisation of the 1980s. Future benefit spending will be driven by the increasing proportion of the population over pension age. The number of persons over the age of 75 in Scotland is projected to rise by over 80% between 2010 and 2035, and the age dependency ratio, the number of 'dependents (those over pension age) per 100 of working age population', is expected to grow over the same period from 60 to 65 (Registrar General for Scotland 2012).

Welfare states and nations

In most countries, as in Britain, welfare states are, as the name implies, operated at the national level. This reflects their origins and how they have grown. Generally speaking, countries provide welfare for their own citizens, and not others. EU member states offer mutual recognition so that workers can move freely from one country to another but welfare benefits, entitlements, contribution records and so on are a jealously guarded national responsibility.

An independent Scotland would no longer be part of the British welfare state, and would make no contribution to it through taxation and, after any transitional arrangements had been made, Scots would receive no benefits from it. Benefits for people living in Scotland would be the responsibility of the Scottish government. Disentangling the UK welfare state would be a major task. Scotland would inherit the present UK system of social security, but would have to decide whether to keep or amend it and whether, for example, to recognise entitlements built up elsewhere in the UK. Whether the same levels of welfare could be afforded is part of the general question of whether an independent Scotland will have the tax revenues to sustain present public services (discussed in Chapter 2). A more complex question is whether there is scope for devolving further aspects of welfare within a continuing UK.

In the last sixty or so years the British people have come to believe that whatever else might divide them, when it comes to public services like health and education, and benefits to safeguard against old age, ill health and unemployment, these should be delivered on the same terms to all citizens irrespective of where they live. Most people believe that the person in Edinburgh should get the same level of social provision and the same form of social protection as the person in Exeter. So widespread is this view that one leading scholar has suggested that a fundamental 'principle' of the UK welfare state is that 'benefits and burdens . . . depend on need, not geography' (Bogdanor 2003). Yet this principle is not quite as fundamental as many believe, since services have not always been delivered on exactly the same terms to all citizens of the United Kingdom. Scotland, for instance, has always had a distinct education system to England. Nonetheless, what differences did exist did not undermine the view that all citizens were entitled essentially to equal treatment. This started to change with the creation of devolved institutions in Scotland, Wales and Northern Ireland over a decade ago. By definition, devolving significant powers over public policy means that services can vary from one part of the UK to the next. And this is precisely what has happened. As a result of devolution, if you live in Scotland today the government will cover the costs of your social care provision, which you would pay for if you lived in England. In Wales, Scotland and Northern Ireland prescriptions are free, in England they are not. And a student in England applying to study at an English university will face a charge of up to £9000 per year, unlike a Scot applying to study at a Scottish university, where fees were abolished.

In other words, as a consequence of devolution, the rights enjoyed by UK citizens now vary according to where people live. And the prospect of further constitutional change means there is scope for them to vary even more. Under the Scotland Act 2012, for instance, it is possible that Scots could pay a higher or lower level of income tax than people in the rest of the UK. If there were some form of 'devolution-max' in operation it might be possible for welfare benefits such as pensions to be different across the UK.

Does it matter if social policy varies across the different parts of the UK?[2] The idea of social citizenship rights emerged at the time of the creation of the post-war welfare state, but devolution has affected our understanding of social citizenship, and further constitutional change could have implications for a shared sense of social citizenship.

Ideas about social citizenship are 'at heart ideas about the territorial scale at which citizens express solidarity with one another' (Jeffery et al. 2010). Typically, this has been a nation-state: taxes are shared across the nation to provide common social welfare, and not across neighbouring countries – even within the EU, there is no assumption that, say, German taxes automatically flow to Greece to pay benefits there. But policy variation which reflects the preferences of one particular UK community, say Scotland, to pursue a distinctive agenda may imply that solidarity is expressed at that level. Similarly, a sense of UK-wide solidarity argues for some policies to be delivered uniformly across the UK. Belonging and sharing go together.

The current devolution settlement treads something of a middle line, with core welfare entitlements (in the form of benefits) reserved to the UK level, and therefore held in common, while other aspects – provided as public services – are devolved, with few legal constraints. Social citizenship rights are therefore shared between the Scottish and the UK levels. The most important question about the idea of significantly more devolution is whether social welfare provision could be managed solely at the Scottish level, or whether responsibility should continue to be shared between the Scottish and UK governments. These debates in turn have important implications for fiscal policy: if social rights are to be expressed at the Scottish level then this would require a substantial degree of fiscal autonomy to pay for them (see Chapters 4 and 6). They also raise fundamental questions about the role and purpose of the union in a more devolved UK, and in particular consideration of the idea of a 'social union'.

T. H. Marshall and social citizenship rights

'Social citizenship rights' was an idea developed by T. H. Marshall, the academic who coined the term. In a short essay delivered in 1950 Marshall identified three distinct but inter-related features of citizenship, which had evolved from the eighteenth century onwards (Marshall 1950). First came civil rights, a necessary precondition for individual freedom, including rights protecting free speech, religious freedoms and property rights. These in turn became a platform for the achievement of political rights, most notably the extension of suffrage in the nineteenth and twentieth centuries. Together these paved the way for the establishment of the social rights embodied in the welfare state. These social rights guaranteed each citizen access to a basic level of welfare – comprising both access to public services like health, education and housing, and cash benefits which protected individuals against things like unemployment – necessary, in Marshall's words, to 'live the life of a civilised being' (Marshall 1950: 11).

Central to Marshall's thinking was the belief that these civil, political and social rights would be exercised by all citizens equally, irrespective of their income or status. That is not to say that Marshall believed that they would 'make everyone the same', but it did mean that citizenship rights would be distributed equally in an otherwise unequal society (Greer 2009). This conception of equality had important *territorial* implications too, since it was believed these social rights were 'national', meaning that they had to be delivered on the same terms to all citizens wherever they happened to live. In practice this meant that if social rights were to be exercised equally across the UK then welfare services and benefits had to be delivered centrally by the UK government. Hence the big push in the post-war years to create a 'national' welfare state, as demonstrated by the passing of the *National* Insurance Act, which established a comprehensive system of social security and the creation in 1948 of the *National* Health Service.[3] The other crucial element to this story is the way these social rights were to be funded: not solely from social insurance schemes, where access depends on contribution, but substantially out of general taxation, which further explains why the British public expected services to be delivered uniformly across the UK.

Social citizenship rights were thus firmly equated with *British* citizenship rights, and the locus of social solidarity was Britain (more accurately the UK) – or to put it another way, the welfare state assumed that the 'sharing community' upon which it was built was Britain. The flip-side of this position is that allowing social rights to vary geographically was anathema to the Marshallian account of citizenship. Indeed, it was precisely because of concerns about the geographical inequities of the localised patch-work provision of welfare that characterised the pre-1945 era that led policy-makers to insist on uniformity. And why Nye Bevan, the health secretary in Attlee's Labour government, rejected proposals by Herbert Morrison, his cabinet colleague, for a network of municipally controlled hospitals instead insisting that equity and universal access to health could only be achieved through a health service administered in London (Campbell 1987: 169–70). To make his point Bevan famously said that he wanted the sound of a bedpan dropping on the floor at Tredegar general hospital to reverberate in the corridors of Whitehall.

And while this Marshallian account of social citizenship rights has been widely criticised (for example, Greer 2009) it is difficult to exaggerate its influence. In particular Marshall's ideas have underpinned the powerful assumptions that welfare services and benefits *should* be delivered on the same terms to all UK citizens. However, like all ideas that acquire mythical status, the closer they are scrutinised the more mythical they appear. The fact is that UK citizenship rights did vary – to some degree at least – by place, it's just that no one really acknowledged it.

To start with, we can observe empirically that the post-war central state often failed to achieve equity in public service provision. The Black Report (Townsend and Davidson 1982) shattered the illusion that a centralised health service would automatically deliver uniformity by exposing significant variations in health outcomes across the country. Since then, the extent of the information on geographical inequalities in public service quality and consequently outcomes has grown enormously, as evidenced, for example, by reports from audit bodies. Scholars who have studied welfare provision have repeatedly shown that rich people living in affluent areas tend to have access to better schools and better hospitals than poor people living in poor areas. In other words some discrepancies in provision were accidental (hence the 'lottery' element of the pejorative term 'post-code lottery'), demonstrating the limits of centralised bureaucracies. However, differences were often the product of conscious choices. Jim Bulpitt's pioneering work on territorial politics within England drew attention to the existence of what he called a 'dual polity' in which central government focused on 'high politics' – things like defence and macroeconomic policy, leaving local government to busy itself with the 'low politics' of social welfare (but not health: Bulpitt 1983). It wasn't really until the 1970s that 'low politics' became the preoccupation of central government, and it did so in response to a public fretting about the varied geographical quality of public services. When Prime Minister Jim Callaghan called for a 'Great Debate' on education in 1976, in response to public concerns about the quality of education, central government began to take seriously delivery of a major local public service. 'Low politics' became 'high politics' and it provoked a number of policies designed to exert central government's grip on local services. Callaghan's speech was followed by Margaret Thatcher's introduction of a national curriculum (in England and Wales) in the 1980s. If central government was to be held responsible for improving local services then it was going to try to control them: and it has not stopped since.

But most obviously social rights varied across the four nations of the UK. Marshall was blind to this because he ignored the experience of Scotland, Wales and Northern Ireland in his analysis. When he conceived citizenship rights to be 'national' he essentially conflated England with Britain. Such conflation contributed to the view that the UK was a unitary state, but this has been convincingly challenged by a number of scholars who point out that the UK is better described as a 'union-state' (Rokkan and Urwin 1982). Whereas a unitary state implies rigid uniformity and standardisation, the concept of a union-state recognises that the UK came about as a result of a series of historic unions, with each constituent nation continuing to retain its own distinctiveness (Mitchell 2006a: 154). Most obviously Scotland continued to have distinct education and legal systems after union with England in 1707.

In the twentieth century this territorial distinctiveness was maintained through a period of 'administrative devolution' when Scotland, Wales and Northern Ireland were governed by separate territorial offices.[4] These were part of the UK government (run by ministers appointed by the prime minister, and accountable to Parliament) but which nevertheless exercised considerable discretion over policy. The degree of policy autonomy differed between the three offices, reflecting the different historic patterns of territorial integration. Wales had been more thoroughly absorbed into England than Scotland, and the Welsh Office started eighty years later than the Scottish Office and exercised fewer powers (Mitchell 2006a: 159).

Returning to Marshall's three-fold typology of rights we can see that even in an era of administrative devolution there existed some important differences in how these were experienced across the UK. That Scotland ran its own distinct legal system ensured some (minor) variation in civil rights (for example in relation to the law on divorce). In Northern Ireland, the Stormont rule was abandoned precisely because the civil rights of the Catholic minority were being ignored. Political rights were exercised almost uniformly, but even here some territorial differences arose, for instance Scotland and Wales were deliberately over-represented in the House of Commons (McLean 1995). Social rights varied to some degree because the territorial offices had responsibility for the administration of public services like health and education. Important here too is the fact that spending per head was in recent decades higher in Scotland, Wales and Northern Ireland than it was in England (courtesy of a block grant sent by the Treasury to the territorial departments), which meant administrative discretion was buttressed with money (McLean 2005). The net result of all this, writes Mitchell, is that 'even before devolution a common citizenship across the UK was attenuated by the existence of separate institutions with separate histories' (2006a: 163).

But because of the cover provided by the operation of a single UK-wide government what diversity there was in social provision – and it would be wrong to exaggerate the degree of divergence, as no basic rights differed – occurred *sub rosa* and the idea of 'need not geography' was allowed to prevail (Wincott 2006: 172). And whatever variation there was it was never sufficient to disturb the powerful post-war discourse that liked to present the welfare state as an expression of UK-wide solidarity. Indeed the immediate post-war era was marked by a number of 'nation-building' projects like the creation of the NHS and the nationalisation of industries that did much to bind together the nations of the UK.

Of course another reason why Marshall's influence resonated so strongly is because in one very important respect, policy – and thus citizenship rights – did not vary at all. When it came to what economists call 'redistributive policies' – policies relating to taxes, benefits and social security that have a direct redistributive impact on citizens – there was no territorial difference at all. So while the Secretary of State for Scotland was responsible for the health service in Scotland and over how to spend the health budget, decisions on the taxation used to fund the health service were set by the UK Chancellor. Nor did the Scottish Office administer any cash benefits.[5]

Devolution and social citizenship

The main thrust of political devolution in the late 1990s was to democratise these pre-existing territorial arrangements. In doing so it had a number of important implications for public understanding of social citizenship. Most obviously it created a new political space – or sharing-community – in which social citizenship rights could be articulated and expressed. If the locus of the post-war welfare state was Britain, it was now Britain *and* Scotland. And not only did devolution provide the impetus for greater divergence across the UK, it also meant that any divergence that did take place would do so in the open, imply-ing that UK citizens would for the first time be made aware of how their social rights varied by territory.

The scope for divergence was considerable in two important respects. Firstly, the devolved institutions were given complete legal control over devolved public services. Unlike in other federal systems, the UK government attached no conditions when it devolved powers or transferred finance in relation to health or education. There are no state-wide framework laws covering devolved matters, no insistence that citizens living in the devolved territories should be entitled to a minimum level of service provision or UK-wide common standards. Secondly, such policy autonomy was matched by the remarkable degree of discretion the devolved institutions exercised in relation to their budgets. The UK government imposed no constraints on how the devolved administrations spent the block grants they were allocated. As the Calman Commission acknowledged '[d]evolution . . . would in principle allow for a fundamentally different welfare state in Scotland, at least in relation to health or education' (Commission on Scottish Devolution 2008: para. 4.60).

What devolution did not do, however, was allow for a different model of social security to operate in Scotland. Responsibility for the redistributive policies described above remained with the UK govern-ment. So while the Scottish government is free to do what it likes to the health service, it cannot introduce a separate scheme of Scottish pensions. Control of social security reserves to the UK a very signifi-cant aspect of the welfare state. And because the Scottish Parliament originally had so few tax powers it had no control over the overall size of its budget, which acted as a further constraint on what it could do in practice. Another potential constraint arises by virtue of the way the block grant works; since changes to the grant are determined by changes in *English* spending, this means that if English spending goes down, so too does Scottish spending. In other words policy choices made in England affect the scope of the Scottish government to use the powers it has distinctively. This is of course changing as the Scotland Act 2012 introduces a Scottish Income Tax (see Chapter 3).

Nonetheless even with these limits, it is clear that the creation of new centres of political power has allowed for territorially distinctive policies to emerge across the four nations of the UK. We listed a number of the best known examples at the start of the chapter, including the differing policies for student fees and social care in different parts of the UK. Beyond these headline differences, devolution prompted important changes in a number of other policy areas (see Lodge and Schmuecker 2010 for a comprehensive assessment of the main areas of difference). Ironically, the driving force behind such differentiation has often proved to be England, and not the devolved administrations. The last decade has witnessed a number of major reforms to the way English public services work, such as academy schools or foundation hospitals, which mark England out: none of these policies has been pursued by Scotland, Wales or Northern Ireland.

Strikingly, however, it appears that not all the architects of devolution anticipated that it might result in devolved governments doing things differently to each other and the Westminster Parliament. In his diaries Paddy Ashdown recalls an exasperated Tony Blair telling him 'you can't have Scotland doing something different from the rest of Britain' with regard to tuition fees (Ashdown 2001: 446). Perhaps the framers of the devolution settlement were more focused on trying to placate the forces of separatism than they were with thinking about the consequences of policy divergence for UK citizenship rights. Time was spent therefore on designing an electoral system for Scotland that would prevent the SNP (or any other party) from winning a majority of seats on a minority of the vote (a plan which failed rather spectacularly in 2011), but not on establishing the common entitlements all UK citizens were entitled to in a devolved context. Or perhaps it reflects the fact that at the time the devolved institutions were established Labour was the dominant political force across the UK, in power in London, Edinburgh and Cardiff, leaving them to believe that policy would broadly converge (neither free care for the elderly or the abolition of student fees were policies of the Scottish Labour party; and were only introduced as a consequence of a coalition deal with the Scottish Liberal Democrats).

If the UK government did not itself expect policy to diverge then it should not surprise us to know that they did very little to prepare public opinion for the likelihood that the substance of UK citizenship rights would begin to vary geographically. For a while this didn't matter: devolution was born in economically and politically benign times with spending rising across all four nations of the UK, and with Labour's hegemonic status ensuring cordial relations between the UK and devolved governments. Things began to change when English public opinion, in particular, started to realise that they were being denied a number of generous universal policies available to Scots (and to a lesser extent Welsh) voters. Parts of the London media became increasingly animated by what they perceived to be the fundamental unfairness of devolution. 'UK's apartheid in medical care' screamed a typical headline in *The Sun*. 'The NHS is unable to guarantee the same level of care for everyone in the UK. Yet this was one of the founding principles when . . . set up in 1948' (*The Sun*, 10 January 2008). That Scots benefited from free social care and did not have to pay tuition fees inevitably drew attention to the level of funding going to the different nations of the UK. Spending per head was significantly higher in Scotland than in England. The unfairness argument developed another layer: Scots, it was believed, were only able to enjoy these policies because they were being subsidised by the English taxpayer.[6] Whether true or not – the SNP argued back that Scotland was a net contributor to the UK exchequer – this became the conventional wisdom within England. For instance, the number of English voters who say that Scotland gets 'more than its fair share' of public money has doubled in the last ten years (Wyn Jones et al. 2012). What compounded this situation was that no one could mount a convincing defence of the Barnett Formula, a spending arrangement which was not based on any principle of need or equity, but whose results appeared arbitrarily to favour Scotland over England (Chapter 8).

Of course awareness of a perceived problem does not automatically imply high salience. English voters might have become more irritated by devolution-inspired policy divergence, but it was obviously not their number one political concern.[7] Nonetheless, that policy was starting to vary and to do so in such a conspicuous way meant that UK citizens could no longer be assured of the post-war promise of common standards. At the same time the benign conditions into which devolution was born gave way to a period of significant economic and political turbulence. The global financial crisis plunged the UK into its deepest and longest recession since the 1930s, prompting the coalition government to enact severe cuts in public spending, which have significant implications for devolved budgets and which put questions about territorial resource allocation high on the public and political agenda. Political dynamics have also changed substantially: in 2007 nationalist parties entered government for the first time, in coalition with Labour in Wales (until 2011) and as a minority government in Scotland. The next big change came in 2010 with the formation of a Conservative-Liberal Democrat coalition and in 2011 with the election of a majority SNP administration, meaning that for the first time different parties hold the reins of power in London, Edinburgh and Cardiff (the party political system has always differed in Northern Ireland). Arguably these political shifts have created centrifugal pressures on the UK as a whole, with each nation increasingly insulated and set-apart from the others (Jeffery 2012).

Devolution then undoubtedly represents a significant challenge to the Marshallian account of citizenship. While civil rights remain uniform across the UK – not least because of the passing of the UK Human Rights Act, which incorporates the European Convention of Human Rights into UK law – the political rights of UK citizens now vary: Scots, Welsh, and Northern Irish citizens have a right to vote for devolved institutions (which exercise different types of powers, using different electoral systems), which is not the case for English citizens (though Londoners have a devolved mayor and assembly). And just as the establishment of UK-wide political rights in the nineteenth and twentieth centuries became a platform for UK-wide social rights after World War II, so the political rights created by devolution have become a platform for the articulation and expression of social rights at the devolved level. In respect of core public service entitlements, these social rights now vary across the UK. Social rights are now expressed at different territorial scales. Where they remain common to all UK citizens is in the field of social security. Could these also be devolved?

What kind of Union? Welfare Unionism vs Welfare Nationalism

Would it matter if pensioners in Scotland were paid more generous pensions than those in England? Or if unemployment benefits were higher in London than in Dundee? The answer is: it might, but that depends on the wider set of beliefs about community and solidarity that citizens might have. It depends in particular on understandings of 'union' in the UK – and what role and purpose is attached to union after devolution. Should there be some limits to (or in certain cases no) variations in policy outcomes by territory, so that the commonality gives meaning to an overarching sense of British community? Or should that policy vary from one part of the UK to the next in line with the differences in preferences that Scottish, Welsh or Northern Irish communities have, as expressed through devolved democratic processes? We look at these two normative accounts of union, which we refer to as 'welfare unionism' and 'welfare nationalism', below, exploring both their strengths and weaknesses, before considering how UK citizens themselves think about these debates.[8]

Welfare unionism

The Calman Commission provides the clearest exposition of the welfare unionist position. Not only did Calman put forward some important options for strengthening the powers of the Scottish Parliament, it also emphasised the need to protect a number of shared UK-wide entitlements as part of what it called a 'social union'. This term is really a new name for an old idea. The old idea is that the people and nations that comprise the United Kingdom benefit from being able to pool resources and risks across a larger and more resilient political and economic community than that provided by the constituent nations alone. Historically, this justification for Union was made with reference to advancing the security and economic interests of England and Scotland. The creation of an Anglo-Scottish Union, it was argued by the eighteenth century deal-makers on both sides, would put an end to centuries of disruptive and expensive warfare. Once established it was assumed that economic benefits would flow to both nations: in return for securing the border, Scots would gain access to English markets and its lucrative overseas colonies, allowing both to thrive (McLean and McMillan 2005: Chapter 2). The Calman Commission reframed this idea in the context of the common welfare (hence the 'social' element) by arguing that:

> there are areas where the people of Scotland have over many years shared rights and responsibilities, and pooled risks and resources, with the rest of the Union. These are areas of common welfare. The most notable is social security – old-age pensions, benefits paid to people seeking work or those unable to do so, and allowances and

credits supporting children and families. Even in federal states, however, it is common (though not universal) for social protection of this kind to be a federal, rather than state or provincial, responsibility. This makes both economic and social sense: economic sense because one part of the country may be differently affected, or affected at different times, by economic change or shocks; social sense because providing people whose circumstances are the same with the same financial support wherever they are in the UK shows solidarity and mutual support. At present social protection is financed by UK-wide resources. Tax revenues are pooled and shared out on the basis of need to individuals (and thus indirectly, to different parts of the UK). This seems to us to be a *fundamental part of the Union* [emphasis added] . . . The risks, and the resources to deal with them, are shared. It has a very explicit expression in the form of National Insurance, which is linked to benefit entitlements. But it is also seen in pooling other taxation like income tax or VAT and even in the pooling of windfalls like taxes from oil revenues and other natural resources. (Calman 2009: 2.24–2.25)

Thus for welfare unionists the essence of union is a belief in maintaining the UK as the principal sharing community with UK benefits paid for out of UK taxes and allocated according to some measure of need. Such a position is perfectly compatible with enhanced devolution (as evidenced by Calman) but there are limits: it has no truck with those who advocate devolving the redistributive aspects of the welfare state. To do so would in the words of the Calman Commission 'break the bonds of common social citizenship' (Calman 2009: 3.207).

The logic of pooling risks among individuals and regions and across generations within the largest possible geographical area is widely recognised in the economic literature. Economic shocks tend to be asymmetric, affecting individuals and regions in different ways and at different times. So, in a state comprising several territories, if one part endures a period of economic hardship it can be supported if it can call on the resources of the other regions in addition to those at its own disposal. This can be seen, operating in both directions, in Scotland's history. As we saw at the beginning of this chapter, Scotland has in recent decades benefited from relatively high levels of welfare spending from the UK pool. But similarly oil revenues from what would be Scottish waters contributed very substantially to that UK pool during the 1980s. In a similar way different parts of the country have age structures which create different profiles of demand for pension payments over time, but will to some degree average out one with another.

The taxes used to pay for welfare are also volatile, and some more so than others. Chapter 7 shows how much revenue from North Sea oil can change from year to year. Recent experience has proven how vulnerable some funding streams can be in adverse economic circumstances: during the global financial crisis revenue from corporation tax and stamp duty collapsed. Welfare unionists point out that resource-pooling at the UK level provides UK citizens with the safety-valve of a broader and more versatile tax base to cope with such unpredictability.

It might however seem odd to emphasise social security as a means for expressing UK-wide social citizenship. Important though benefits are, it is the NHS which is considered the 'apotheosis of *nationalised* social citizenship' (Wincott 2006). If something as sacrosanct and popular as the NHS, which is considered for some the truest expression of Britishness (most recently demonstrated by Danny Boyle's opening ceremony at the Olympics), can be devolved, why shouldn't social security be devolved as well?

Of course this reflects the history of devolution: the administration of the NHS has always been decentralised in the UK. Although the UK has clearly been among the countries which seeks greater uniformity in living conditions via welfare, this has never been an explicit, still less a constitutional, requirement. It was considerations like these which led the Calman Commission, in championing a 'social union', not merely to argue in favour of retaining social security as a UK-wide function. They also argued that 'certain social rights . . . should also be substantially the same, even when it is best that they are separately run in Scotland' (Calman 2009: Executive Summary para. 20). In their final report they called on the Scottish Parliament and the UK Parliament to 'confirm that each agrees to the elements of the common social rights that make up the social union' such as a commitment that health and education be open to all free at the point of use. In other words Calman was suggesting some form of explicit, agreed, constraint on devolved (and UK) policy, analogous to what is seen in other federal systems, but conspicuously absent in the design of UK devolution policy. This has not however been taken forward: it was perhaps unlikely that governments with sharply differing constitutional views would agree to it.

The idea of common social citizenship has however recently been taken further by former Prime Minister Gordon Brown, in a series of speeches (see, e.g., www.bbc.co.uk/news/uk-scotland-26510735). He argues that the defining characteristic of the UK as a Union is that it provides for 'social justice between [its constituent] nations'. This is shown in common UK-wide state pensions and benefits, guaranteed from shared UK tax income, but also, he argues, in pooling of resources to support devolved services in each part of the UK so that what he calls 'covenanted rights' to free health care and schooling can also be guaranteed, irrespective of the tax income available to the devolved governments. This explicit welfare unionism, Brown argues, should be acknowledged as a principle of the UK's territorial constitution. These ideas were picked up in the Labour party's Devolution Commission discussed in the previous chapter.

Welfare nationalism

Welfare nationalists believe that the Scottish nation – and not the UK state – should be the main sharing community for welfare provision. Many believe that devolution has allowed Scots to pursue a more distinctly Scottish welfare approach with greater emphasis on universalism than that in England. Keating believes that this is evidence of a 'rescaling' of the territorial community at which citizens seek to express solidarity with one another (Keating 2011). On this reading, nations within the state are perceived as a better locus for guaranteeing social rights than the state as a whole. Indeed there is some evidence to suggest that Scottish support for devolution in the run-up to the 1997 referendum was based on a desire of Scots to insulate themselves from UK governments which did not share Scottish traditions of social solidarity (Henderson and McEwen 2005).

This of course is to assume that there exists a distinctive Scottish welfare model that reflects traditional Scottish – and by implication not British – values. Keating points to the emergence in Scotland of a distinct policy community that is more committed to traditional social democratic form of welfare provision than that pursued for England by various UK governments (Keating 2011). Similarly in Wales, the former First Minister Rhodri Morgan invoked the imagery of 'clear red water' to distinguish between the prevalence of traditional Labour values with the more pro-market policies of New Labour. For welfare nationalists, the point is to challenge the idea that social rights have to be the same across the state and to argue instead that they should differ where values differ. However, the apparent differences identified between political elites north and south of the border are not reflected at the popular level. Public attitudinal research suggests that the Scots and the English are not very different at all when it comes to support for means-testing, equality and redistribution (Curtice and Ormston 2011).

There is a similar pattern in Quebec in Canada of seeking to contract out from the social policy jurisdiction of a central government no longer seen as trusted to deliver traditional understandings of social rights. By contrast, in other places the perceived problem is not the centre, but other devolved regions, typically where economically stronger regions – e.g. Flanders, or Bavaria, or parts of northern Italy – resent 'their' tax revenues being transferred to other regions in the interests of guaranteeing common, state-wide social rights (Jeffery et al. 2010). In each case a smaller scale of 'sharing community' is presented as more in the interests of the devolved region than a state-wide one.

The 'insurance' argument suggests welfare is better protected and delivered at a larger territorial scale. But alternatively it can be argued it might make more sense for contribution rates and levels of benefits to be set in Scotland so they take account of local conditions, such as the cost of living (which they do not when set by the UK government for all UK citizens). It might also be sensible to link benefits with the current powers of the Scottish Parliament to maximise the effect of the policy levers it has at its disposal. For instance while the Scottish government is responsible for housing policy, it has no control over housing benefit. Without control of maternity and paternity benefits there are limits to the family policy it can enact. Moreover, there is a literature in political economy that suggests that small states may be better equipped to develop generous welfare than large ones (Katzenstein 1985; Garrett 1998).[9]

So they might – but it may come down to what they can afford. And this is the critical issue facing welfare nationalists. If the redistributive component of the welfare state were devolved, then, that means there would be no redistribution within the UK any more. Welfare spending would have to be covered by Scottish tax revenues alone (implying a significant amount of tax devolution). For Scotland this may just be possible (see Chapter 4), but for a country like Wales, which has a weak tax base, it would be impossible. Even in the case of Scotland it is at least possible that in some years it would struggle to meet the cost of its welfare bill. What happens then is a moot point: would Scotland have to make cuts? Or would the UK government step in to meet a shortfall? If the latter on what basis would the UK government justify such a transfer? This would, to a large extent, depend on whether under a model of devolution-max there would continue to be an attachment to a common UK citizenship, perhaps based on a common minimum level of social entitlement.

Welfare-unionism and welfare nationalism offer important, and polarising, perspectives on how to conceive social citizenship in a devolved UK, but do they reflect the views of the public?

Public attitudes

Looking at attitudinal data[10] we find support for both welfare unionists and welfare nationalists: there is evidence to suggest that Scots increasingly see Scotland as their 'sharing community': the community which they are most attached too, and which they believe should exercise responsibility for policies that shape that community (including social security). Yet, we also see the gravitational pull of Marshall: while Scots might want powers devolved to the Scottish Parliament, they do not support the idea of policies and benefits varying across the UK. Jeffery and the CANS teams term this the 'devolution paradox'.

As we saw in Chapter 4 there is, according to opinion poll data, an appetite for more devolution in Scotland. This applies to welfare also: as Table 5.3 shows, a majority in surveys support devolving taxation and social security. These data represent a direct challenge to welfare unionists who believe both should be retained as a UK-wide responsibility so as to insure individuals and communities against risks such as unemployment (Curtice and Ormston 2012).[11] Table 5.4 confirms that a majority of Scots would apply this to old-age pensions. According to this data, the only area that a majority of Scots believe should be the responsibility of the UK is defence and foreign affairs. As John Curtice and Rachel Ormston argue:

> So it appears that – whatever way the question is asked – there is majority support in Scotland for devolving responsibility for the bulk of the country's domestic affairs, including the key areas of taxes and benefits, to the devolved institutions. (Curtice and Ormston 2012)

On the other hand, it is less clear that Scots want this to lead – as it logically ought – to differences in policy outcomes. Tables 5.5 and 5.6 report on a broadly phrased question fielded across Great Britain, with variations in Wales and Scotland in 2003, showing that the English are most in favour of policy uniformity, but also that majorities in

Table 5.3 Which institution should make important decisions about . . .?

	Scottish Parliament	UK Government at Westminster	Local councils in Scotland	EU
	%	%	%	%
Health service	66	26	5	*
Schools	62	14	23	*
Welfare benefits	62	25	9	1
Defence and foreign affairs	31	63	1	3
Taxation	57	37	3	*

Source: Scottish Social Attitudes 2010

Table 5.4 Which institution should make important decisions about . . .?

	Scottish Parliament	UK Government at Westminster
2011	%	%
University fees	86	10
Basic income tax	68	29
Government old-age pensions	65	33

Source: British Social Attitudes

Table 5.5 Attitudes towards territorial policy variation in Britain 2003 (%)

	Should be the same in every part of Britain	Should be allowed to vary
England		
Standards for services such as health, schools, roads and police	66	33
Scotland		
Standards for services such as health, schools, roads and police	59	40
Level of unemployment benefit	56	42
University tuition fees	56	40
Wales		
Standards for services such as health, schools, roads and police	55	44
Level of unemployment benefit	57	41
University tuition fees	58	40
Cost of NHS prescriptions	63	37

Table 5.6 For or against variation?

The level of benefits for unemployed people should be . . .	2003 %	2010
. . . the same everywhere in the UK	56	55
. . . the Scottish Parliament should be allowed to increase or decrease these in Scotland	42	42
Sample size	*1,508*	*1,495*
University tuition fees should be . . .	**2003** %	**2010**
. . . the same everywhere in the UK	56	50
. . . the Scottish Parliament should be allowed to increase or decrease these in Scotland	40	47
Sample size	*1,508*	*1,495*
Level of taxes people pay should be . . .		**2010**
. . . the same everywhere in the UK		58
. . . the Scottish Parliament should be allowed to increase or decrease these in Scotland		39
Sample size		*1,495*
Old-age pensions should be . . .		**2010**
. . . the same everywhere in the UK		63
. . . the Scottish Parliament should be allowed to increase or decrease these in Scotland		35
Sample size		*1,495*

Wales and Scotland are too, even in areas like tuition fees (Scotland) and prescriptions (Wales) where different devolved policies have been introduced. This is the 'devolution paradox': citizens appear to want devolved institutions to have more powers; yet they appear also to be uncomfortable with territorial policy variation.

Of course the population are entirely entitled to give contradictory answers to pollsters, and indeed it would be surprising if they did not: these are snap responses to questions posed in a particular way, rather than considered views, formed after looking at the pros and cons of the options and the trade-offs they involve. The challenge for policy makers and political leaders is both to interpret and inform public opinion, rather than blindly follow poll findings, which are often contradictory. Do international comparisons offer any guidance?

International comparisons: welfare and nations

In making the argument for welfare unionism the Calman Commission drew attention to the fact that the argument for larger risk pools meant welfare was typically a national rather than a sub-national function. Indeed in almost all other federal states, even those in which considerable powers are devolved to the sub-state level, social security is typically the responsibility of the central government. Table 5.7 shows which level of government has legislative responsibility for various aspects of welfare provision in a number of federal states, with Scotland for comparison.

In most of these federations welfare is primarily a national, federal function, and in none is it solely operated at the sub-national level. In some cases, for example Germany, history shows a programme of gradual centralisation to provide universal and uniform benefits, even when implementation responsibilities fall on sub-national governments. If a country, such as the US, does not regard variation in the circumstances of individuals or families as unacceptable simply because they live in different states, then it has more scope to devolve aspects of welfare provision. By contrast, if there is a belief (or even a constitutional requirement, as in Germany) in harmonisation of living conditions across the national territory then nationally run welfare systems emerge. Even in the most decentralised of these countries however welfare is at most a shared responsibility, with responsibility for insurance-based systems of welfare, especially pensions, always discharged at the national level. In this sense, the present UK arrangements are therefore typical: social welfare is largely a national responsibility, though sometimes shared with states or provinces, as in Canada.

As we noted above, states provide welfare for their own citizens, and jealously guard this privilege, for example in the European Union context. This is partly because providing social welfare is not just a function of the state, but a way of binding it together. In Britain, after World War II the creation of universal welfare was very much a national project – as we have seen to harmonise provision across the country, but also to bind different social groups (not, at that time, so much nations within the UK) together in a common understanding of what it meant to be British. The provision of welfare has also been a way of nation building elsewhere – often self-consciously. In Germany, for example, in the late nineteenth century the welfare state developed by Bismarck was designed 'to provide momentum for the internal foundation of the Reich after [its] "territorial consolidation"' (Obinger 2005). More recently, in Canada, the Canada Health Act 1984 was designed to buttress a common Canadian citizenship across divergent provinces.

Table 5.7 Legislative responsibility for aspects of welfare in various federal countries and Scotland

	Australia	Austria	Canada	Germany	Switzerland	USA	Scotland
Old age, survivors and disability	Commonwealth	Federal	Shared	Federal	Federal	Federal	Reserved
Unemployment	Commonwealth	Federal	Federal	Federal	Federal	Shared	Reserved
Work injury	State	Federal	Provincial	Federal	Federal	State	Reserved
Family allowances	Commonwealth	Federal	Shared	Federal	Federal	Shared	Reserved
Social assistance	Commonwealth	Shared	Provincial	Federal	Cantonal	Shared	Reserved
Health	Commonwealth	Federal	Shared	Federal	Federal	Shared	Devolved

Source: Obinger et al. (2005) Table 1.6, extended

Table 5.8 Very attached 'region' and state, comparative (%)

	a) % 'region'	b) % state	A) – B)
Scotland	80	43	37
Wales	69	49	20
Catalonia	55	25	30
Brittany	65	49	16
Thuringia	57	42	15
Galicia	58	44	14
England	44	31	13
Bavaria	53	42	9
Alsace	60	60	0
Vienna	52	61	−9
Salzburg	52	64	−12
Upper Austria	51	62	−11
Lower Saxony	36	51	−15
Castilla la Mancha	33	52	−19
Ile de France	26	53	−27

Source: CANS 2009; FoES 2011

One author describes Canadian welfare as 'nation building in a federal welfare state' (Banting, in Obinger 2005).

So deciding on welfare is not just a practical, utilitarian calculation about risk pooling or resource sharing. It has an emotional dimension too. Belonging and sharing march together. We are more willing to pool resources with those with whom we have a common bond of identity or citizenship: but sharing risks and resources is one of the ways of creating that common bond. Nationalists, understandably from this perspective, will press for sharing resources and a community of solidarity at a purely Scottish level. For those who want to emphasise a continuing British identity or give it some effect, a pooled welfare system will be a powerful tool to demonstrate that this identity is real. Certainly Scottish identity has increased in salience in recent years, and more Scottish residents are likely to see themselves as more Scottish than British, than in the past. As Table 5.8 shows, Scots are more likely to prioritise their Scottish over their British sense of belonging than people in other regions of European countries.

Whether this feeling of identity should lead to changes in social welfare is the question. There might be different ways of sharing responsibility for welfare across the different levels of government. International experience suggests that most patterns are peculiar to the circumstances of different nations, and reflect how welfare services grew up. The only general point that can be made is that of the great scholar of federalism, Ron Watts, who pointed out the obvious: that the more homogenous society is the stronger the power of central government, and vice versa (Watts 2008). It may be that the UK is becoming a less homogenous society, and this is reflected in existing devolution, and could be reflected in more, perhaps some greater sharing of power for welfare. But any such scheme would have to be carefully constructed to be financially and operationally stable. It will be of little comfort to Scots, if welfare provision fails, to be told that it nevertheless reflects their Scottish identity. This suggests any changes like to be incremental rather than radical. Those who seek radical change in this area will no doubt argue for independence.

Notes

1. For an account of the development of the welfare state in Britain, see for example Fraser (2003).
2. This material develops themes from Jeffery, Lodge and Schmuecker (2010).
3. Paralleled by the National Heath Service (Scotland) Act 1948.
4. And between 1922 and 1972 Northern Ireland was governed by Stormont, a devolved parliament.
5. Somewhat anomalously, for historical reasons, social security was and still is devolved in Northern Ireland: but this is in name only – GB policies are always applied and financed by a transfer from the UK Exchequer.
6. A twist arising out of student funding added another layer. Because in some policy areas the EU prohibits member states from discriminating against EU citizens but not within member states it meant that while English students studying in Scotland would be charged tuition fees, Scottish students and non-English EU citizens were not. This double-whammy of a combined devolution and EU inequity provided grist to the mill of *Daily Mail* leader writers.
7. Scotland, Wales and Northern Ireland represent just 15% of the UK population, so it is rare for events there to catch the attention of the English.
8. We are grateful to Professor Daniel Wincott for prompting us to use the terms 'welfare unionists' and 'welfare nationalists'.
9. Though equally a strong theme in the literature that decentralising welfare tends to make it less generous overall (Obinger 2005).
10. The authors would like to thank a) Professor John Curtice and b) the CANS team at Edinburgh and Cardiff Universities for providing us with these data.
11. These findings are corroborated by IPSOS Mori who also found strong support among Scots in favour of devolving social security. Available at<http://www.futureofscotland.org/wpcontent/uploads/2012/06/Future-of-Scotland MORI-Poll-Briefing.pdf/>(last accessed 16 November 2012).

6

The Principles of Fiscal Federalism

IN EARLIER CHAPTERS we looked at tax sharing arrangements between Scotland and the rest of the UK. Such arrangements would be needed under either the Scotland Act 2012 – the default in the event of a No in 2014 – or some as yet undefined scheme for more devolution, on one or other assumption of how much of the present social union of the UK is retained. In the process, we have introduced concepts of fiscal gaps and equalisation. The purpose of this chapter is to pull these discussions into one place for reference. We aim to show how thinking systematically about fiscal federalism may help to clarify the difficult issues surrounding any scheme from the Scotland Act regime up to 'full fiscal autonomy' short of independence – however that fashionable but vague term might be defined.

The name 'fiscal federalism' is misleading. It is the study of fiscal – that is, tax and public-expenditure – transfers between two levels of government. The two levels could be in a federal system, as in Switzerland, or as 'devolution-max' might turn out to be for Scotland. But they need not be. There is equally a fiscal relationship between central and local government in unitary states such as England. The Calman regime for Scotland (Chapter 3), while not creating a federal state, would certainly involve fiscal transfers. Actually, so would Scottish independence on anything like the terms being suggested by the 2011 Scottish government, under which Scotland would still be a member of the EU, would use the pound sterling as its currency, and would seek agreements on sharing of financial regulation, defence and overseas spending with the rUK. Such arrangements would involve financial transfers to pay for common services. So an understanding of fiscal federalism will help us to understand the issues behind any of Scotland's possible choices.

Vertical fiscal imbalance

The key concepts to grasp are *vertical fiscal imbalance* (VFI) and *horizontal fiscal equalisation* (HFE). Vertical fiscal imbalance occurs when one level of government raises most of the tax and another level does most of the spending. Usually national government does most of the taxing and local or provincial government more spending than taxing. Table 6.1 shows the current situation for the UK compared with other relevant members of the OECD – the rich-country club that keeps comprehensive economic statistics on its member states.

We first calculated VFI [column VFI (1)] by averaging the difference between central revenue and central expenditure, and the difference between local revenue and local expenditure. In federal countries such as Canada, Switzerland or the US, 'local' includes the middle tier of government – provincial, cantonal, State, etc. The year 2009, the most recent available, was one in which every country spent more than it raised, so the two differences do not just mirror one another.

On this measure, the UK has only moderately high VFI. But this may be misleading, as countries where expenditure most exceeded tax receipts may on that measure appear to have an artificially low VFI. So we rely on a cruder measure, labelled VFI (2) in Table 6.1. This is simply the share of GDP accounted for by sub-national government expenditure minus the share of GDP accounted for by sub-national government receipts. In most countries, the central government does most of the taxing; in all countries, local governments do a fair proportion of the public spending. On this measure, the UK has one of the higher scores for VFI among OECD member states.

A country may have high VFI because local governments undertake a high proportion of public spending (such as Denmark) or because they have weak tax capacity (such as Mexico), or both. In this respect, the UK is closer to Mexico than to Denmark. Unless or until the Scotland Act 2012 comes into force, all UK taxes except two are collected centrally. The only two that are not are the two property taxes, council tax and business rates, and even there the UK and Scottish governments lean very heavily on local authorities to hold these taxes down. The old (pre-Calman) Scottish Variable Rate of income tax of 3 pence in the £ would have been counted as a local tax if it had ever been levied; but it never was.

Is VFI necessarily bad? One might say that the central government is usually the most efficient tax-collector. Things or people can move.

Table 6.1 Vertical fiscal imbalance, selected OECD countries 2009, as % of GDP

Country	Central revenue	Provincial/ local revenue	Central spending	Provincial/ local spending	VFI (1)	VFI (2)
Denmark	39.66	15.94	21.17	37.24	19.90	21.30
Netherlands	40.97	5.06	33.94	17.48	9.72	12.42
Belgium	40.34	7.91	34.39	19.94	8.99	12.03
Spain	22.69	12.16	23.35	22.62	4.90	10.46
United Kingdom	**36.36**	**4.20**	**37.36**	**14.49**	**4.65**	**10.29**
Mexico	20.15	2.04	12.18	11.34	8.63	**9.30**
Italy	38.61	8.07	35.76	16.18	5.48	**8.11**
Canada	17.48	21.06	15.13	28.92	5.10	**7.86**
Poland	30.42	6.74	29.98	14.42	4.06	**7.68**
Hungary	41.32	4.80	38.61	11.88	4.89	**7.08**
Finland	37.67	15.79	33.86	22.48	5.25	**6.69**
Sweden	33.62	20.60	28.96	26.22	5.14	**5.62**
Czech Republic	32.39	7.78	33.55	12.38	1.72	**4.60**
USA	15.96	15.02	22.57	19.61	−1.01	**4.59**
Austria	36.76	12.04	35.80	16.52	2.72	**4.48**
France	40.14	8.31	44.43	11.59	−0.50	**3.28**
Slovak Republic	29.52	4.08	34.37	7.15	−0.89	**3.07**
Switzerland	18.81	16.14	14.88	18.87	3.33	**2.73**
Germany	29.41	15.07	30.07	17.44	0.85	**2.37**

Source: OECD (2012) Section B, Tables 2 and 4; authors' calculations
Countries selected: all OECD member states at least as large as Scotland for which data exist, excluding Greece

Some can move more easily than others. People can move from one area to another. Rich people may have more than one house and can claim to live in whichever leads to them paying less tax. Factories cannot move easily, but companies can move their head offices very quickly if there are tax advantages in doing so. Online activities can move instantaneously. Of course they can move between countries: a factor that may depress the maximum the state can take in tax. But they can also move within countries. That is why it may be most efficient to collect taxes on personal and company income (such as, in the UK, income tax, national insurance contributions and corporation tax) at national level, wherever the money is spent.

The taxes that are best collected locally are taxes on stuff that doesn't move, such as land and unextracted oil. The Scottish government already controls three bad land taxes (Council Tax, Business Rates, and Stamp Duty Land Tax (SDLT)). It already has an opportunity to improve things and has taken a tentative step by proposing a Land and Buildings

Transaction Tax in place of SDLT (available at<http://www.scotland. gov.uk/Publications/2012/06/1301/3>, last accessed 21 March 2014). The Scotland Act offers it some more small tax bases that do not move.

Then there is the issue of expenditure taxes such as VAT and excise taxes. Many of the countries in Table 6.1 where local revenues are relatively high are large, or thinly-populated: people in these countries may be unwilling to move a long way in order to pay a little less tax. So a large country can allow, for instance, sales taxes to be set and collected locally, because not everyone would drive across a provincial boundary just to pay a few cents less on their purchases. For instance, the only conurbation in Canada that is on a provincial boundary is Ottawa (although several are close to the US boundary, which also imposes limitations on their freedom to tax). By contrast, if Scotland becomes independent, or gains control over such tax bases as VAT and excises (e.g. petrol, cigarette, and alcohol duty), then a huge retail shed will spring up alongside the A74 at either Gretna (if Scottish tax rates are lower) or Carlisle (if English rates are lower). If the relative rates fluctuate, there will be two hypermarkets; but at any one time, one of them will be derelict. This effect may be mitigated by the thinly populated Anglo-Scottish border. But some people *do* jump in their cars to travel 100 miles and save a few pence on petrol or alcohol.

Some people (for instance, Sharma 2011) do not like the term 'vertical fiscal imbalance', preferring the more neutral 'vertical fiscal gap'. They argue that a gap is inevitable, and therefore cannot be called bad, because personal and corporate income tax is better collected at national level, and property tax at local level. But VFI is a real problem. If one level of government does a lot of the taxing, and another does a lot of the spending, the incentives facing both of them are distorted. The taxing government, usually the upper tier, usually tries to put conditions on the money the lower tier spends, which defeats some of the point of having regional or local governments. This distortion has not arisen in the UK under the Barnett Formula, which does not attach strings to the substantial sums that it transfers from the UK taxpayer to the three devolved administrations. But the other side of the coin has the same feature in the UK as everywhere else: that the lower tier enjoys spending money it has not raised, which is always more fun than spending money it has had to raise itself.

The problem is more acute in the present UK than the OECD statistics in Table 6.1 reveal. None of the parliaments of Scotland, Wales, or Northern Ireland has any serious tax-raising powers. Wales and

Northern Ireland have none; Scotland has some but has not used them. But they all spend. Because the three together amount to only 15% of the UK, that does not show up as a separate effect in Table 6.1. But it is an acute problem, which the Calman proposals (Chapter 3) were designed to address. Devolution-max and independence would also make the Scottish Parliament fiscally responsible. All of Scotland's possible choices point in the same direction on this matter.

Horizontal fiscal equalisation

Unlike VFI, horizontal fiscal equalisation (HFE) is a perfectly normal, indeed desirable, feature of taxing and spending in every democracy. Rich people tend to cluster in certain areas, and poor people in others. These clusters can be self-reinforcing. Rich people tend to cluster along with other rich people, perhaps because they are good at supplying services for one another, or because the places where they live are good at providing Porsche dealerships or Michelin-starred restaurants. This very trend also creates its complement. Rich people living in places where most people are poor will want to move out. Poor people have to live somewhere; the places where other poor people live will have more affordable housing than you can get above a Porsche dealership or a Michelin restaurant.

All modern democracies have some concept of a social union (see Chapter 5). In the UK this is borne out by near-total support for the concept of the NHS as a universal service open to all, free at the point of access, and on approximately the same terms for all. When people are prompted to think about it, they also tend to say that welfare benefits such as state pensions or unemployment benefits should be paid at uniform rates throughout the country. Data on public attitudes were given in Chapter 5.

The other side of the coin is equally obvious. Rich places have more taxable capacity than poor places. The possible tax bases are either people, or enterprises, or property, or sales. All of these, including property, are worth more per head in places where rich people live than in places where poor people live. A possible exception, namely taxation of mineral rights, is probably not applicable in the UK except in relation to the taxation of oil revenues (Chapter 7).

It follows that every democracy must have transfers between rich people and poor people; and hence transfers between rich places and poor places. Some of these transfers occur automatically. Benefits such as state pensions and unemployment benefits go direct to individuals. But as these individuals live in places, each with a postcode, it is easy to calculate the flow of these transfers on a regional, or sub-national, level. The flow between regions is not a deliberate consequence. But it is part of the social union.

Other transfers are deliberately designed. Since the mid-1970s, funds for the NHS in England have been designed to flow so that the most money per head goes to the regions with the worst health – as measured by death and disease rates (mortality, morbidity, and life expectancy). This system was created by a medically-qualified health minister, David Owen, to replace systems based on inertia and bargaining power, which had ensured a healthy flow of NHS funds to healthy areas of England, including those served by London teaching hospitals (McLean 2005: 102–3).

The other main deliberately-designed transfer is formula funding for local government services. The most important of these, from the point of view of inter-regional fiscal equalisation, are education and personal social services. In these areas, there is a baroquely complicated formula (long known in England as Standard Spending Assessment) that attempts to take account of both the needs and the resources of each authority. 'Needs' are judged by things such as the age structure of the population – young people and old people need more expensive services from the state than do middle-aged people. 'Resources' are judged by the relative ability of councils to raise the revenue they need to spend, through council tax and business rates.

Different formulae are in place in England and Scotland. Very interesting results arise if you apply the Scottish formulae in England, or vice versa (King, Pashley and Ball 2004). The two sets of formulae produce very different allocations, suggesting that 'need' can be defined in incompatible ways, or that the process is captured by interest groups. Or you may use the English formulae to evaluate the relative need of Wales, as did the Holtham Commission. This body (the Independent Commission on Funding and Finance for Wales) was set up shortly after the Calman Commission, and the two commissions worked simultaneously, taking note of one another's findings as they went along. However, the remit of Holtham was narrower than Calman's: to

i) look at the pros and cons of the present formula-based approach to the distribution of public expenditure resources to the Welsh Assembly Government; and

ii) identify possible alternative funding mechanisms including the scope for the Welsh Assembly Government to have tax varying powers as well as greater powers to borrow (Holtham 2010: 3)

The Commission published a working paper in which it calculated how much block grant Wales and Scotland might get if they were treated as regions of England, and the English formulae for distributing health and local-government funds were applied to them:

A formula for calculating relative needs across the devolved administrations that combines simplicity with a high degree of completeness and is based on real world funding allocations by the UK government and the devolved administrations finds that Wales should receive some £115 for every £100 of funding spent on comparable activities in England. At present, Wales receives only £112 for such activities. For Scotland and Northern Ireland, the figures generated by the formula are £105 and £121 respectively, although these estimates would need refinement to take account of different devolved responsibilities.

We propose a straightforward way of aligning relative funding with relative need in the devolved administrations over time. An assessment of the relative needs of each devolved administration would be undertaken at the beginning of each spending review period, using the simple formula. Changes to the block grant would be calculated as at present, with two key amendments:

- Firstly, a multiplicative needs adjustment term would be added to the current funding formula that would align changes in relative funding with relative need.
- In addition, a transition mechanism would be applied to close the funding gap between current relative funding and current relative need in a phased manner. We set out a straightforward mechanism that would achieve this objective. (Holtham 2009: 1)

The model for this exercise was probably the Commonwealth Grants Commission of Australia, which uses similar formulae, which it hopes are game-proof, to reduce inequality across Australia by equalising the amounts available in each State to spend on services for any given citizen in a similar position to an equivalent citizen in another State (the Australian regime is described in McLean 2005: Chapter 9).

However, an Australian regime cannot now be applied across the

UK, because the Calman Report and hence the Scotland Act rejected an Australian egalitarian transfer regime in favour of an essentially Canadian regime of what the Canadians call 'vacating tax points' (explained later in this chapter). The focus of this chapter, therefore, is to establish how much HFE there is in the UK at present, and how much there might be if Scotland takes either the Calman or the devolution-max road. Table 6.2 gives the latest data available at the time of writing.

Table 6.2 updates tables which have been published for several past years, using the same main series of official statistics known as Public Expenditure Statistical Analyses (PESA) (See HM Treasury 2012; McLean and McMillan 2003; McLean 2005: Table 8.2; McLean, Lodge, and Schmuecker 2009. An explanation of how PESA works and how it was improved following our investigation in 2003 is in McLean 2005). They show a consistent pattern of substantial, but declining, advantage for Scotland. The table works as follows. The first column of numbers shows the identifiable public spending per head for the four countries of the UK. Some public expenditure is on things such as repayment of debt interest and national defence, which can only be deemed to be equally for the benefit of all citizens. Other public expenditure takes the form of either transfer payments (such as pensions) or expenditure on services (such as schools or transport subsidies) which can be identified as being for the benefit of people in a particular part of the country.

So, the identifiable spending per head is highest in Northern Ireland, followed by Scotland, Wales, and England. The numbers are indexed in the next column to an average of 100 for the UK. Thus identifiable spending per head in Scotland is 114: in other words, it is 14% higher per head than the UK average identifiable spending.

Nobody would expect the index number to be 100 for all four countries. Some are richer than others, and HFE, whether automatic or intentional, should equalise away some of that difference by providing for higher spending per head in the poor areas. The other side of that equalisation would be shown if the yield of taxes per head in the four countries were known. For the English regions, Northern Ireland and Wales, unfortunately, it is not reliably known; we deal with the comparisons on the tax side between Scotland and the rUK in a moment.

Table 6.2 next looks at the income per head in each of the four countries of the UK. The first measure shown is the main one used by the Office for National Statistics (ONS). This is called Gross Value Added, or GVA. To everybody other than a national statistics aficionado it may

Table 6.2 Identifiable public expenditure per head (2010–11) and gross value added per head, household income, countries of the UK (2010)

	Pub. exp. per head, £	Pub. exp. per head, index (UK = 100)	GVA per head, £	GVA per head, index (UK = 100)	Household income	Household income index (UK = 100)
England	8,634	97	20,974	102	15,931	101
Scotland	10,105	114	20,220	99	15,342	96
Wales	10,017	113	15,145	74	13,783	88
Northern Ireland	10,668	120	15,651	76	13,554	86

Source: Columns 2 and 3: HM Treasury 2012 for financial year 2010–11;
Columns 4 and 5: Office for National Statistics data for calendar year 2010
All data are National Statistics

be treated as the same thing as the more familiar GDP (Gross Domestic Product). Under either label, it is the income arising from economic activity in each part of the UK. An alternative measure is household income, shown in the next column; it includes transfers into the area. We can readily see that the countries of the UK comprise two relatively rich ones: England and Scotland, with a GVA per head of over £20,000 in the sample year of 2010; and two relatively poor ones: Wales and Northern Ireland, each with a GVA per head of about £15,000 in the sample year. The fourth column again indexes these numbers to a UK average of 100. This shows that Scotland (which in these calculations does not include the Scottish part of the North Sea – see below and Chapter 7) is very close to an average part of the UK, so one might expect it to be neither a donor nor a recipient of HFE, in aggregate.

Most people would expect that public spending (supported by HFE) should be higher in poorer areas, and much government spending is indeed directly to relieve poverty: so we do a thought experiment: what if all spending were to relieve poverty (and hence deliver HFE between persons and between regions)? Then we would expect public spending per head to be an exact mirror reflection of GVA per head or income. Where one was above average, the other would be below average. But that is not what the table shows: Scotland is on the UK average for wealth, but spending is not: identifiable public spending per head in Scotland is 14% higher than the UK average. Higher than Wales, which is much poorer, though not as high as Northern Ireland.

Of course GVA or household income do not make good measures of spending need, for all sorts of reasons. Spending is driven by the factors like population structure and income distribution that are included in the distribution formulae we mentioned above: perhaps this is behind the high spending figures in the table? Figure 6.1, taken from a House of Lords study (House of Lords, 2009), shows how Scotland compares with the other countries in the UK on some common measures of need: on some, it is lower than the UK average and on some higher. The Holtham Commission reached a similar conclusion by a different route, applying English distribution formulae to Scottish and Welsh data. Whatever is driving Scottish spending, it does not seem to be HFE within the UK.

Thus HFE, on the expenditure side, is more limited among the four countries of the UK than one might have expected. But the reason is clear. Although money spent in Scotland directly by the UK government – on the non-devolved social security system – is allocated

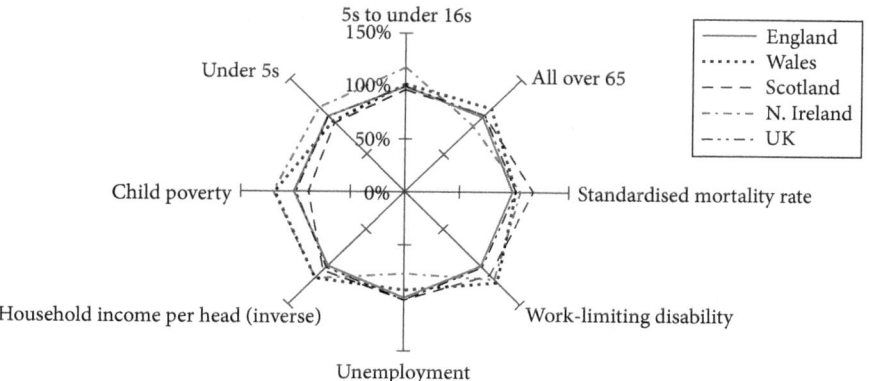

Figure 6.1 Measures contributing to relative need

Source: House of Lords Select Committee on the Barnett Formula, 2009, Chapter 7, Diagram 2

according to need, the transfer to the Scottish government under the Barnett Formula is not. It is population-based, and reduces Scotland's historic advantage per head (see Chapter 8) only very slowly.

There is a great deal of HFE in the UK that is not captured by these figures. That is equalisation within each country. If the exercise of Table 6.2 is repeated for the regions of England, it shows that London does unaccountably well, and the midland and northern regions do unaccountably badly. Likewise, in Scotland, there are notorious pockets of poverty, ill-health, and lowered life expectancy, just as there are pockets of great affluence. Some of this is mitigated by HFE within Scotland. This will continue, to the extent chosen by the Scottish government, whatever choice the people make in the forthcoming referendum. But that there are devastating pockets of poverty and deprivation in Glasgow and elsewhere does not remove the fact that, taking Scotland as a whole, fiscal transfers must largely arise from history or other factors, rather than from poverty. Since Scotland is not unusually poor, poverty cannot be driving any excess of transfers to Scotland.

The picture of HFE is incomplete unless data are available on the tax as well as the expenditure side. As some taxes including the biggest one, income tax, are progressive, there would be redistribution even if all spending programmes were flat-rate. (A tax is 'progressive' if a richer taxpayer pays more on the last taxable pound than a poorer taxpayer.) One set of official statistics, *Government Expenditure and*

Revenue in Scotland (*GERS*), published annually by the Scottish government, attempts to compare tax paid per head in Scotland with public expenditure per head in Scotland. These are sensitive numbers, which politicians will always try to manipulate and spin. Fortunately, *GERS* is protected from partisan spin by its status as National Statistics. The phrase National Statistics, in capitals, is a warranty that the statistics in question are produced by neutral stat-isticians and are immune from political interference. Thus although there have been some technical criticisms of the way the numbers are collated (and there would be, however they were collated), we take the *GERS* numbers as as authoritative as they can be given their inherent limitations.

Nevertheless, they are not as easy to integrate with other official statistics as one might like. Although, on the expenditure side, *GERS* is integrated with PESA, and on the tax side with the Budget Red Book produced annually by HM Treasury, *GERS* compares Scotland with an entity, 'Rest of the UK', referred to throughout this book as rUK, which does not (yet) exist for the purposes of other official statistics. Therefore, producing the data in Table 6.3a, which are drawn from three official statistical sources, required some manipulation to get it into the form shown. For the avoidance of doubt, the manipulation is purely arithmetic and done for the sole purpose of deriving robust rUK numbers.

The first column of figures in Table 6.3a is derived from the 2010–11 edition of *GERS*, but for consistency with the other tables in this chapter we use the data for financial year 2009–10. It divides the UK's tax receipts for the year into three territories: Scotland, rUK, and something called 'Extra Regio'. (Some of us have been complain-ing for years that HM Treasury's Latin is not as good as its macro-economic management: we think it should be 'Extra Regionem'). Extra Regio means offshore, mostly in the North Sea. Its murky origins are explored in Chapter 7. Tax receipts from offshore economic activity amounted to almost £6.5bn in 2009–10, though this is a sum that varies massively from year to year, again for which see Chapter 7. Whether Scotland 'subsidises' or 'is subsidised by' rUK is a hotly contested question, which we do not answer except to say that it depends on the assumptions you make. Table 6.3a works out the answers for 2009–10 according to the two main scenarios offered by *GERS*.

The second column of Table 6.3a is simply the 2010 population, to the nearest thousand, of Scotland and the rUK. As this is an estimated

Table 6.3a Tax receipts and total managed expenditure per head 2012–13: Scotland, rest of the UK and Extra Regio

	Tax receipts £m	Population, 000s	Tax receipts per head excluding Extra Regio, £	Tax receipts per head, assigning Extra Regio per head, £	Tax receipts per head, assigning Extra Regio by geographical share, £	Total Expenditure per head, £	Revenue shortfall per head, assigning Extra Regio per head, £	Revenue shortfall per head, assigning Extra Regio by geographical share, £
Scotland	47,566	5,314	8,951	9,055	10,001	12,265	3,210	2,264
rUK	532,727	58,391	9,123	9,228	9,141	10,883	1,655	1,741
Extra Regio	6,632							
	586,925	63,705						

Source: GERS; PESA; Office for National Statistics

Table 6.3b Breakdowns of Extra Regio

	By population share, £m	By population share per head, £	By geographical share per head
Scotland	553	104.10	1,050.24
rUK	6,079	104.10	18.00

number from the year before a census, the official source (ONS) does not give a more exact number. Column 3 is *GERS*'s estimate of tax receipts from Scotland and the rest of the UK, divided by the population numbers in order to get tax receipts per head. Consistently with Table 6.2, the Scottish figure is just below the rUK figure. This is what one would expect given the intense concentration of top earners in London and the south-east of England, which swamps the lower tax capacity of northern England, Wales, and Northern Ireland. *GERS* then offers two ways of treating North Sea oil revenue. One is to assign it on an equal per head basis to all UK taxpayers, in which case tax receipts per head throughout the UK rise by the same amount – just over £100 in 2009–10 (Table 6.3b). The other, which needless to say is the method the Scottish government prefers, is to assign to Scotland the proportion of tax arising from economic activity that is held to be in Scottish waters. For 2009–10, *GERS* calculates this fraction as 91.4%. This works out at £1136.11 for the given tax year (Table 6.3b), bringing total tax receipts per head on Scotland to £9,162.92, about £1,000 ahead of receipts per head for rUK.

Next, we have to work out the deficit for the year. The year in question was at the depth of the financial crash involving, among others, Scotland's two largest banks, so it is no surprise that there was a substantial deficit per head in both Scotland and rUK. To quantify it, we need, not Total Identifiable Expenditure, the number reported in Table 6.2, but another Treasury number called Total Managed Expenditure (TME). The main difference between these two is that the latter includes expenditure on such things as debt interest, national defence, and overseas representation. These are, in economists' language, public goods. This is not a value judgement. We take no view on whether the UK spends too much or too little or the right amount on defence and overseas services (on debt interest, it has no choice). 'Public good' is just a technical term meaning something which, if provided to anybody, is necessarily provided to everybody. Whatever the benefits of having an army are, they can only be assigned on an equal per head basis to everybody. (This is a different question to one that is often raised, but is much less relevant to this book, namely, where in the UK does the money go, that is spent domestically on defence procurement and housing troops?).

TME per head in Scotland in 2009–10 was just below £12,000, considerably higher than in rUK, as Table 6.2 already led us to expect. The final two columns of Table 6.3a calculate the deficit for the year on each of the two *GERS* scenarios on how oil revenue might be assigned. The table shows that in the year in question, Scotland had a bigger deficit per head than rUK on either assumption about the allocation of North Sea revenue; naturally, however, the gap is narrower on the 'geographical share' scenario.

In summary, Tables 6.2 and 6.3 tell us that there is not very much HFE between Scotland and rUK. This is especially true if oil revenue is assigned to the Scottish government. To a very rough approximation, the North Sea revenue that would accrue to Scotland under a 'geographical share' deal equals the amount transferred under the Barnett Formula. Cancel both of these out, and the degree of HFE does not change much.

However, some caveats remain. Under 'full fiscal autonomy', whatever that is held to mean, Scotland must pay a substantial sum to the UK for common services (foreign, defence, and debt interest). And, while oil revenue might have made up for the withdrawal of the Barnett grant in 2009–10, it will not do so in future years as receipts decline. Therefore an equalisation formula is needed. The Calman Commission did not undertake a needs-based assessment, for the unspoken reason that, however Scotland's needs were calculated, a needs-based grant would be much smaller than a Barnett grant. The Holtham Commission's and our (Table 6.3) calculations confirm this. If Scotland remains in the UK, and there remains a block grant, it will presumably be calculated on a 'resources' basis, as in Canada, which we explore in the next section. The numbers suggest that getting VFI right is a more significant problem than getting HFE right. If Scotland remains in the UK and oil revenue is not assigned, then a needs-based block grant may succeed Barnett (and HFE remains an issue). If Scotland remains in the UK and the oil revenue is assigned, HFE disappears as an issue. If Scotland becomes an independent state, then neither HFE nor VFI with the rest of the UK has any meaning.

Some first principles

The professional discussion of fiscal federalism goes back to those great Scots David Hume and Adam Smith, who first recognised the problem of public goods. In Book V of *The Wealth of Nations* (1776) Smith discusses how to pay for canals and highways, shrewdly noting that it is easier to induce private contractors to keep canals in repair than roads, because once a canal starts to leak, the proprietors lose their income, whereas roads can deteriorate but the toll-keepers still get their money.

By the mid twentieth century, the conventional wisdom in economics was that 'no "market type" solution exists to determine the level of expenditures on public goods' (Tiebout 1956: 416). The problems identified by Smith had been formalised by numerous other economists. Consider, the analysis ran, any of the public goods that might be supplied by a subnational government, such as street lamps or a public park. People cannot be stopped from taking a 'free ride' on any of these, or if they can it is expensive. (For instance, at least a few years ago, the city of Palo Alto, California, maintained a city park in the neighbouring mountains, but kept a full-time guard at the entrance who allowed only parties who could show evidence of residence in Palo Alto to enter.) Therefore a government with compulsory tax-and-spend powers is needed. In a famous paper, Charles M. Tiebout (1956) proposed a rival model. On a set of highly restrictive assumptions, which demand that consumer-citizens can move anywhere at zero cost, and that there are many available local governments to choose from, Tiebout concludes that citizens would vote with their feet for their optimum mixture of taxing and spending, and each local government would supply exactly those services that its citizens wanted, eliminating the free-rider problem.

Tiebout himself saw the model as a piece of pure theory, but some of his (over-enthusiastic) followers have hoped or expected it to be borne out in real life. There has been a bit of Tieboutian loose talk in Scotland, and also in Northern Ireland, by people who assume that they could cut their taxes (whether in or out of the UK) in order to bring in mobile people or capital. That talk lacks a budget constraint. The numbers in this chapter show that, with oil revenues at their 2009–10 level, an independent Scotland would have either to raise taxes or cut services, or both.

However, Tiebout's basic insight is valuable. One of the advantages of all three schemes on offer, or possibly on offer, is that they all allow Scots to make a Tieboutian choice between spending more (and having to raise it in tax) and taxing less (but having to cut services). How might this play out in the three main scenarios?

If Scotland becomes independent within the EU, its tax-and-spend choices will not be unconstrained. As discussed elsewhere in this book, the EU would be in a position to insist on conditions for recognition of its newest member state: These might include membership of the Euro zone at some point, and, probably more important, commitment to the Maastricht criteria – or whatever the criteria would be on the day of accession – that set limits to governments' annual deficits and accumulated debts. Were Scotland to become independent tomorrow it would not satisfy the Maastricht deficit criterion, although nor would most existing member states. Whether or not it satisfied the debt criterion would depend on the negotiations between Scotland and rUK on the division of liability for the UK's national debt at the time of the dissolution of the UK.

Under devolution-max or Calman-plus, the vital thing is to ensure that the Scottish Parliament's *marginal* taxing decision is aligned with its marginal spending decision. The relationship with the UK must be designed in such a way that it is always up to the Scottish, not the UK, Parliament to decide whether to spend a pound more on the services it controls, or to reduce the burden of tax by a pound. This implies that transfers of spending powers and of taxing powers must march hand in hand.

'Devolution-max' implies for sure transferring the biggest tax that is not devolved under Calman, namely national insurance contributions (both employer and employee). At the same time it implies transfer of social protection to the Scottish Parliament. The implications of this for the social union are discussed in Chapter 5. The other big tax, VAT, is more problematic. Not only does the Gretna hypermarket issue arise, but

> the European Commission clearly see regional variations as disruptive to the objectives of a single market, whilst also rejecting the application for a number of regional derogations on the basis they would constitute State Aid. (Calman 2009: para. 3.20)

If Scotland becomes an independent EU member state, it can levy any VAT rate, so long as it observes the EU minimum of 15%, and can decide whether to extend VAT to any of the sales that are lower- or zero-rated in the UK, such as energy, food and children's clothes. Within the UK, it cannot do either. It must accept both the rate and base decided by the UK government. VAT revenue from Scotland may (and under devolution-max should) be assigned to the Scottish Parliament, but it cannot use the VAT rate or base as a policy tool.

The next biggest tax is corporation tax. As noted, there has been heavy pressure to devolve this from politicians in Northern Ireland, who are understandably aggrieved by the low corporation tax rate in the Republic of Ireland. But, unless carefully designed, any devolution of Corporation Tax would simply lead companies to set up shell HQs in the lowest-tax jurisdiction. The whole UK would lose out, even though the lowest tax part of the UK might gain. This issue came sharply into focus with the interrogation of executives from Amazon, Starbucks, and Google by the Public Accounts Committee of the House of Commons in November 2012. The Committee wanted to know why these three companies paid little or no corporation tax in the UK. They found the executives' answers highly unsatisfactory (http://www.publications.parliament.uk/pa/cm201213/cmselect/cmpubacc/716/716.pdf, accessed 26 March 2014). This suffices to show that devolution of corporation tax to Scotland is just about the worst idea on the current policy agenda.

The Scottish Parliament could do inventive things with other, smaller taxes. It already controls property tax, but showed no interest in experimenting until it acquired responsibility for Stamp Duty Land Tax under Calman. The range of possibilities, and strategies to deal with HFE and VFI, may be illustrated by a quick survey of fiscal federalism in Canada.

Some Canadian examples

The leading scholar on fiscal federalism, Wallace Oates, follows Tiebout (to some degree) when he says:

> Decentralized levels of government have their raison d'être in the provision of goods and services whose consumption is limited to their own jurisdictions. By tailoring outputs of such goods and services to the particular preferences and circumstances of their constituencies, decentralized provision increases economic welfare above that which results from the more uniform levels of such services that are likely under national provision. (Oates 1999: 1121–2)

Canada is a possible model for devolution-max or the implementation of Calman or Calman-plus. The two leading experts on fiscal federalism in Canada, Robin Boadway and François Vaillancourt, were both advisers to the Calman Commission and its report accordingly carries a Canadian stamp. But there may equally be Canadian lessons for the other constitutional options. Much fuller (though now somewhat out-of-date) descriptions of fiscal federalism in Canada may be found in Boadway and Watts (2000) and McLean (2005: Chapter 10).

Canada is the second-largest country, by area, in the world. It is normally regarded as comprising five regions:

- The Atlantic region (Newfoundland, Prince Edward Island, Nova Scotia and New Brunswick: collectively known as the Maritime provinces)
- The central region (Quebec and Ontario)
- The prairies (Manitoba, Saskatchewan, Alberta)
- The Pacific coastal region (British Columbia)
- The sparsely inhabited north

Most of the population inhabit a narrow strip relatively close to the US border. It is hard to imagine Canada being governed in any other way than as a federation. The provinces vary enormously in population, area, and GDP per head. Table 6.4 contains basic details.

The two largest provinces, Ontario and Quebec, contain more than half of Canada's population between them. The four small Atlantic provinces (and the three northern territories) together contain fewer people than each of the four largest provinces. The three territories are vast in extent but tiny in population (about 100,000 in all three put together), so they are excluded from Table 6.4 for simplicity. The range of GDP per head among the ten provinces is greater than among the four countries of the UK (although smaller than the range if England is broken down into its nine standard regions, with London being more out of line than Alberta).

Comparing Table 6.4 with data collected from the same sources for 2003–4 (McLean 2005 Tables 10.1 and 10.5), we can see that two provinces – Newfoundland and Saskatchewan – have moved rapidly up the table in recent years, in both cases because of natural resources. This contrasts with the very stable relative position of the four countries of the UK.

Table 6.4 Canadian federalism: some basic numbers

	Population 2011, 000	GDP per head 2008, C\$	% of average	Federal support per head 2011–12, C\$	Equalisation funding 2011–12?
Newfoundland	515	38,181	96.8	2,293	N
Prince Edward Island	140	30,003	76.1	3,418	Y
Nova Scotia	922	30,942	78.5	2,827	Y
New Brunswick	751	30,939	78.5	3,322	Y
Quebec	7,903	34,521	87.6	2,187	Y
Ontario	12,852	40,677	103.2	1,325	Y
Manitoba	1,208	35,108	89.1	2,715	Y
Saskatchewan	1,033	40,889	103.7	1,175	N
Alberta	3,645	52,814	134.0	922	N
British Columbia	4,400	37,412	94.9	1,183	N
CANADA	33,477	39,425	100.0	1,698	

Source: Statistics Canada; Finance Canada, websites, various years
Note: Data for Territories not shown

Canada has an elaborate HFE programme. As in other federations, this programme aims to compensate for the lower tax capacity of the poorer provinces: in the language of s. 36 of the Constitution, to make 'equalization payments to ensure that provincial governments have sufficient revenues to provide reasonably comparable levels of public services at reasonably comparable levels of taxation'. Note that this is equalisation for unequal resources only: Canada does not attempt to equalise for differential needs, or for the cost of providing public services in the ten provinces. (It does, however, make a needs-based grant to each of the three territories.) To this extent, Canada's HFE arrangements are much more restricted than Australia's, which are perhaps the most elaborate and egalitarian in the world on the needs side. On the resources side, however, Canada's procedures are elaborate and distinctive.

Canada makes three main transfers from Ottawa to the provinces. Two of these are conditional, and are labelled CHT/CST (Canada Health Transfers and Social Transfers). These transfers reflect the fact that Canadians see health as a consistently important political issue for them; that there seems to be a cross-Canada commitment to nationally uniform (or at least comparable) standards and a commitment to uniform rights for all Canadians. Health and social services (which in Canada include higher education) are provincial responsibilities, and the federal transfer to the provinces requires the provinces to adhere to the 'five principles of the Canada Health Act'. These principles are:

1. Public administration (health care insurance plans to be administered and operated on a non-profit basis by a public authority);
2. Comprehensiveness (of provincial health care insurance plans);
3. Universality (all residents of a province or territory to be entitled to medically necessary health care services);
4. Portability (of cover for all Canadians anywhere in Canada); and
5. Accessibility (all Canadians to have access to insured health care services, without any barriers – particularly financial barriers).

These principles are a Canadian expression of the concept of a social union. All provinces, even rich Alberta and culturally distinct Quebec, receive CHT and CST transfers. Some of these transfers are, in Canadian terminology, transfers of tax points on personal and corporate income tax in 1977: that is, the withdrawal of the federal government from some of its capacity to tax personal and corporate incomes, allowing the provinces to fill the gap. Vacation of tax points reduced VFI and helped ensure that provincial governments matched the last dollar in spending against the last dollar in taxing. This idea substantially influenced the Calman Commission and helped to shape its main recommendation. The federal government and the provinces argue about whether or not the federal government should count this vacation of tax points every year when it accounts for the CHT and CHT payments to each province. Non-Canadians do not need to get into that argument.

The third component of Canadian federal-provincial transfers is equalisation. Unlike Australia, Canada equalises for resources only, not for both resources and needs. This means that it considers prov-inces' tax-raising capacity, but not either relative needs for provincial services nor relative costs of providing them. The federal Department of Finance examines each tax base, estimates the average per capita yield of the tax, and compensates those provinces where the per capita yield is below average. It does not explicitly withdraw funding from provinces where the per capita yield is above average (although, since money is fungible, there must be an implicit withdrawal from them). Unlike the Commonwealth Grants Commission in Australia, it does not look either at indicators of need (such as age structure, or population sparsity) or at relative costs of providing public services.

On the expenditure side, Canada has relatively few direct federal employees. Only the post office and the Royal Canadian Mounted Police (who supply police services under contract to some provinces) employ substantial numbers. There is no unified public sector pay bargaining in Canada. Each province negotiates its own pay arrangements with its employees. Federal pay rates are equal throughout Canada, but that has limited knock-on effects given that, typically, federal and provincial employees are in different trade unions (unlike in the UK, where national wage bargaining is still the norm). Consequently, provincial pay rates and hence the cost of delivering public services are lower in poor provinces than in rich ones. This seems to be one reason for the surprisingly small role of 'needs' claims in Canadian intergovernmentalism. With the UK government thinking aloud in the 2012 Budget about differential public-sector pay, and perhaps considering lowering it in low-wage areas, this could provide an interesting contrast with Canada.

In contrast to both Australia and the UK, the Canadian evidence on the cost of public services does not always suggest a heavy weighting for sparsity of settlement (except in the special case of the territories). All provinces except Prince Edward Island have sparsely populated hinterlands. It is open to a province to reduce the cost of public services to remote areas by encouraging migration within the province, as might happen anyhow for economic reasons (e.g. the migration of Newfoundlanders from 'outports' to the Avalon peninsula around St. John's). Because provincial governments control their own wage bills, these are lower in low-GDP than in high-GDP provinces. So are accommodation costs.

Lessons for Scotland

When the Calman Commission was taking evidence, it heard both from the chair of the Commonwealth Grants Commission and from Professor François Vaillancourt, an expert on Canadian fiscal federalism (Commission on Scottish Devolution 2008). As noted above, another such expert, Robin Boadway, was a member of the Commission's Independent Expert Group on fiscal issues. It was therefore exposed to both the Canadian and the Australian approach to equalisation. The Canadian approach, to simplify, is to address VFI by vacating tax points and to address HFE up to a point, by equalising for tax capacity, but not for needs or for cost of providing public services. The Australian approach, again to simplify, is to equalise for both needs and resources, but to do so in a way that as far as possible is immune to gaming and strategic plays by the States. Calman opted for a more Canadian than Australian approach. This was predictable and well advised. If the UK remains in existence but moves from the Barnett arrangements to a needs-based one, the block grant to Scotland would surely fall sharply.

But choices have consequences. If, under Calman or devolution-max, Scotland moves to a regime more like Canada's, some Canadian consequences may follow. One predictable one would be the decoupling of public-sector wages and conditions from those in England. If the Scottish Parliament has both the marginal power to tax and the marginal power to spend, it will be under pressure to exit from UK-wide arrangements and make its own. This may surprise some readers; but it is a consequence of fiscal autonomy. Needless to say, it is also a consequence of a vote for independence.

Another consequence is that Scotland and the UK will both have to look carefully at tax-collection arrangements to make sure that the cost, both to taxpayers and to governments, does not shoot up. In Canada, compliance costs are particularly high in Quebec (Commission on Scottish Devolution 2009) as, for political reasons, successive provincial governments have been at best unwilling partners in federal tax collection.

Under any arrangement short of independence, the UK seems certain to become more like Canada than it already is. Given the strong cultural links between the UK (notably Scotland) and Canada, this should be palatable, like buttered scones for tea.

7
Oil

BUT FOR NORTH SEA OIL, Scotland would probably not now be facing the choices it is. Oil fuelled the SNP's second wave of popularity in the early 1970s; helped it to its peak of Westminster seats in the October 1974 General Election; and set in motion the changes that (despite an 18-year stasis from 1979 to 1997) have put today's constitutional options on the table. And of course oil revenues are still important for Scotland's fiscal position today. An independent Scotland would/will be considerably better off with access to North Sea oil than it would have been without (see the chapters in Mackay 2011, especially Cuthbert 2011). However, this chapter will also show that there are two big problems with Scotland's oil today. The first is that, when oil revenues really did form a significant proportion of the UK's tax take, no sovereign wealth fund was created, but the oil revenue was used to support current spending. A sovereign wealth fund is a state-owned fund that (in countries such as Kuwait and Norway) invests the tax receipts from natural resource taxation. One of its purposes is to supply a stream of revenue that will be available when a natural resource such as oil is exhausted. The second is that future oil revenue is inevitably decreasing and will be significantly reduced by the oil companies' right to offset their decommissioning costs against their tax liability.

Oil and the first triumph of the SNP

The first wave of electoral success for the SNP crested with Winifred Ewing's sensational by-election victory at Hamilton in 1967. It probably represented Labour Scotland's disenchantment with its Labour government. The option of voting for the official opposition, the Conservatives, was apparently closed off for many Scots by their image as a southern and lairds' party (Conservative archives CCO 180/29/1/2, 4, quoted by McLean and McMillan 2009: 21). The SNP topped the local government poll in 1968 (McLean and McMillan

2009: 18). The wave receded in 1970. Mrs Ewing lost her seat, although Donald Stewart made the SNP's first General Election gain in the Western Isles. However, soon after the 1970 General Election, the SNP found its winning slogan: *It's Scotland's Oil.* Possibly the most effective poster in the series had a haggard-looking elderly lady on a gable-end-sized poster, with the full caption reading *It's Scotland's Oil: so why do 5,000 people in Scotland a year die from hypothermia?* (McLean and McMillan 2005: 161). The campaign coincided with the quadrupling of the oil price in the wake of the Arab–Israeli war of 1973. It helped the SNP to win seven seats (out of the then 71) in the Commons in the General Election of February 1974. Incoming Labour Prime Minister Harold Wilson, who had previously arranged for the issue to be batted into the long grass of a Royal Commission, realised that the threat to Labour's hegemony in the whole UK was serious. He forced the unwilling Labour Party in Scotland to reverse its previous anti-devolution stance (no devolution in the internal workings of the Labour Party in those days: for an account of the Dalintober Street coup of 1974 see McLean and McMillan 2005: 162). In the October 1974 General Election the SNP made a further advance, to 11 Westminster seats, and 30% of the Scottish vote. The electoral system frustrated it, and saved the unionist parties for the time being, as the Conservatives won more seats in Scotland on fewer votes than the SNP. But all parties were forced to think about devolution, and indeed independence. The Wilson (later Callaghan) government embarked on the ill-fated Scotland and Wales Bill that was to be the occasion of bringing it down in 1979. Tam Dalyell started asking the West Lothian Question (Dalyell 1977).

'It's Scotland's Oil' is a great slogan. The SNP was in no position, in the Parliament of 1974–9, to turn it into a policy. But debate began on three issues which remain important to Scotland's current choices:

- Is it Scotland's oil?
- If it is, on what terms would (or should) the UK government surrender control of the tax receipts to Scotland if it remains in the UK?
- If it is, should the tax revenue be used to pay for current expenditure or to create a sovereign wealth fund against the day the oil runs out?

We now trace how each of these arguments has evolved.

Is it Scotland's oil?

When oil was first discovered in the North Sea, a statutory instrument specified that installations south of the latitude of the Anglo-Scottish border where it meets the sea north-west of Berwick-on-Tweed came under the jurisdiction of the English courts; those north of that line, under the jurisdiction of the Scottish courts (Continental Shelf (Jurisdiction) Order 1968; SI 1968/892). However, as the issue suddenly went live, Scots lawyers rushed to deny politicians' claims that all the oil north of Berwick was Scots:

> The SNP have argued that it is Scotland's oil. Whatever the merits of this assertion on a political or moral basis, the claim has no legal basis whatsoever ... [But] Scotland would have a legal claim to the hydrocarbon deposits off her coast immediately on independence ... The real problem is not whether an independent Scotland would have title to an area of the Continental Shelf, but rather the extent of shelf that would fall to Scotland ... [I]n the absence of special circumstances justifying another line, the boundary is to be the median line between the two states ... The best that the government of an independent Scotland could hope for is the straightening and the lengthening of the fictional baseline from which the median line is drawn. Scotland would fare better with a line drawn from, say, Peterhead to Great Yarmouth than with a line drawn from, say, Dunbar to Bamburgh. Nonetheless, whatever baseline were chosen, the median line would ... place the Argyll, Auk, and Josephine fields into the English sector ... [and] put the Montrose field in jeopardy, despite the fact that it is located about 140 miles due east of Peterhead. (Grant 1976: 87–9; for the current situation see Fig. 7.1)

This nicely illustrates that a coastline is a fractal: if it is not straight at one scale, increasing or reducing the scale does not make it straight either. If Scottish independence had come in the 1970s, there would have been long and hard bargaining between the Peterhead-Yarmouth government of Scotland and the Dunbar-Bamburgh government of the rest of the UK (rUK). A median line is defined (*OED*, 'median line', sense b) as a line joining points equidistant from, in this case, the English and Scottish shorelines; but the fractal nature of these shorelines means that there is not a unique median line.

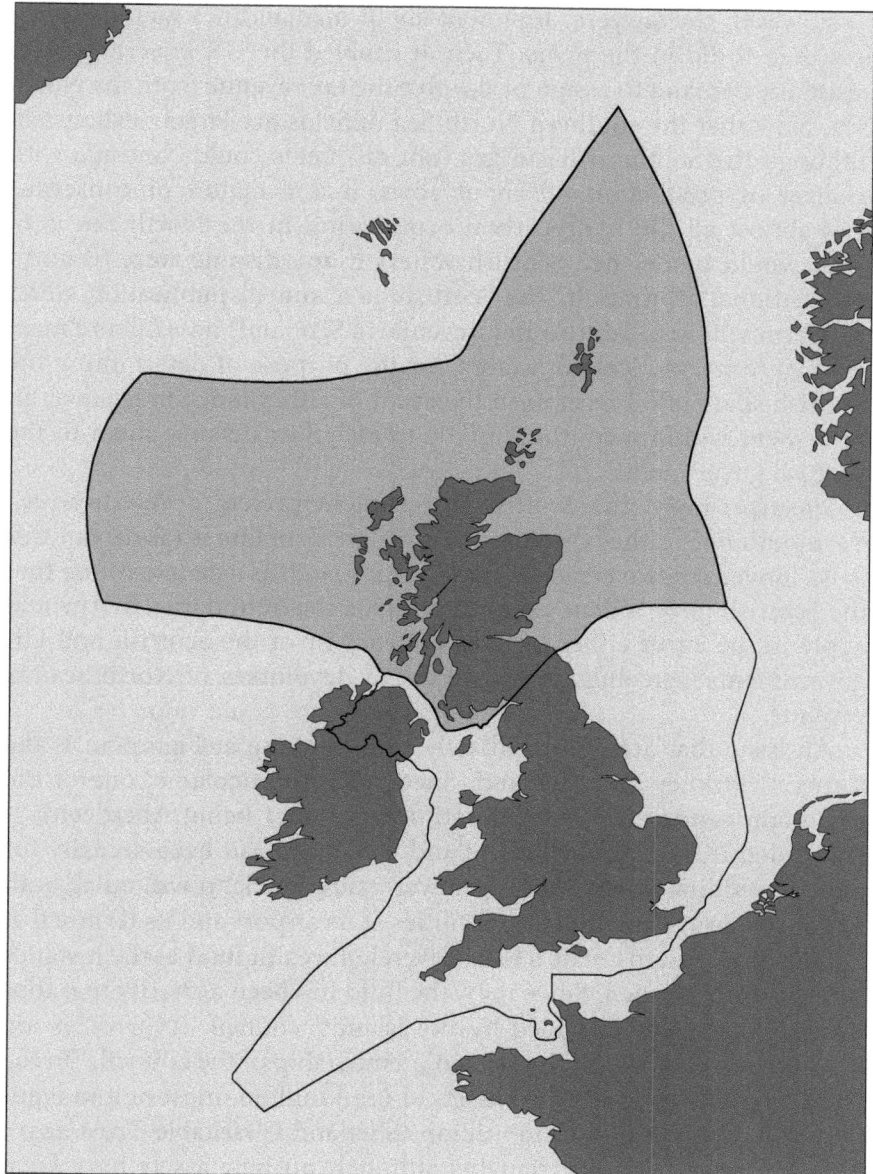

Figure 7.1 The UK's continental shelf and Scotland's share of it

Source: Scottish Government, *GERS 2010–11*, Table 4.1. Crown Copyright

However, the lawyers' argument about median lines matters much less than it did in the 1970s. Then, it enabled the UK government to resist any demand to assign or devolve the tax revenue from the North Sea. Now that the southern North Sea oilfields are largely exhausted, although the Southern Basin gas (not oil) fields could continue with a sliver of production till about 2040, it is a matter of consensus that almost all the hydrocarbon exploitation in the North Sea is in what would be deemed Scottish waters if any dispute were to go to international arbitration. The Scottish government publication *GERS* (Government Expenditure and Revenue in Scotland) now offers a map, see Figure 7.1, of 'Scottish waters' for the purpose of determining the Scottish share of oil receipts in the event of either independence or an agreement within a continuing UK to assign or devolve them to the Scottish government.

Unsurprisingly, the Scottish government prefers a Peterhead-to-Yarmouth line as the one from which its median line is taken. But this is no longer controversial, as far as we know. It is safe to assume that the Scottish government's map represents the boundaries that would apply in the event either of independence or of the Scottish and UK governments' agreeing an assignment or devolution of North Sea tax revenue.

An issue that arises immediately from looking at Figure 7.1 is the status of Orkney and Shetland. Shetland in particular is one of the two main centres for oil exploration (the other being Aberdeen). It was ceded from Norway to Scotland in 1471 (it had been security for a royal wedding dowry that was never paid). Shetland was quick both to get into providing industry facilities at its airport and its terminal at Sullom Voe, and to create a local sovereign wealth fund at the instance of the county council. Since 1997, the fund has been a charity that tops up public services provided by the islands' council. Its trustees are almost coextensive with the elected membership of the council. On the latest available figures, it had assets of £220 million, most of it in equities, and expenditure of £16 million (Shetland Charitable Trust 2011). This substantial balance remains although no new assets have been paid in since a change in the agreements between the council and the oil companies in 2000.

During the 1970s, there were disputes as to how much of Scotland's oil was in fact Shetland's. In a debate on the Scotland and Wales Bill, Mrs Ewing (now back in the Commons and SNP leader) said:

[P]erhaps I may spell out SNP policy on the subject. Since my party was founded fifty years ago we have recognised that the two groups of islands are unique. We have said that they should have as much autonomy as they want. Our policy in that respect has never changed. Hon. Members have tried in this House to introduce a red herring by saying that if the islands were given their independence, or if they went back to Denmark, that would be against the SNP because the SNP wants the oil. I say 'No'. They can have the oil. They can all be billionaires if they want.

Unfortunately, her colleague Iain MacCormick (SNP, Argyll), arriving later in the debate, intervened to say:

The only islands in Scotland with a genuine case for independence are the Western Islands. In the Shetland and Orkney Islands there is not one person who can speak in the language that they blether about as being their national language. (*Hansard* 26 January 1977)

SNP policy on Shetland independence remained unclear. Subject to that, there is no longer any dispute. It is Scotland's oil. The proportion of North Sea revenue that would accrue to Scotland if the oilfields were divided according to Figure 7.1 is given annually in *GERS*; since 2000, it has lain within the range of 72 to 92%.

On what terms would the UK government concede control over North Sea oil revenues?

The short answer in the 1970s was, over its dead body; in the 2010s the situation may have changed somewhat. During the preparation of the Scotland (and Wales) Acts 1978, the UK government issued several White Papers on the subject. For most issues at stake, the tone was one of resignation (from Whitehall departments that did not like the idea at all, but whose foot-dragging was limited by the fact that devolution was government policy). But when the SNP claim to Scotland's oil was discussed, the tone changed completely:

There are some who argue that oil revenues should be controlled directly by those parts of the United Kingdom off whose shores the oil is found, whatever the effect elsewhere. Let there be no

Table 7.1 Total North Sea revenue: UK 1980–1 to 2012–13 in real terms (£2011)

Year	£ million	Year	£ million	Year	£ million	Year	£ million
1980–1	12,616	1988–9	6,835	1996–7	4,957	2004–5	6,234
1981–2	18,654	1989–90	4,810	1997–8	4,754	2005–6	11,042
1982–3	21,780	1990–1	4,118	1998–9	3,489	2006–7	10,055
1983–4	23,098	1991–2	1,712	1999–2000	3,500	2007–8	8,083
1984–5	30,971	1992–3	2,195	2000–1	5,909	2008–9	13,866
1985–6	26,687	1993–4	2,038	2001–2	7,147	2009–10	6,801
1986–7	10,780	1994–5	2,617	2002–3	6,522	2010–11	8,786
1987–8	10,471	1995–6	3,548	2003–4	5,332	2011–12	11,600
						2012–13	6,906

Source: GERS 2010–11; RPI from ONS; authors' calculations

misunderstanding: such a proposal – whether its advocates realise it or not – would mean the break-up of the United Kingdom. (Lord President of the Council 1975: para. 97)

As noted above, Treasury civil servants were working on the scheme which created the region called 'Extra Regio' in order to head off that demand. With the SNP at the peak of its Westminster numbers, the Wilson government made it clear that this was a red line it was not prepared to cross. Rather, the Scottish Office was to be funded from a block grant under what would later become known as the Barnett Formula (paras 98–105). Although the Scotland Act collapsed, the Barnett Formula took wing, as described elsewhere in this book.

Thus, oil revenues were entirely at the disposal of the UK during the 1980s, when they were at their highest. Table 7.1 shows government tax receipts from the UK Continental Shelf since 1980. The numbers, which *GERS* presents in current money, have been rebased to show receipts in real terms, expressed in 2011 pounds. Figure 7.2 shows the calculations made by the Official Historian of North Sea Oil and Gas as to how much revenue would have accrued to Scotland if, instead of the creation of 'Extra Regio', the government of the day had conceded that it was Scotland's oil.

Oil revenues were really significant in the 1980s, for two reasons. One was that the price of oil was at a real-terms historic high, after two political shocks in 1973–4 (caused by the Arab–Israeli war) and 1978–9 (caused by the Iranian revolution). In 1979 the marker oil price reached a peak of US $93 per barrel at today's prices. This price has only been exceeded twice in history: once at the dawn of extraction in the 1860s, and once in 2007–8 (source available at<http://www.

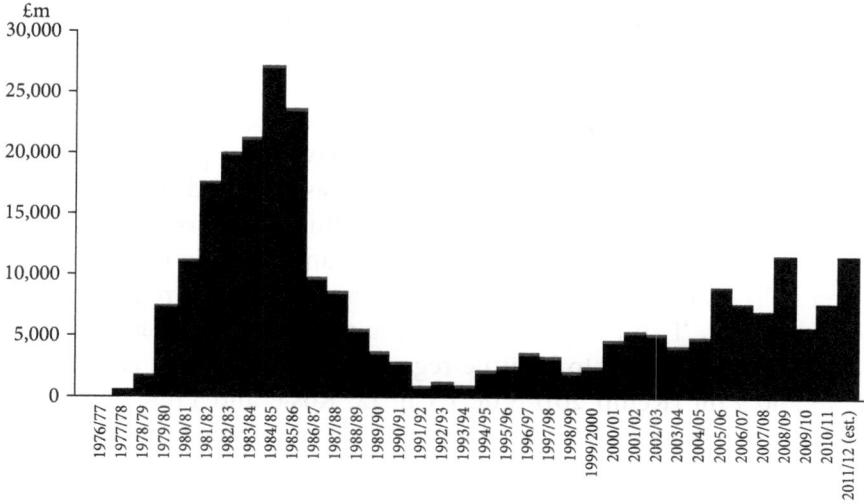

£m

Figure 7.2 Hypothetical tax revenue from Scottish share of UK continental shelf 1976–2012 (£m. at 2009/10 prices)

Source: Kemp (2012), Chart 1

forbes.com/2008/05/13/oil-prices-1861-today-real-vs-nominal_flash2. html>last accessed 16 November 2012). The other was that North Sea production came on stream rapidly, with the easiest fields, of course, being exploited first.

That combination has never been repeated. Table 7.1 shows that Continental Shelf revenue plummeted, beginning in 1986 and reaching a nadir in 1991–2, when the benchmark price reached a trough of US \$23.25 in present-day money. When the oil price is low, high-cost production areas such as the North Sea reduce production at the expense of fields where oil can still be profitably extracted. In the most recent years for which data is available, oil and gas revenue recovered at the recent peak in oil prices, but to less than half, in real terms, of the revenue received annually between 1984 and 1986. As the oil price drops, so does the tax yield from the North Sea.

The numbers in Table 7.1 and Figure 7.2 also show how nationalist and unionist politicians can come to totally opposite conclusions about the same set of facts. For many years, with the help of information from carefully planted Parliamentary Questions, the SNP has maintained that Scotland subsidises England, Unionist politicians of all parties claim the opposite. It all depends on the baseline. *If* you assume that all the oil off Scotland is Scotland's, *and if* your baseline period starts at or just before tax years 1984–5 and 1985–6, you can make a case that Scotland subsidises England; otherwise not.

Without being politically partisan, one can certainly make a case that the windfall of those years ought to have been put into a sovereign wealth fund for the UK or Scotland, as Shetland did in a small way. This is discussed in the next section. But it was not. The milk (or rather the oil) was spilt a long time ago, and there is no use crying over it. The Treasury's decision to create a new artificial region (called, in bad Latin, 'Extra Regio'), for the regional accounts was driven by a perceived need not to let it be regarded in the national accounts as Scotland's oil (Kemp 2011 Vol. I Ch. 12; Rosie and Linklater 2009). As will be argued below, whatever political advantage this may have given to unionist governments, it meant that a chance for a serious discussion of sovereign wealth funds was lost.

Devolving or assigning oil revenue to Scotland may no longer need to be a red-line issue for the UK government. Neither the Labour nor the Coalition government have taken the unyielding line that any such idea would necessarily lead to the break-up of the UK, though they have not canvassed the possibility. Whereas a typical well-informed academic survey in 1990 (Heald 1990) does not even mention assignment or devolution of oil taxation as an option, the Calman Commission's independent expert group (IEG) discussed it extensively. Recall from Chapter 3 that the Calman Commission was set up by a vote of the three unionist parties in the 2007 Scottish Parliament and supported by the then (Labour) UK government.

The IEG's discussion of the issue is the most authoritative discussion to date, as its lead author was the acknowledged expert on these matters, Professor Alex Kemp of Aberdeen University. Professor Kemp is a member of the Scottish government's Council of Economic Advisers and the Official Historian of North Sea Oil and Gas (IEG 2009, para. 2.2).

Taxation of natural resources has several unusual features. In one aspect, it is a taxation of economic rent, which may be defined as the excess return that an asset earns over and above the normal returns to other assets. In lay terms, whoever can secure an economic rent is exploiting a monopoly and can therefore charge higher prices. Economists since the classical days of Adam Smith and David Ricardo two centuries ago have argued that taxation of economic rent is one of the best forms of taxation, because unlike all other forms of taxation, it does not discourage the taxed activity, which can still be more profitable than the alternatives.

Furthermore, as the IEG explains:

> 9.1 Taxation of natural resources has some correspondence to property taxation. One key element of the tax base is that it is clearly immobile, and this in itself makes this an attractive tax base for a devolved government. As we have previously noted, however, the necessary co-operant factor (capital) is highly mobile. Without capital and labour the potential revenues cannot be realised.
>
> 9.2 In principle a devolved Scottish government could have separate taxation powers over that part of the UKCS [UK Continental Shelf] which was deemed to come under its tax jurisdiction. The devolved government would then inherit an established system with many investors operating at all stages in the chain of exploration appraisal, development, production and decommissioning. Disturbing the arrangements would add greatly to investment uncertainty.

This explains, first, that oilfields share with houses, landfill sites and airports the property that they do not move. This makes them the best sort of tax bases for devolved government, as explained in Chapter 6. However, it adds a warning that the cooperation of capital is required. Nevertheless, it is not only a devolved or independent government that might be tempted to disturb the tax arrangements on which oil companies have planned their investment decisions. The UK government did just that, by imposing surtax in the 2011 budget. As the IEG points out with examples, there are many federal countries in the world where the tax base of natural resources is shared between the central government and sub-national governments. This can include offshore natural resources, as for instance in Nigeria and Brazil. Even where the tax base is not shared, it is perfectly possible to use the 'derivation' principle to assign revenues. The derivation principle assigns proceeds to the part of the country in which the relevant taxable activity takes place (that is, it is another word for what this book calls 'tax assignment'). In the case of Scotland and oil, it would be the 'geographical share' shown in recent issues of *GERS*.

For decades the UK Treasury has set its face against the principle of derivation, for that raises the spectre of 'hypothecation'. It is a spectre that haunts the UK taxman, even if nobody else is spooked. A tax is hypothecated if the proceeds are earmarked in some way related to

Table 7.2 Value of a hypothetical Oil Fund for UK (2008–9), on assumption that given percentages of North Sea revenues had been allocated to it since 1980

	Annual return (£bn)		
assuming nominal rate of return of:	3%	5%	7%
Annual investment (% of total revenues)			
10%	24	33	47
20%	47	66	94
30%	71	99	141

Source: Scottish Government (2009), Table 2

the tax base. The nearest thing the UK has to a hypothecated tax is the Television Licence Fee, which is used to fund the BBC. In the current area, it would mean that the proceeds of oil revenue were hypothecated to Scottish spending, even if Scotland remained in the UK. But, if Scotland remains in the UK, that can be dealt with, as it is for instance in Australia (IEG 2009: para. 5.4.2), by adjusting the formula for the block grant to compensate.

The real problem for Scotland is not the idea that North Sea oil taxation could be devolved, or assigned, or become a significant tax base for an independent Scotland. Of course it could. It is the problem of whether the proceeds should be regarded as part of the proceeds of general taxation or put into an 'oil fund'. And this relates to the second problem: what happens when the oil runs out?

In 2009, the Scottish government published *An Oil Fund for Scotland: taking forward our National Conversation* (Scottish Government 2009c). It seized on points made by the IEG report just discussed, especially that natural resource tax proceeds are more suitably treated as a fund out of which future spending can be financed than as a source for current expenditure. An interesting section discusses 'how much a hypothetical UK Oil Fund would have been worth had the UK government invested a proportion of oil tax revenue over the past three decades' (Scottish Government 2009c, para. 3.26). The answers, on three different assumptions about the annual investment, and three different assumptions about the nominal rate of return, are shown in Table 7.2.

These are large numbers. If 10% of UK tax receipts from the North Sea had been put into an oil fund starting in 1980 and continuing until 2008, and if the nominal return had been 7%, the value of the fund would be £47 billion: 'This would mean that the value of the fund would be at least twice as large as the total amount of revenue raised in 2008–9 from the North Sea' (Scottish Government 2009c, para. 3.28). For comparison, total identifiable expenditure in Scotland by the Scottish and UK governments put together in 2008–9 was £48.3 billion (*GERS* 2010-11, Table 5.8).

However, before readers are dazzled by the large numbers, they must consider:

- As the Scottish government admits in a footnote, 'Of course, this would have implied that less money would have been available for funding government expenditures without an increase in net borrowing or taxation for such years';
- The presentation encourages confusion between stocks and flows. A stock is an amount of capital (such as an oil fund, or the stock of infrastructure in Scotland). A flow is an annual amount (such as the income from an oil fund, or the annual proceeds of North Sea oil taxation). Presenting stocks and flows in the same paragraph invites confusion;
- Building up an endowment (a stock of capital that yields returns in perpetuity) is slow and expensive. Charities estimate that the proportion of an endowment that can be spent annually while preserving its real value is somewhere between 3% and 4%. The lower figure is probably realistic in current conditions, and is the one used by the Scottish government in its calculations (para. 3.34). Thus an oil fund worth, say, £1 billion could generate annual expenditure of about £30 million, which would be about 0.1% of the Scottish government's own-account current spending (£28.5 billion in 2008–9).

None of this is to say that an oil fund for Scotland is a bad idea. It is a very good idea, for reasons to be explained in a moment. But recall that the whole exercise is hypothetical. The Scottish government's tables illustrate what *might* have happened if the UK government had set up an oil fund in 1980. But it didn't. Perhaps it should have done, but it has always spent North Sea receipts on provision of goods and services – and the other taxes to support them were in short supply in much of the 1980s. It has not booked them for capital formation or replacement. In the 1980s, oil revenues were available to take up the costs of soaring unemployment linked with the industrial policies of the 1979–87 governments.

Building up an endowment is something politicians would often agree is a good idea. But they rarely do it, except in resource-rich countries that are running a fiscal surplus. The reason is very simple. A politician in a democracy must be re-elected in, at latest, five years' time. An endowment must be built up, unspent, for much longer than that if it is to yield anything worth having. The classic example concerns social protection: pensions, unemployment and sickness insurance. When Lloyd George was planning a national insurance scheme in 1911, his advisers insisted that it must be actuarially sound. That would imply that the fund would build up over many years and could not start out paying serious amounts for a generation. The political imperative was quite different: it had to be a pay-as-you-go scheme, in which current benefits are paid out of current receipts. Lloyd George understood the arguments perfectly well. His civil service henchman recalled:

> I had carried all day in my golf coat with the golf balls a piece of paper with some boiled down figures showing the effect of interest on accumulative insurance, such as sickness insurance necessarily is, with sickness occurring mainly in later life . . . L.G. said he had read my paper and did not understand it, nor the necessity for interest. Was it real interest? I managed to convince him that one way or another it was, and had to be paid . . . After about half an hour's talk he went upstairs to dress for dinner, saying over the banisters: 'I am inclined after all to be virtuous.' (Braithwaite 1957: 126–7)

But he did not keep his resolution. National insurance has been a pay-as-you-go scheme from the beginning, with benefits from those who are currently old and sick being paid from the contributions of those who are currently young and healthy, with a substantial top-up from the proceeds of general taxation. There is a nominal National Insurance Fund, but no real one. National insurance contributions are simply a disguised form of income taxation.

The 1911 scenario was repeated with the national insurance scheme set up during and after World War II in response to the Beveridge Report. William Beveridge, who had been one of Lloyd George's advisers in 1911, again recommended a genuinely contributory scheme. The political pressures to turn it into a pay-as-you-go scheme again proved overwhelming.

Therefore it is no surprise that the Scottish government talks about an oil fund. But all its statements on tax-and-spend implicitly assume both that it's Scotland's oil, and that the proceeds will be used for current spending. The Scottish government's fiscal commission recommended an oil fund, but only in the medium term as the money was needed for current expenditure at present (Scottish government 2013a).

The SNP has a powerful rhetorical point to make: the UK government *should have* created an oil fund in the early 1980s, rather than use the receipts to spend on current services and transfers. It will predictably deploy this argument during the referendum campaign, and in any subsequent bargaining with UK ministers. But, as mentioned above, the milk remains spilt. What was done in the 1980s cannot be undone retrospectively.

The reason why it would still be good for the Scottish government to create an oil fund relates, again, to stocks and flows. The stock of oil in Scottish waters is finite. The industry estimates that 24 billion recoverable 'barrels of oil equivalent' (boe) remain to be extracted from the UK, compared to the historic total of 40 billion boe extracted since 1970. The amount extracted in 2010 was 810 million boe (Oil and Gas UK 2011). Although technical advances mean that more of it can be extracted than was expected in the 1980s, it will run out one day. Tax receipts on a finite natural resource ought to be used for capital formation, not for current spending. If used for the latter, there will be a painful crunch as the resource runs out: in the case of oil, probably well before it runs out, as companies can offset their heavy decommissioning costs against their tax liability. A government that has been using oil revenues to pay teachers' and doctors' salaries will quite quickly have to tax more, or spend less, or both.

In summary, then:

- In a change from the 1970s, recent UK governments have signalled that they are prepared to accept that oil in the Scottish sector of the UKCS is Scotland's oil.
- If Scotland becomes independent, the principles of international law mean that roughly the area shown in Figure 7.1 will be accepted as Scotland's continental shelf.
- If Scotland votes for 'devolution-max', discussions between the Scottish and UK governments may ensue, as a result of which the proceeds of North Sea oil taxation are either assigned or devolved to Scotland.
- However, oil revenues are both volatile and in long-term decline.
- It would be desirable to set up an Oil Fund, but money put into such a fund cannot at the same time be used for current spending. To

build up a useful endowment, it would have to remain in the fund for a long time without being touched.

A policy mistake and two unfortunate legacies

As noted above, UK governments in the 1970s and 1980s made both public and behind-the-scenes moves to ensure that it was not treated as Scotland's oil. But whosoever oil it was deemed to be, the policy of treating the tax receipts as a windfall to set against current expenditure was a bad policy mistake, akin to, but arguably worse than, creating national insurance as a pay-as-you-go scheme while retaining the pretence that it is a funded insurance scheme. Oil and gas in the North Sea are part of the nation's capital stock: *which* nation's is disputed; but certainly *some* nation's. To tax this stock and spend the money in a flow of current expenditure is to deplete the stock. Rather, tax proceeds on capital receipts should be reserved in some form for capital expenditure or for creating a fund to permit future current expenditure once the stock of capital is depleted. As noted above, Shetland did this but the UK did not, when the oil receipts were really substantial. Figure 7.3 shows that the fiscal balance of the UK would have been much worse than it already was in the 1980s if the windfall had not occurred. If, hypothetically, an oil fund had been created then, either public expenditure would have had to be cut severely, or other taxes increased, or government borrowing massively increased (or some mixture of all three). As every household will know, borrowing to build up a savings fund makes little economic sense. That's why the UK did not do it in the 1980s, and Scotland could not do so now without first cutting spending.

The failure to set aside oil receipts in that period of course benefited Scotland as well as the rest of the UK in the short run, as more public services were delivered, social security payments made and/or other taxes were lower, than would otherwise have been the case. But two unfortunate legacies remain. One is that, however much or little oil remains in the North Sea (to be discussed in the next section of this chapter), the amount that can now be put into any sovereign wealth fund is a fraction of what it might once have been. The other is that projected tax receipts will fall off much faster than will projected North Sea production. An important part of the reason is that oil the industry is under an obligation to reinstate the North Sea to its original condition once they have finished sucking the oil out. The estimated cost of doing this is uncertain, but big. A figure of £30 billion has been suggested.

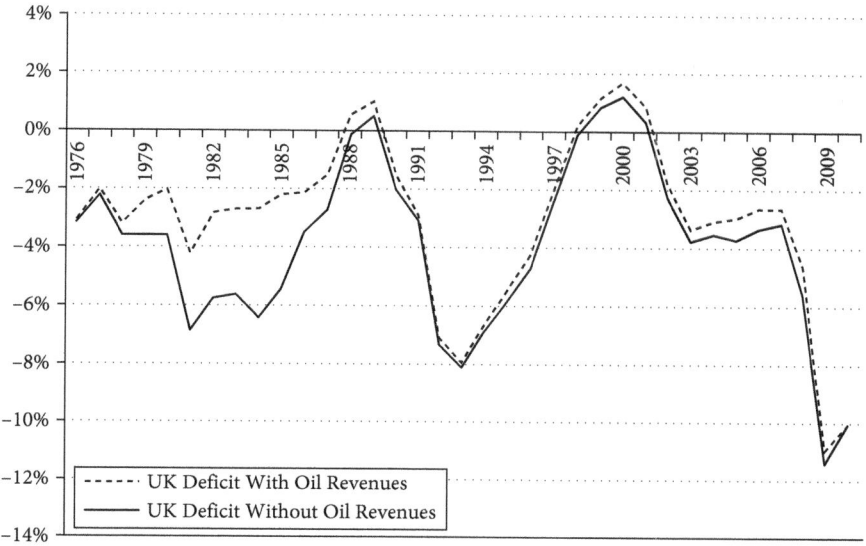

Figure 7.3 UK fiscal deficit with and without oil revenues

Source: Royal Society of Edinburgh and British Academy (2012) Figure 7

The industry has recently been negotiating with the UK government on how this large future cost will be offset against taxation (petroleum revenue tax and/or corporation tax). They are currently negotiating complex agreements to get some certainty that they will get tax relief on the spending. But this expenditure will be incurred quite probably many years after the tax has been paid to the (currently UK) government. Also, in many cases in the North Sea the big operators are selling on the wells to smaller companies. Those smaller companies may be less financially secure, and less able to pick up the decommissioning costs, which may fall back on the bigger companies. So the original big operators have an incentive to strike a deal with the UK government to give them some kind of legal protection (a complex quasi contractual arrangement called a deed) to the effect that they will get tax relief on any decommissioning expenditure they have to pick up in those circumstances as well.

The effect of this is that HM Revenue and Customs have included in their accounts for the most recent year a charge of £20 billion for or lost tax in future as a result of the relief on decommissioning. The effects of this on UK public finance projections are dramatically shown by the

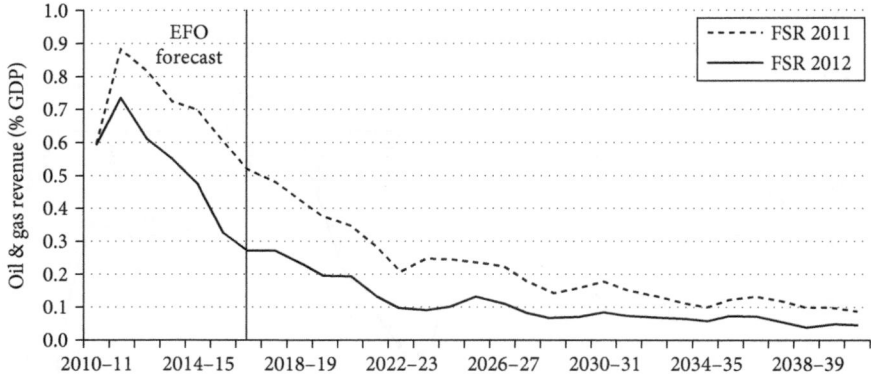

Figure 7.4 UK oil and gas sector revenue projections 2011 and 2012
Source: Office for Budget Responsibility, *Fiscal Sustainability Report*, annual

revision of the Office for Budget Responsibility's drastic downward revision of revenue forecasts (Figure 7.4).

In a single year, the projected government revenue from oil and gas has been drastically downgraded because of the expected decommissioning allowances against tax liability that the oil companies will be able to claim.

To what extent would this obligation to give relief be transferred to an independent Scotland? From the oil companies' perspective, a deal struck with one government should be honoured by its successor, especially when it concerns long-term tax liabilities and claims; although promises about taxation might well be hard to enforce in any court, independence or not. It's pretty clear however that the post-independence Scottish government would argue that since it was the UK that made these promises, and had the benefit of the tax revenue, it should be the rUK that inherits the obligation to give the companies tax relief. But as this would be relief on tax they would no longer be liable to pay to the rUK, it is not clear how that could happen. The result is that this is bound to be an issue in the negotiations (see Chapter 9).

Economic activity in the oil economy will not decline as rapidly as tax receipts. Decommissioning will be a long-drawn-out and expensive process, and it will continue to generate employment in the parts of Scotland where the oil industry is concentrated, just as the long process of decommissioning the nuclear reactors at Dounreay will continue to provide employment in the Thurso area for some years to come.

Likewise, oil industry expertise may remain as a strong invisible export from Scotland even after the oil runs out.

How long will the oil last?

Nobody knows. Exploration in the North Sea is still going on. But it is not just a matter of finding oil; it is also a matter of deciding whether or not it is worth bringing to the surface, transporting, and refining. That depends on the future of oil prices, which nobody knows. It also depends on the future price of things that are sufficiently like oil to be substitutes for it. The most obvious of these is gas. Here there is an important recent development. In the US, one of the world's most profligate energy consumers, the price of gas has plummeted because of the recent development of a new technology called hydraulic fracturing ('fracking'). Fracking is highly controversial in the UK, where it may or may not ever be used on a large scale. But in the US it is a proven technology, where it has dramatically reduced gas prices. (Unlike oil, gas can have widely different prices in different countries.) It is predictable that it will spread to other countries with extensive gas reserves, if they are geologically suitable and (in democracies) if the population will stand for it.

The price of oil depends on demand, which in turn depends on multiple things: the state of the world economy; the relative price of substitutes such as gas, coal, and renewable energy; government policies on carbon taxation or pricing; future technology in transport, power generation, and the chemical industry; and many others. It also depends on the rate of the US dollar against other currencies, as oil is traded in US dollars (and will remain so whatever the constitutional future of Scotland).

All other things being equal, the higher the oil price, the longer North Sea extraction is likely to continue, because the higher the oil price the more it is worth exploring for new reserves. The data we present in Figure 7.5 (from Kemp and Stephen 2011) therefore represent just one of the thousands of projections that could be made on different assumptions about the future price of oil and gas, and the many other variables in the underlying equations that give rise to the chart. In this particular 'medium price' scenario, oil and gas production is predicted to have halved by 2042. In a typical 'high price' scenario, with oil at US $90 a barrel and gas at 60 pence a therm, production increases from 2012 levels to a plateau of about a third more than at present from

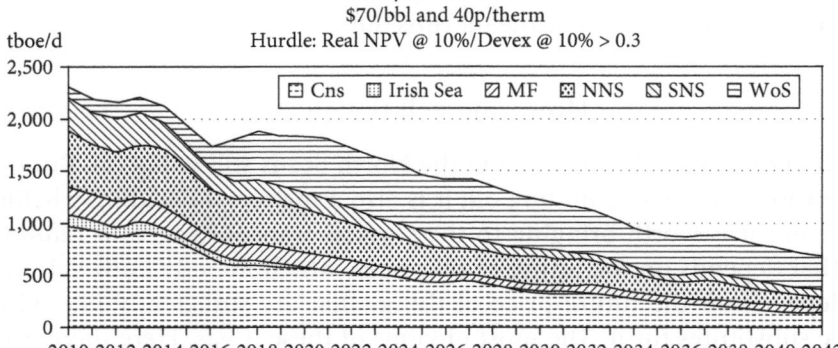

Potential Hydrocarbon Production
$70/bbl and 40p/therm
Hurdle: Real NPV @ 10%/Devex @ 10% > 0.3

Legend:
$70/bbl: real oil price per barrel in US dollars
40p/therm: real gas price per therm
tboe/d: thousands of barrels of oil equivalent per day
Real NPV @ 10%/Devex @ 10% > 0.3: a measure of the threshold at which an oil company will think
it worth investing in new exploration

Figure 7.5 Potential oil production, UK continental shelf, on low price and low rate
of return on capital assumptions

Source: Kemp 2012 (Chart 2)

2018 to 2028, whereupon, as in the medium price scenario, it declines
by 2042 to half the current level (Kemp and Stephen 2011, Chart 35;
Kemp 2012).

Tax receipts will not follow the same path. At any given level of
production, tax receipts in future years will be lower than in past years,
because the oil companies will be allowed to offset their (extensive)
decommissioning costs against their taxable profits.

These numbers are necessarily uncertain. However, they make it
clear that it would be a foolish Scottish government that planned future
public expenditure on the basis of current tax receipts from North Sea
oil and gas. If it puts a substantial proportion of the tax receipts into a
sovereign-wealth fund (as it certainly should), then under either independence or devolution-max it will face an unpalatable choice between
increasing non-oil taxes and cutting current public expenditure. Or
both.

8

Devolution and Separation in the United Kingdom since 1707

THE CHOICES WHICH Scotland faces in 2013 are not new. The same dilemmas have arisen a number of times in the history of the United Kingdom, and have been resolved – or not resolved – in similar ways. In this chapter we look at what that history can tell us.

There has been more than one union in the United Kingdom. Much of Wales was united with England by conquest more than 1000 years ago, and after revolts in the mountainous north and west, was assimilated, without seeking Welsh consent, to the English administration by the Laws in Wales Acts of 1536 and 1543. Then came the union of England and Scotland, enacted by their Parliaments in 1707, which created Great Britain. There is also a union of Great Britain and Ireland, on terms enacted by their Parliaments but partly vetoed by the king in 1800–1, to create a United Kingdom. Most of Ireland left that union in 1921 after a guerrilla war, a Treaty, and legislation in the UK and the then Irish Free State. Northern Ireland of course remained, but with its own domestic Parliament.

Similarly the history of devolution does not begin in Scotland. Before Irish independence, UK governments made three attempts to offer devolution to Ireland. One was defeated in the Commons (1886); one was defeated in the Lords (1893); and the third derailed by vetoes from the Lords, the monarch, and parts of the Army (1914–20). This may be studied in many monographs (see for example, Jackson 2003; McLean 2010). In this chapter, we are interested less in the history than in the properties of the three Home Rule bills: could they have worked if they had not been vetoed by what McLean (2010) calls the 'Unionist coup d'état' of 1911–14? This chapter is not a history of UK devolution since 1707 – that would be a big book, and has already been covered in several (for instance, Bogdanor 1999; Devine 1999, 2003; McLean 2005, 2010, 2012; McLean and McMillan 2005; Mitchell 2003; Whatley and

Patrick 2006). We review this history (only) insofar as it helps readers understand the issues facing devolvers and independence campaigners in the UK today. These include:

- Why the Scots Parliament voted for union in 1707. Were they a parcel of rogues? Were they right, given their values, to give up their independence?
- Why the Government of Ireland Bills and Acts 1886 to 1914 failed. Does their failure show that the consent of the English is needed, or that they were badly drafted, or both?
- How Northern Ireland worked, and how it failed to work, as a devolution-max regime from 1920 to 1972.
- The various proposed solutions to the 'West Lothian Question': should a devolved nation have no representation, or reduced representation at Westminster, or can there be some scheme for it to represented on some matters and not others? W. E. Gladstone dropped his 1886 and 1893 proposals for dealing with the question. Is there any other viable solution?
- What the English think of Scottish independence today. Have the problems of obtaining consent, that derailed Irish Home Rule, been overcome, and/or replaced by a different set of problems?

1707 and all that

There have been many interpretations of the Union of 1707. In the heyday of the British Empire, Scottish commentators, along with the few English commentators who noticed it, tended to regard it as a great piece of statesmanship which laid the foundations of the empire. Since the end of empire, the dominant interpretation in Scotland has probably been that of Robert Burns:

> We're bought and sold for English gold/Such a parcel of rogues in a nation! (In Hogg 1817: I, 56–7)

True, some of the votes of the members of the last Scottish Parliament were bought by an English promise, known as the 'Equivalent', to redeem at par the worthless stock of the disastrous Company of Scotland (the Darien expedition to establish a Scottish trading company in Panama, which had collapsed ignominiously). The original finance for Darien was raised by the Bank of Scotland, created in 1695 as Scotland's central bank; the 'Equivalent' compensation was handled by the Royal Bank of Scotland, created in 1727 for that purpose. These two banks were thus born at the Union. They died, as independent entities, in 2008: which may or may not be a good omen for Scottish independence.

However, Scots MPs who were known Darien stockholders were no more likely to have voted for union than the rest (McLean and McMillan 2005: Table 2.6). This suffices to show that, although there was naked bribery, it cannot explain why some people who were not known Darien stockholders voted for union. If the parcel of rogues explanation thus fails, what then made both Parliaments vote for union? The Scottish Parliament elected in 1703 is the more puzzling. Early in its life it passed fiercely anti-English legislation. In 1704 it issued a naked threat in the Duke of Hamilton's Resolve: 'Not to name the Successor [to Queen Anne, who had no heirs] till we have a previous Treaty with England for regulating our Commerce, and other Concerns with that Nation' (quoted in McLean 2010: 54). The English Parliament had already chosen the elector of Hanover to be their next king. The Resolve threatened that the Scottish Parliament might vote to restore the Stuarts, thus splitting the 1603 Union of Crowns. This brought the English to the table. The unreliable Hamilton proposed that the Queen should appoint both her English and her Scottish commissioners: a puzzling move that weakened his own anti-union cause; but an eye-witness, Sir John Clerk of Penicuik, stated that Hamilton was 'so unlucky in his privat circumstances that he wou'd have complied with anything on a suitable encouragement' (Clerk 1892: 57).

Our analysis of the flow of votes in the last Scottish Parliament (McLean and McMillan 2005, tables in Chapter 2) shows that, beyond simple bribery, two main motives led Scots MPs to switch from anti-union to pro. One of the swing vote bloc, (more elegantly, the *Squadrone Volante* as it was labelled at the time) the Earl of Roxburgh, described them as 'Trade with most, Hanover with some'. Here, *Trade* is shorthand for the fiscal and economic mess that Scotland was in after the Darien disaster. Many on the Union side joined Clerk in believing that there was no realistic alternative. *Hanover* is shorthand for protecting the Presbyterian establishment of the Church of Scotland. In 1689, when there was no king because of the flight of James VII and II, the Presbyterians seized control of the Convention Parliament they had called, (which the Episcopalians had boycotted). They offered the Scottish throne to William of Orange and his wife Mary on condition (which they accepted) of recognising the Presbyterian Church as the sole established church there. William hailed from another Presbyterian land, the Netherlands. But relations between William and the Scots quickly soured, when the infamous Massacre of Glencoe (1692) was followed by Darien. Scots plans to establish a colony in Panama cut across William's statecraft of making an alliance with Spain (which claimed to control the whole of Latin America) against France.

The crucial move in turning the Scottish Parliament was to insist on incorporating the Act of Security, protecting Presbyterian establishment, in the final Act of Union. The Scots made their approval conditional on the English accepting it. Hence the final Act, that created Great Britain, that is still in force, and that will have to be repealed in the event of Scottish independence, contains two contradictory sections, each referring to the 'true Protestant religion' which is Presbyterian in Scotland and Anglican in England. One might have thought that at most one Protestant religion can be true. But this logical inconsistency secured the Union in Scotland. The *Squadrone Volante* ('Flying Squad') flew across the floor and the Union was enacted.

This leads to the question: why did the *English* Parliament, and English ministers, ratify the Union? The Union of 1707 was a genuine treaty, not a takeover. The English had to concede for the first time that they could not impose their church or legal system on Scotland; the Scots secured trading and bargaining privileges. If 1707 had been a takeover, the acceptance of Presbyterianism in Scotland would have been quite inexplicable. Our answer (McLean and McMillan 2005; McLean 2010) is essentially military. In 1637 the English had tried to impose their religion on Scotland, and failed. In 1643 the Scots had tried to impose their religion on England, and failed. The only successful imposition was by Oliver Cromwell in 1650, and that died with him. The Union of 1707 marked a military standoff. Each country accepted that it could not impose its religion, nor its monarch, on the other. The Union was a middle ground between an English conquest of Scotland (unachievable) and Scottish independence (no longer fiscally sustainable).

The Union was none the less insecure for four decades. Episcopalians were a large minority, who resented what they saw as the 1689–90 coup d'état of the Convention Parliament. Few Scots at the time were Catholic; the Catholic, Jacobite, Stuart claimant the 'Old Pretender' and his son the 'Young Pretender', aka Bonnie Prince Charlie, relied on Highland and Episcopalian support. The Risings of 1715 and 1745 had some military success. In 1745 the Edinburgh militia melted away, despite the efforts of Scottish Enlightenment thinker Adam Ferguson. And Bonnie Prince Charlie set up court in Holyrood before his victory at Prestonpans. However, his invasion of England petered out in Derby, and his retreat ended in military defeat at Culloden.

The Jacobites had initially done better in Parliament and the courts than on the battlefield. In *Greenshields* v. *Magistrates of Edinburgh* (1711) Robertson 12, the House of Lords, sitting as a court (and well stuffed with Church of England bishops) allowed the appeal of James Greenshields, who had been jailed for conducting an Episcopal service in Edinburgh. Two Acts followed, in a Parliament controlled by the Tories in which the Jacobites were at their peak strength: the Toleration Act (allowing Episcopal services) and the Patronage Act (restoring rights of lairds to nominate ministers, which had been cancelled in 1690). The latter was to cause two centuries of trouble, leading to the Disruption in 1843. It was repealed in 1874, but its shadow lived on until the Church of Scotland Act 1921, in which Parliament bound itself to keep out of the courts and discipline of the Kirk.

These events are less well known than Prestonpans and Culloden. But unlike those, they matter to today's debate. For they raise what is now known as the West Lothian Question: can Parliament properly legislate for just one part of the UK when the MPs from that part oppose it? Although the Jacobites were at their peak strength in 1711–12, a majority of Scottish MPs opposed both Acts. And the *Greenshields* appeal, like the Patronage Act, appeared a clear breach of the Act of Union, which both protects the rights of the Church of Scotland and denies appeals from the Scottish courts to 'a court at Westminster Hall'. First Minister Alex Salmond's recent attacks on the UK Supreme Court for intervening in Scottish criminal cases on human rights grounds (see for example McHarg 2011) echo the controversy in *Greenshields*, exactly three centuries later.

But the Jacobite challenge disappeared at Culloden. Remarkably quickly, two things happened. First, the British state turned highland clans into the frontline troops of the British empire. Highland soldiers were exempted from the general banning of the kilt after Culloden. By the time of the French Revolutionary and Napoleonic wars Scottish, and specifically Highland, regiments formed a disproportionate number of the troops of the Empire. The sentimental Highlandisation of Scotland came later: with the visit of George IV to Edinburgh in

1822, orchestrated by Sir Walter Scott, and Queen Victoria's purchase of Balmoral in 1852.

Secondly, the economic and other advantages of the Union started to appear. The Union negotiators created a free trade and free movement area. That was not their prime concern, but it led Adam Smith to write to his publisher in 1760:

> The Union was a measure from which infinite Good has been derived to this country. The Prospect of such good, however, must then [during the Jacobite risings] have appeared very remote and uncertain . . . No wonder if at that time all orders of men conspired in cursing a measure so hurtful to their immediate interest. The views of their Posterity are now very different[.] (To William Strahan, 4 April 1760, quoted in McLean 2006: 65)

The free movement of people mattered even more than the free movement of goods. First, it gave the Scots unimpeded access to the whole Empire. Because Scottish schools and universities were better than Oxford and Cambridge (then the only English ones) at training servants of the Empire, they opened a career path for doctors, administrators and ships' engineers. The latter are deeply immersed in popular culture – think of Rudyard Kipling's epic poem *McAndrew's Hymn* and reflect why the Chief Engineer in *Star Trek* is called Scotty.

The Union must also have facilitated the Industrial Revolution. The free trade granted in 1707 turned Britain into a single market for James Watt's steam engines and, later, Henry Bell's steam ships. It opened trade between Scotland and America, and helped shift the economic power of the country from east to west and from south to north – Liverpool and Glasgow being closer to America than London and Bristol. Above all, the Union made the Scottish Enlightenment possible. It had the double effect of protecting the Church of Scotland and removing from it the power to hang blasphemers, as religious leaders had last ensured for Thomas Aikenhead in 1697. Only sixty years after that, Smith published his *Theory of Moral Sentiments* (1759) which says that morality cannot be derived from religion (and hints that Stoic morality is superior to Christian); in only another twenty years David Hume's *Dialogues on Natural Religion* and Smith's eulogy on Hume's death revealed Hume's atheism (McLean 2006: 19–20). The weak state and the weak church of the mid-eighteenth century made the Scottish Enlightenment possible.

Thus began what Colin Kidd (e.g. Kidd 2008) and others have characterised as the era of 'banal unionism': that is, an era in which the Union was so much in the background that its advantages were assumed rather than discussed. However, banal unionism was perfectly compatible with cultural nationalism. The same Walter Scott who stage-managed George IV's visit to Edinburgh also created the mythical Scottish history that all Scots used to learn in primary school, in *Waverley, Rob Roy*, and *Tales of a Grandfather*. Together with Burns and Hogg, Scott cast a romantic glow over the Jacobites – managing also to cast a romantic glow over the opposite religious extreme, the Covenanters. At least they both fought the English Crown, as well as one another. The same Walter Scott, a Tory who owed his baronetcy to the government of Lord Liverpool, wrote in the *Letters of Malachi Malagrowther* (Scott 1826) a polemic on behalf of Scottish banknotes so passionate that they are with us yet – even those issued by the Bank of Scotland and the Royal Bank of Scotland.

During the era of banal unionism, however, there was another Union that was far from banal: the Union of Great Britain and Ireland (1800–1). The Irish Parliament, like the Scottish Parliament, voted itself out of existence in exchange for seats at Westminster and integration into the UK's free trade and free movement economy. Adam Smith helped William Pitt the Younger design it. One condition of union, which persuaded some swing voters in the last Irish Parliament, was civil rights for Irish Catholics – 'emancipation' as it was called. But Ireland had started from a very different place. The Irish Parliament represented only the 'Ascendancy' of Anglican landowners and Protestant Dublin lawyers. Both Catholic and Presbyterian Ireland were totally excluded. But Catholic civil rights were vetoed by King George III after the Irish Parliament had already dissolved itself. He lost Pitt, his best Prime Minister (Hague 2004: 463). More important, he doomed the Irish Union from the outset. The vast majority of the Irish population were Catholic. They got emancipation in 1829, but by then it was too late. Two waves of demands for Irish devolution ensued, split by the disaster of the Great Famine of the 1840s. Daniel O'Connell 'The Liberator' (1775–1847) was never pivotal in Parliament and so could not force his demands for repeal of the Union on to the floor of the Commons. But Charles Stewart Parnell (1846–91) and his successors were, and could, and did. From 1885 until 1918, the Irish Party created by Parnell never held fewer than eighty seats in the Commons. It was pivotal in the Parliaments of 1885–6, 1892–5, January–December

1910, and from December 1910 until the all-party wartime coalition of 1915. In each of these Parliaments, it could insist on devolution ('Home Rule') reaching the floor of the Commons.

Parnell's party won almost every seat in three of Ireland's four historic provinces, and about half of the seats in the Province of Ulster (i.e. present-day Northern Ireland plus Cavan, Monaghan, and Donegal). But Protestant Ulster never supported the Irish Party. Under slogans such as 'Home Rule is Rome Rule' it furnished the bitterest opponents of Irish devolution. The Conservative Party had a material interest in Ireland because many of its leading members were Irish landowners. But that alone did not make it an ally of the Ulster Protestants, who mostly belonged to a different social class and a different religion. For instance, the Conservative Lord Lieutenant of Ireland, Lord Carnarvon, struck a deal with Parnell in 1885 that led Parnell to encourage the Irish in Britain to vote Tory in return for concessions. The Conservative leader Lord Salisbury repudiated Carnarvon's deal after the votes had been cast, but was saved from his embarrassment when W. E. Gladstone's son stupidly revealed that his father had been converted to Irish Home Rule, allowing Salisbury to resign and setting in train the events of the next subsection.

Although, as we shall see, the Conservatives ('Unionists' – a title referring to the Irish Union, not the Scottish Union) fought tooth and nail against Irish devolution, protection of the material interests of Irish landowners cannot have been the dominant reason. Successive Unionist administrations were happy to 'kill Home Rule with kindness' in their own phrase, by expropriating landlords and making rural Ireland outside Ulster a land of peasant proprietors. The great houses of Ireland fell into their long decay.

Irish Home Rule 1885–1921

After Salisbury's resignation, Mr Gladstone formed his third government in January 1886 with Irish Party support. The bungled announcement that he favoured Home Rule led some leading Liberals to refuse to serve, and others, including Joseph Chamberlain, to resign quickly. The Government of Ireland Bill was defeated in the Commons in June 1886 by ninety-three Liberals voting against it, and Gladstone's government resigned. A number of leading Liberals including Chamberlain and Viscount Goschen, now labelled 'Liberal Unionists', became ministers in the Unionist governments that followed until 1905, with a break between 1892 and 1895. It was in 1885 that the maverick Conservative Randolph Churchill (father of Winston) had said, 'If the GOM ['Grand Old Man' – disrespectful nickname for Gladstone] goes for Home Rule, the Orange card will be the card to play. Please God it will be the ace of trumps and not the two' (Quinault 2010). The Unionists played the card more and more until 1914. In the short-term game it was the ace of trumps. Looking back with the advantage of hindsight it has been a total disaster.

But there was more than Unionist obduracy to the failure of Gladstone's 1886 bill. He worked on it largely on his own, and though he was the unquestioned master of Victorian parliamentarianism, he failed to solve the two questions that dog devolution to this day: representation and finance. On representation, Gladstone took as his model the British North America Act of 1867, which had given what was then called 'responsible government' to Canada. Like the thirteen colonies of the US, Canada had no representation at Westminster, and Gladstone proposed the same for Ireland. This had the low advantage that it would have taken the Irish Party, which had mastered the arts of obstruction, out of the Commons Chamber. However, the powers proposed for the Irish Parliament were more akin to those of the Canadian provinces than to those of the Canadian Federal Parliament. It was to have some assigned and devolved taxes, but was not to have complete control over Irish taxation. Therefore, the Irish were offered taxation without representation. It had not worked in Boston in 1776, and it would not have worked for Ireland in 1886.

The starting point on finance for all four Home Rule Bills (including the only one that came into effect – the Government of Ireland Act 1920) was that Ireland must pay an 'Imperial Contribution' for the services that would still be delivered from Westminster – defence and foreign affairs in those days. Macroeconomic management is a modern issue which did not trouble Mr Gladstone.

But Ireland lacked a tax base out of which to pay even for local services, let alone an Imperial contribution. To an approximation, the Irish economy in 1886 was: commercial agriculture in some parts of the country; subsistence agriculture, with zero taxable potential, in the rest; the capital-goods industries of Protestant Ulster; and Guinness. The possible tax bases were income, capital, real estate, and sales. All of these were relatively weak. Probably the most robust was real estate, but the great landowners with their seats in the House of Lords and the heart of the Unionist Party were in a strong position to minimise that.

As discussed in Chapter 3, there are in principle three ways to pay for devolved services: by a block grant, by the assignment of taxes, or by the devolution of taxes. The difference between assignment and devolution is that with assignment the Imperial Parliament retains control of rates and bases, but hands over the proceeds to the devolved Parliament for it to pay for local services. With devolution, the Imperial Parliament also hands over control of rates and bases. Tax devolution was out of the question for Ireland in 1886. (Gladstone had proposed devolution of customs and excise, but was defeated by his Cabinet: McLean 2005: 41.) That left assignment or grant.

In 1888, Unionist Chancellor George Goschen came up with a scheme that purported to be assignment, but ended up as grant. It was to cast a long shadow, in Scotland as well as Ireland. Goschen announced that the proceeds of probate duty (estate tax on personal property – later absorbed in Inheritance Tax) would be assigned to England (including Wales), Scotland, and Ireland in the proportions 80:11:9. This was nominally an assignment to pay for Irish domestic services, but in practice they were paid out of general UK revenues. As Ireland was poorer than Britain, this meant that from the beginning the Goschen Proportion concealed a transfer rather than an assignment. For Scotland, it was to set a floor. Throughout the life of the Goschen Formula, which lingered into the 1960s, Scottish Ministers and civil servants could always argue that Goschen set a floor, never that it set a ceiling (Mitchell 2003, Chapter 7). Scotland's population dropped below 11/80ths of that of England and Wales in the early twentieth century and it has continued to drop. So the Goschen Formula became redistributive. That is why it was succeeded by the Barnett Formula, which was intended to correct what the Treasury perceived as overspending in Scotland and Northern Ireland.

But these matters (fully discussed in Mitchell 2003 and McLean 2005) take us ahead of our story. If Ireland could not be fiscally independent, it became obvious to Gladstone that there must be Irish MPs. He continued to toy with the subject until the 1892 General Election returned a hung Parliament in which the Irish held the balance in the House of Commons. The two unelected chambers – the monarchy and the House of Lords – were unremittingly and bitterly Unionist. Queen Victoria vainly, for the fourth time, tried to block the leader of the largest party, whom she called 'that dangerous old fanatic thrust down her throat' (Matthew 1999: 579). Nevertheless, Gladstone became Prime Minister for the fourth and last time. He introduced a second

Government of Ireland Bill. Even if he had not wanted to, which he did, he had no choice, as the Irish Party could have blocked all other Commons business.

Gladstone's main idea, with which he had been toying since 1886, was an 'in and out' plan. Irish MPs would attend Westminster when Imperial business, including taxation, was under discussion. They would not attend for purely domestic business affecting England, Wales, and Scotland. Unfortunately, the 'in and out' idea had two fatal flaws, which Gladstone himself saw as clearly as anybody. In his notes-to-self, usefully collected by Bogdanor (1999: 30–5), he wrote at various times:

> Ireland is to have a domestic legislature for Irish affairs. *Cannot come here for English or Scotch affairs* . . .
>
> [The distinction between Imperial and non-Imperial business] cannot be drawn. I believe it passes the wit of man.
>
> Irish members *cannot ordinarily* sit in the Imperial Parliament . . . Painful Party relations of later years recommend a period of intermission.
>
> How then is Ireland to be taxed? . . . [if Irish MPs were to come in only for budget votes] some inconvenience in this, as there might be intrigues with the Irish to overthrow a ministry through its Budget?

So Gladstone dropped 'in and out' in favour of a plan to reduce Ireland to less than its population share of MPs, but for those MPs' sitting and voting powers to be unimpaired. This drew a devastating criticism from his colleague Sir William Harcourt:

> [T]hough it may lessen the *amount* it does not really touch the *principle* of the objection . . . When parties are pretty equally divided fifty Irish votes may be as decisive as 100 . . . and when you have once conceded the objection to Irish interference you don't get rid of it any more than the young woman did of the baby by saying it's such a little one . . . (quoted in Bogdanor 1999: 33)

The 1893 Bill passed the Commons. The Lords threw it out by 419 to 41, without serious debate. Soon after, Gladstone resigned; his successor Lord Rosebery did not attempt to revive the bill.

The debates that Gladstone had with himself and with Harcourt (probably the only two people willing to listen) resonate today. If

Scotland is to remain in the UK under a Calman or devolution-max scheme, it must be represented at Westminster. But how? Mr Gladstone's in-and-out has been revived recently under the heading *English Votes on English Laws* (EVOEL). But under any EVOEL scheme that the wit of man has so far devised, the two fatal (in the view of at least one of the authors) objections that Gladstone pointed out to himself remain. First, an intolerable burden would be thrown on to the House of Commons authorities to determine what was 'reserved' and what was 'devolved' legislation. As party fortunes would depend on the answer, there is a risk that party fights on policy would be diverted into unedifying party fights on the Speaker's rulings that such-and-such business was devolved (and out of scope for Scottish MPs) or reserved (and in scope).

Second, under EVOEL, there might be intrigue with the Scots to overthrow a ministry through its budget, or any other domestic matter. If, as in the Parliament of 2010, the Conservatives have a comfortable majority of seats in England, but lack one in the UK, under EVOEL the government would be able to implement the Conservative manifesto on all English business, but not on British or UK business. Who would then form the government?

It is not surprising that Gladstone was forced back to the 'reduced representation' argument. Despite Harcourt's pungent criticism, it might end up as the last argument standing. All of these options show that the West Lothian Question, discovered (although not under that name) in 1711, is just about the most difficult problem of devolution if Scotland stays in the UK and, as we saw in Chapter 4, becomes more pointed the more devolution there is.

Irish Home Rule slumbered until the Irish Party was once again pivotal. This occurred at the General Election of January 1910, which was forced by the Lords' rejection of the 1909 'People's Budget'. As Roy Jenkins aptly says in his monograph on the constitutional crisis, 'as is so often the case when the House of Lords is engaged in reaching a peculiarly silly decision, there were many comments on the high level of the debate and on the enhancement it gave to the deliberative quality of the chamber' (Jenkins 1968: 101). It was a peculiarly silly decision for the self-interest of the Unionists. Any reform of the Lords was bound to bring Home Rule back on the table as soon as the Irish Party became pivotal again. The General Election forced by the Lords' veto duly immediately delivered that very result: poetic justice for the Unionists, one might think.

The Parliament Act 1911, forced through the Lords by a (very reluctant) king promising to threaten the creation of peers so that the Commons would get its way, created the relationship between Lords and Commons that essentially still exists in the UK. The Lords have a 'suspensory veto' as it was called at the time. If a Bill is presented by the Commons in identical terms in three (since 1949 two) successive sessions, then it may become law without Lords' consent. This structure determined the Parliamentary timetable for 1912, 1913, and 1914, and much else besides. Like its predecessors, the Government of Ireland Bill 1912 made no special provision for Ulster. This time, the Unionists played the Orange card with vigour. In each session the Lords dismissed the Bill without engaging with it (except to lament the fate of Ulster, by which they meant Protestant Ulster: in the December 1910 Parliament Nationalists actually held the majority of seats in Ulster in the elected house). Under the Parliament Act, the Bill had to be re-presented unamended, which gave the Unionists a further chance each time to say that the wishes of the people of 'Ulster' were being cast aside. Meanwhile, paramilitary preparations were under way. At first they were bluff, but two events in spring 1914 turned them into reality. One was the Curragh mutiny, in which Protestant officers in the British Army camps in Curragh near Dublin said that if ordered to protect arms dumps from paramilitary raids, they would resign their commissions. The other was the Larne gunrunning, in which 30,000 rifles and three million ammunition rounds, bought from a dealer in Hamburg, were landed with the forces of law and order being held back by mass intimidation.

The Government of Ireland Bill was enacted in September 1914. By then World War I had broken out, and the Act, together with disestablishment of the Anglican church in Wales, was immediately suspended. During the war, it became clear that any scheme of devolution would have to contain an opt-out for the Protestant parts of Ulster, although how to draw the boundaries remained, as it still does, intractable: Winston Churchill gave a memorable description in a Commons speech in 1922:

Then came the Great War. Every institution, almost, in the world was strained. Great Empires have been overturned. The whole map of Europe has been changed. The position of countries has been violently altered. The modes of thought of men, the whole outlook on affairs, the grouping of parties, all have encountered violent and tremendous changes in the deluge of the world, but as the deluge subsides and the waters fall short we see the dreary steeples of Fermanagh and Tyrone emerging once again. The integrity of their quarrel is one of the few institutions that has been unaltered in the cataclysm which has swept the world. (HC Deb 16 February 1922 vol. 150: cc1270)

All sides must be grateful that there is no boundary problem between England and Scotland. The boundaries of Northern Ireland have caused hundreds of deaths; which they would have done wherever they were drawn.

Devolution in the UK since 1920

In the end, Northern Ireland was left with the most arbitrary of boundaries: the old Province of Ulster minus Cavan, Monaghan, and Donegal. Fermanagh and Tyrone had Catholic majorities and other areas, including south Armagh and west Belfast, were Catholic-majority. The boundary has a very peculiar shape. The Government of Ireland Act 1920 offered two minority protections, both carried over from earlier Home Rule bills. One was that there must be no established church in Ireland, including Northern Ireland. This provision, copied from the First Amendment to the US Constitution, had been in every bill since 1886 and has been repeated in all subsequent Northern Ireland constitutional law. The other was that elections to the Parliaments (including an abortive Parliament of southern Ireland) must use the Single Transferable Vote (STV) in multimember constituencies. In Northern Ireland, this was swept away by the Unionist government, unconstitutionally, in 1929, and finally restored under the Good Friday Agreement in 1998.

These measures were introduced to combat the effects of sectarianism. They were only partly successful. There is no analogy with Scotland, where sectarianism is much less of an issue. But on Mr Gladstone's other bugbear, finance, the failure of the Stormont regime – the Unionist-dominated Parliament of Northern Ireland that sat from 1921 to 1972 – was more complete. Although this story is much less well known, the Scottish analogy is much more compelling.

In form, the 1920 Act repeated the formulas of all its predecessors. Northern Ireland should raise its own revenue for domestic services, out of which it should pay an 'Imperial Contribution' to Westminster for common services. But consider both the politics and the public finance. In politics, the Northern Ireland government was a one-party state, governed by those Unionists who had imported 30,000 rifles from Hamburg to defy that home rule they were given in 1920. A centrepiece of their politics was that Northern Ireland was British, and therefore it should have British standards of welfare spending. In public finance, Northern Ireland has been, since its creation, one of the poorest parts of the UK. The skills that built the *Titanic* did not lead to wealth after 1920. Hence, in James Mitchell's summary:

> [W[hat transpired was the opposite of that which had been intended by the 1920 Act. Instead of Stormont having sources for raising revenue from which it funded services (a revenue-based system), Stormont's expenditure determined levels of income as agreed with the Treasury (an expenditure-based system). (Mitchell 2006b: 58)

Given Ulster Unionist ministers' desire to match British welfare standards and UK ministers' wish to minimise sectarian trouble in Northern Ireland, the former simply asked the latter for whatever it would take to make up the gap between taxes raised in Northern Ireland and welfare expenditure at the uniform UK level. The latter always obliged. When the idea of devolution to Scotland revived in 1973, nobody proposed the Stormont model of public finance. Nevertheless, Scotland has not yet broken away from an expenditure-based system, either. The Goschen Proportion was intended to be a revenue-based assignment; it speedily turned into an expenditure-based block grant. Its successor, the Barnett Formula, has never pretended to be revenue-based. However, all the proposals now on the table, even the Calman proposals, involve some attention to the revenue base.

On representation, Northern Ireland got Gladstone's 'housemaid's baby' plan, now that neither he nor Harcourt were around to comment. It had twelve seats at Westminster rather than its population share of about eighteen. It had reduced representation on the grounds that it had Stormont for internal business. Unlike Parnell's troops, the twelve Westminster MPs from Northern Ireland were never pivotal. In a 1979 political deal, the Northern Ireland contingent was returned to its population share after the abolition of the Stormont Parliament. It has not been reduced again after the Good Friday Agreement and the creation of the Northern Ireland Assembly.

The idea of devolution to Scotland was dormant from the mid-1920s until the early 1960s. One reason for this has already been mentioned: the success of the British Empire, and Scots' material stake in it. But lack of interest in changing the Union of 1707 outlived the fall of Empire. It occurred, fundamentally, because the UK was now a Welfare State, a welfare state implies some sort of social union (Chapter 5), and a social union, in turn, is much easier to achieve on an expenditure-based system than on a revenue-based system of public finance.

This may usefully be traced by studying the evolution of thought in the Labour Party, which was the dominant party in Scotland from the decline of the Unionists until 2007. The first two generations of Scots Labour leaders were Home Rulers, for Scotland as well as for Ireland. In 1888 (the year not only of the Goschen Proportion but also of the Mid-Lanark by-election), Ramsay MacDonald wrote to his fellow-Scot Keir Hardie to congratulate him on running in Mid-Lanark as an independent for 'the cause of Labour and of Scottish Nationality' (quoted in McLean and McMillan 2005: 120). One cause, not two. The 'Red Clydesider' (that is, independent-minded left-wing Labour MP) George Buchanan took the same view when he sponsored a Government of Scotland Bill in 1924. The Church of Scotland Act 1921, a successful piece of devolution, which protects the Church from any possible repetition of the events of 1711–12, was a necessary precursor for Presbyterian unity in Scotland. On that, Buchanan said:

This House will be called upon to deal with the Union of the Scottish Churches ere long. I must confess, for my part, I am very open in my views. I have never committed myself on that question to either one side or the other, but what I feel is that on a purely Scottish question, a question dealing with the religious feeling and aspirations of the Scottish people, members largely alien to our views should not be called upon in the main to decide a question of which they have no knowledge or thoughts. (HC Deb 09 May 1924 vol. 173: cc791–2).

But social welfare was a bigger question for Buchanan and the rest of the Labour Party. The Glasgow that he represented was in a long recession after the post-war restocking boom ended in 1921. Socialism by now demanded social union. Buchanan's last job in politics was as chairman of the National Assistance Board from 1949–53. The National Assistance Board administered the part of social protection that was explicitly paid for out of general taxation, not out of national insurance contributions: that is, the most social part of the social union. From the 1920s to the 1960s, Scotland had become more and more like Northern Ireland in at least one respect: that it requested, and got, substantial transfers from the Exchequer to justify generous social spending (Mitchell 2003; McLean 2005). An Edinburgh Ph.D. student, Gordon Brown, put the social-union case for Unionism as clearly as anybody in his thesis on Labour in Scotland when he wrote of Buchanan and his contemporaries:

> No theorist attempted in sufficient depth to reconcile the conflicting aspirations for home rule and a British socialist advance. In particular, no one was able to show how capturing power in Britain – and legislating for minimum levels of welfare, for example, could be combined with a policy of devolution for Scotland. (Brown 1981: 527, quoted by Mitchell 2006b: 55)

Despite his edited *Red Paper on Scotland* (Brown 1975), Dr Brown came no nearer than Buchanan to squaring this circle when he became Chancellor of the Exchequer and Prime Minister.

Thus when the minority Labour government of 1974 started considering devolution to Scotland, it was simply as a reaction to the first wave of SNP success. The SNP had won its first by-election when Winifred Ewing took the 'safe' Labour seat of Hamilton in 1967. In the 1970 General Election it did not do very well, losing Hamilton albeit gaining the UK's smallest seat – the Western Isles. However, within a couple of years the SNP was the first political party to realise the potential of North Sea oil – 'It's Scotland's Oil' the hoardings proclaimed, and the Scottish people seem to have agreed, whatever the international lawyers thought. In the General election of February 1974 the SNP won seven Westminster seats, and its fortunes continued to rise. (In October, after Labour's shotgun conversion to devolution, the SNP would progress to eleven seats and 30% of the Scottish vote.)

Prime Minister Harold Wilson's main motive seems to have been fear of losing control of future UK governments, as his Labour government, with a tiny majority, depended on its seats in Scotland. Accordingly, over the summer of 1974 he railroaded the Scottish Labour Party into reluctant support for a devolved Parliament for Scotland. A 'me-too' commitment to devolution for Wales was added rather absent-mindedly (McLean and McMillan 2009). Labour won a narrow overall majority in October 1974 and prepared a scheme for devolution. Probably because the overriding motive was, and was known to be, political expediency, it faced enemies on all sides. Tam Dalyell, then MP for West Lothian, first raised what became known as the West Lothian Question in his honour. The Treasury, which had long resented what it saw as Scottish overspending protected by the Goschen Proportion and by Wilson's vigorous Scottish Secretary Willie Ross, brought its new scheme into effect. This was later named the 'Barnett Formula' after Lord (Joel) Barnett, who was Chief Secretary to the Treasury. Lord Barnett did not name it after himself, and he has recently disowned the name, as he argues that the outcome is still over-generous to Scotland. The Treasury's other weapon was a Needs Assessment by which it intended to assess the relative needs of each of the four countries of the UK. In normal circumstances, the Barnett Formula would lead to convergence. That is, if allowed to run unhindered, and if relative population did not change, it would end when public spending per head was equal in all four countries of the UK. The Treasury's cunning plan, clearly, was to allow Barnett convergence to run until such time as Scotland's and Northern Ireland's public spending was reduced to their 'needs' as assessed by the Needs Formula, and then to switch to that. This never happened, because of the fall of the Labour government in 1979.

But that fall was precipitated by the many other enemies of the Scotland and Wales Bills. The most lethal were in the North-East of England. As the Scotland and Wales Bill (later two separate bills) made its way through Parliament, a 'Geordie revolt' built up. The North-East of England was a strong Labour area. Its MPs for sure believed in a social union for the same reasons as the late George Buchanan and the early Gordon Brown. An area with high poverty and high unemployment, some of it structural due to the long decline of mining and shipbuilding, it was poorer than Scotland. But regional statistics released for the first time in that era (Northern Region Strategy Team 1976) showed that public spending per head in the region was lower, not higher, than in Scotland. To add a devolved assembly in Scotland, Geordie politicians thought, was to add insult to injury and to entrench Scotland's advantage. They therefore coordinated a rebellion on a guillotine motion in February 1977. The rebellion succeeded, and killed off the first bill (Guthrie and McLean 1978). Later bills were introduced separately for Scotland and Wales. Further backbench rebellions forced a referendum requirement with an unrealistically high threshold. A Yes was not to be implemented unless 40% of the electorate had voted Yes. But no government since 1945 had obtained the vote of as much as 40% of the electorate.

In March 1979 the referendum in Scotland resulted in a narrow 'Yes' which fell well short of the 40% threshold. This led to a motion of no confidence in the Labour government, which lost. As a result the 1979 General Election was forced. The ensuing Conservative victory led to all plans for devolution being shelved, and a surprising, maybe ominous, silence fell in Scotland.

As in 1886, 1893, and 1914, the failure of devolution can be put down to a mixture of bad drafting and English resentment. The Bill was badly drafted in the face of a Whitehall mutiny, where UK departments fought tooth and nail to prevent any of their functions from being devolved. The result was an enumeration of powers to be devolved that legal experts thought would have been quite unworkable if the Scotland Bill had been brought into effect (Bradley and Christie 1979). But that was not the reason for the Geordie revolt. It showed that devolution had to be acceptable in England as well as in Scotland. That lesson is as important today.

Only after the third Conservative General Election victory in a row, in 1987, did Scottish civil society stir from its post-1979 torpor. The 1983–7 Parliament had witnessed one of the more striking instances of the West Lothian Question. The Poll Tax legislation for Scotland had been enacted against the votes of the large majority of Scottish MPs. Although a prelude to the roll-out of the Poll Tax in the rest of the UK, this Act affected only Scotland, and was even more in defiance of Scottish MPs' wishes than the Patronage Act 1711.

In 1989 the Scottish Constitutional Convention finally started work under the chairmanship of the Episcopal clergyman Canyon Kenyon Wright. Its first act was to issue a 'Claim of Right', echoing documents of the same title in 1689 and 1842. All three were claims to Scottish self-determination – over religion and the monarchy in 1689; over religion, again, in 1842, and over domestic policy in 1989.

Both the SNP and the Conservative Party kept out of the Constitutional Convention, but its proceedings have been remarkably influential. Many of its recommendations were carried over, largely unaltered, into the Scotland Act 1998. They therefore determine the shape, functions, and make-up of the Scottish Parliament. The features most relevant for this book, and for the decision that Scots now have to take, are these:

- *The Scottish Parliament is elected for fixed terms by a mixed-member system of proportional representation.* It has a four-year term, except that the Parliament elected in 2011 will run until 2016, to keep deliberately out of step with the recently changed timetable for elections to the House of Commons. The mixed-member system (MMS) comprises a number of Members of the Scottish Parliament (MSPs) elected in single-member constituencies, and a number elected by region in a way that makes the total representation from each region as near as possible proportionate to party vote shares in the region. Donald Dewar, the originator of the system, called it 'the best example of charitable giving this century in politics' (House of Commons 06 May 1998) because it deprived his party, the Labour Party, of the majority it would otherwise have got in the first Scottish Parliament. However, because of various minor flaws and features, it enabled the SNP to win a majority of seats in 2011 on a minority of votes.

- *The Scottish Parliament has powers to tax.* In addition to powers over the taxes collected by local authorities (that is, council tax and business rates), the Scottish Parliament has always had power to vary rates of income tax. From The Scotland Act 1998 until the Scotland Bill 2012, this tax power has been restricted to varying the standard rate of employment income tax up or down by 3 pence in the pound. It has never been used. The new regime under the Scotland Act 2012 will force the Scottish Parliament to set an income tax rate every year. This is explored in other chapters of this book.

- *Unlike the abortive 1978 Act, the 1998 Act starts with a short list of reserved powers; all else is devolved.* There is elaborate machinery for resolving devolution disputes, where the Scottish and UK governments disagree on whether an Act of the Scottish Parliament (would) stray into reserved matters. This machinery has not been tested. As explained in Chapter 1, even the politically opposed Scottish and UK governments have agreed on a mechanism to ensure that the upcoming independence referendum has legal force: namely, an order under Section 30 of the 1998 Act.

Most independent commentators seem to think that the Scottish Parliament has worked very well since its first sitting in 1999 (Calman 2009). However, the Scottish Constitutional Convention ducked the two most important issues for any continuing Union, and accordingly the Scotland Act 1998 does likewise. Readers who have got thus far will not be surprised that those matters are, as they were for Gladstone, public finance and representation at Westminster.

Sorting out finance and representation

The Scots can vote unilaterally for independence. They cannot vote unilaterally for 'devolution-max'. Any changed relationship short of independence requires the consent of the rest of the UK as well as that of the Scots. What does this mean for finance and representation?

On finance, it means that Scots cannot themselves cast a binding vote in favour of a particular pattern of transfer of block grant. That will have to be negotiated between the Scottish and UK governments. The Constitutional Convention did not tackle this because it might well have brought divisions to the surface. It was content for the Barnett arrangements to continue. Under the Scotland Act 2012 scheme, they will continue at a reduced rate. Under devolution-max or independence, they will have to stop.

Whatever decision is taken about finance, if Scotland remains in the UK, will have a consequence for the future of Scottish MPs at Westminster. They must surely, as an implication of devolution-max, be reduced in number below Scotland's population share. Very likely, their powers to vote on English-only legislation may be amended, although we suggest above that this is difficult.

But Scots need to be aware of the West Lothian Question (WLQ). The WLQ is sometimes wrongly described as the problem of a government legislating for the whole country when it does not have a majority in some parts of the country. That is incorrect. The true WLQ arises only when a government legislates for just one part of the country without the consent of the legislators elected from that country. In the past, Scotland, Wales, and Ireland have suffered from this. Now, only England can. That is because Scotland, Wales, and Northern Ireland all have devolved assemblies; therefore the UK does not pass legislation affecting only them. But it does pass legislation affecting only England. There has to be some mechanism to ensure that, if the union continues, the votes of Scots MPs do not determine the outcome of England-only proposals. Devolution-max, in this as in other respects, requires the consent of the English as well as the Scots.

9

After the Vote

THE VOTE OF the people in the referendum will decide whether
Scotland stays in the United Kingdom, or leaves to become a
separate, independent country. In either case, there will be a great deal
of consequent activity. If Scotland votes for independence, the terms
of separation will have to be negotiated. There will then be complex
work to disentangle Scotland from the UK and set up the institutions
of a separate state. If Scotland votes to remain within the UK, then the
Scotland Act 2012 will be implemented. But some further devolution
will also be planned, which is likely to require negotiation between
the UK government and the devolved Scottish government. In this
chapter we explore what would have to be done in each case. There are
of course many uncertainties here, but it is important that voters have
some understanding of what might happen afterwards when making
their choice.

A vote for independence

If a majority of those voting in the referendum opt for independence,
then Scotland will leave the UK. But it won't happen straightaway, as
the process of separating from the UK, setting up the institutions of
an independent state, and establishing its place in the world is likely
to take some time, certainly a couple of years. There will be extensive
negotiations, mostly with the UK government, but also with international organisations of which Scotland wishes to become a member.
These, together with planning the new constitution, laws and public
organisations of the new nation, will all require a great deal of time
and effort. This has been done before elsewhere. British experience
includes a long history of decolonisation, and of course Ireland became
an independent country in the first half of the last century (see Chapter
8). More recently, there may be lessons to be learnt from the split of
Czechoslovakia in the early 1990s (see Chapter 2). But none of these

offers a recipe to follow: circumstances were significantly different in each case.

The first question is 'who negotiates?' It might seem obvious that this would be the Scottish and UK governments, and they will have to be the dominant parties to any negotiation. There are however some difficulties. First, on the UK side, the UK government presently represents the whole of the UK, and indeed includes Ministers representing Scottish seats. In the negotiations it will be their responsibility to represent the interests of the UK apart from Scotland. This is one of the reasons UK Ministers have given for not negotiating on possible terms of independence prior to the vote, though they made an exception in setting out their position on currency issues. On Scotland's side, although the Scottish Parliament and government are elected only by Scots, they are not the only representatives with a democratic mandate in Scotland. Scottish MPs can also claim that too. Additionally, at a technical level, there is the problem that the Scottish government, although in these circumstances it would have a very strong political mandate, does not have the formal legal powers to conduct these negotiations (see Chapter 1).

In practice, both sides will have to nominate negotiating teams, who will have to be given the task of agreeing how to put into practice the decision taken by the Scottish people. The UK side will have to be sure that it can agree terms which safeguard the interests of the rest of the UK and secure a vote in Parliament at Westminster on that basis. On the Scottish side, the Scottish Parliament is the only body which can in practice represent the Scottish interest (if need be, having been given the technical legal powers to do so, to avoid any risk of court challenge). The Scottish government will have to take the lead in the negotiations, but an important question for it will be how inclusive to be in putting together a negotiating team. Once a decision has been made, even those who opposed independence might be willing to contribute to making a success of it, and should be given the chance to do so.[1]

The negotiations will involve hard bargaining, and at least some of the process will have to be behind closed doors. Both sides will have outcomes they wish to secure, but a great deal of goodwill will be needed to reach an acceptable outcome, especially one which minimises disruption during the transition.

In parallel with the negotiations with the UK government, there will have to be conversations with international organisations of which Scotland hopes to become, or remain, a member (see Chapter 2). The most important of these is the EU, and it is inevitable that the UK government will also participate in those discussions. Relations with the UK would be wholly different if an independent Scotland were not an EU member. Similarly, if Scotland wishes to remain a member of NATO, discussions will have to proceed in parallel, and again the UK will be present at that table also. The question of NATO membership will be critical to the Scottish/UK negotiations so far as defence is concerned. The length of the negotiations is hard to predict. The Scottish government White Paper suggests that they can be completed in less than eighteen months so that the elections scheduled in 2016 for the devolved Scottish Parliament would instead become the first to a new independent Parliament. This might look neat. It is in the interest of the present Scottish government, as it guarantees it is they who would complete the negotiations, which they would not do if they lost office in 2016. But it also looks a remarkably ambitious timetable, as the list is long and some items are contentious. Hard bargaining takes time, and this period also includes a UK General Election and potential change of government. If EU entry negotiations are to be completed before independence takes effect then time will need to be allowed for the ratification of the necessary treaty changes by all EU member states. It is even possible that referendums about it could be held in some member states. So Scotland being independent and an EU member before May 2016 is hard to see.

The issues to be negotiated

The list of issues is formidably long: the negotiators will have to find a way to disentangle the institutions of the British state. Little attention will need to be given to devolved issues such as justice, health, or schooling. But many public services operate on a UK basis: defence and foreign affairs, economic and monetary management, tax collection, banking and financial regulation, social security benefits and pensions, citizenship, immigration and border control, energy regulation, the BBC, university research and many others. Economic and fiscal issues will loom large. A decision will be needed on currency and monetary policy, and the UK's national debt will have to be shared out, as will its other future obligations, like pensions, and other things such as the government stake in the big Scottish banks. It is not possible to say how these negotiations would turn out, but it may be helpful to explore some of the major issues which will be on the table.

Membership of the European Union

As we discussed in Chapter 2 it is likely that an independent Scotland would wish to be in the EU, although the way in which this would be secured is not completely clear. The most likely legal framework is that the UK would be the continuing member state and Scotland would apply to 'accede' as the jargon has it, under the Treaties. But the EU might not treat Scotland as just another accession state, as it is already within the EU, and its people are EU citizens. Other member states might want to use the negotiations to secure their own aims, and while it seems unlikely that Scottish membership would in the end be turned down, conditions might well be attached.

Some of the issues to be negotiated would be procedural or formal: how many Scottish members would there be in the European Parliament? Would Scotland have the right to nominate a member of the European Commission? What about voting rights? Answers to these questions could be obtained relatively easily. (Smaller EU member states get proportionately more MEPs so Scotland might, for example, have twelve or thirteen MEPs, compared with six at present; Denmark, with 5.5 million people, has thirteen MEPs, while Ireland, with 4.2 million people, has twelve MEPs.) Similarly small nations get greater voting power than their size would suggest in the European Council – which is where governments negotiate deals, and is probably the most powerful European institution. In both cases, the rUK might get less than now.

It is common in EU negotiations that apparently unconnected issues are brought to the table. Countries like Spain – dealing with their own secessionist movements – might want to set conditions with an eye to domestic pressures. The conditions of membership could be important, both in their own right, and because they would influence important aspects of the negotiations with the rUK. Immediate Euro membership may be unlikely but Scotland might well be required to give a commitment to join at some point in the future. It is also possible, though on balance unlikely, that Scotland would be obliged to participate in the Schengen agreement: that would enable Scots to travel to France or Germany without passport control, but paradoxically would require passport controls at the borders with England or Ireland. If neither of these conditions is imposed, that makes it possible for Scotland to discuss a currency union with the rUK, and maintenance of the Common Travel Area in the British Isles. Other issues such as fisheries or the British rebate could well be raised in these negotiations.

Economic issues

It is inevitable that economic and financial issues will dominate the negotiations between Scotland and the rest of the UK. The UK is a highly integrated economy, and Scotland is on many measures typical of it – economic activity per head is close to the UK average, Scottish unemployment and employment levels are similar to those of the UK, and both tend to change in response to external events in roughly the same way (ONS 2012). Goods and services move freely across the UK, as do people to seek employment. This means, as we discussed in Chapter 2, that the United Kingdom today meets many of the criteria of an 'optimal currency area'. A single currency can readily be used in all parts of the country, with a single central bank, the Bank of England, running monetary policy, regulating banks and acting as a lender of last resort to them.

The Scottish government's policy remains to retain Sterling in a currency union but that is not a decision Scotland can make for itself. Senior UK politicians have gone to some lengths to rule out currency union. If they stick to that position one major issue has been taken off the negotiating table. It has been argued sometimes by Scottish ministers (for example, Barnes 2012) that the UK could not prevent Scotland from using the pound sterling. In a strict sense this is true, as some countries simply allow the currency of another nation to circulate within their borders. This is how Panama uses the US dollar, and Montenegro the Euro. That is not however a currency union, but rather a decision to have no monetary policy of one's own. It does not allow for the operation of a sophisticated banking and financial services system of the sort Scotland already has.

A single currency implies a single monetary policy, and almost certainly an integrated system of banking regulation. As current experience in the Eurozone very clearly shows, it works well only if there is also close integration of fiscal policy, because the amounts which governments spend and borrow have a very significant effect on monetary policy and interest rates.

If the rUK were, despite the position Ministers and other politicians have taken, willing to consider a currency union, it is therefore highly likely that the UK would seek to have extensive influence over Scottish fiscal policy before agreeing to it. How far that influence would extend beyond limits on Scottish borrowing and into tax policy, and how much Scottish influence over monetary policy the UK would be willing to cede in return, would be for negotiation.

If the Bank of England was to act as lender of last resort for Scottish financial institutions, it is highly likely that the UK would want significant constraints. This is because it will not wish to subject its own economy and currency to unnecessary risks from fiscal decisions over which it has no influence. The UK might also seek constitutional guarantees that the currency union was permanent and irreversible. These conditions will be difficult to negotiate, and could be hard for an independent Scotland to accept.

Scotland leaving the UK would precipitate a division of the UK's assets and liabilities. International law suggests that it should be on a 'fair and equitable basis' (which like much legal advice, is no great help in making practical decisions). Some things would be straightforward. Physical assets like government buildings which lay inside its borders would readily transfer to Scotland's ownership, but the allocation of financial items would be more complex. The most significant of these is the UK's national debt. It is over £1 trillion at present and is expected to grow further before declining (Office of Budget Responsibility 2014). Scotland would be expected to take a share of that, as it has benefited from the borrowing. The share might be on a per capita basis (about £33,000 per household), or on some other basis such as GDP or share of tax revenues, which might more fairly represent Scotland's ability to pay.

The UK government have issued the national debt, and have made clear to the markets that they will stand behind it, but expect Scotland to take on a fair share of the liabilities. (Scotland would make a payment to the UK for the agreed amount.) The Scottish government agree that Scotland should take on a share of national debt, though they have suggested that it might be less than a per capita share to reflect the fact that oil revenues have contributed significantly to UK finances in recent decades. But they have also said that if the UK rejects currency union then they will not take on a share of debt. They argue that both assets and liabilities should be divided, and the currency is one of the assets. There is some shadow boxing going on here, obviously, and these issues would surface in the negotiations. The technicalities however shed some light onto what the outcome might be. The UK's legal argument that as the continuing state it will automatically inherit state institutions implies that it will inherit the Bank of England as an institution (even though the Bank's assets and liabilities, including reserves, notes and coin, etc. would be part of the overall share out). A currency depends on the state which backs it: and is not so much an asset as a system for transactions, savings and so on. So it cannot be split up and shared out as an asset can. Armstrong and Ebell (2014) argue that it is essentially a state's reputation which backs a currency, and that is not something that can be split up and shared out.

The UK's liabilities also include promises and commitments of other kinds. The most significant of these is public sector pensions. Personal liabilities are estimated at about £1 trillion, mostly from unfunded government pension schemes, which are essentially promises made to people like health service workers or civil servants. A formula would have to be agreed for Scotland's share of this (perhaps in proportion to the number and seniority of public servants), and Scotland would be responsible for paying the continuing pensions. Then there would also need to be agreement on dividing up other UK liabilities, such as the payments on PFI deals (£32 billion) and nuclear decommissioning (£60 billion) (Office of Budget Responsibility 2014).

Responsibility also has to be agreed for the assets and liabilities arising from the UK's direct interest in some financial institutions, including the Royal Bank of Scotland and Lloyds Banking group. The government shareholding in these bodies is formally an asset, but the various promises and guarantees which it has made to ensure that these banks can continue to operate, and losses which are likely to be made on realising some of the banks' assets, are potential liabilities. What these will be on the date of independence will depend on economic performance over the next few years. The UK might argue that for banks registered in Scotland, all these responsibilities should pass to the newly independent country; alternatively assets and liabilities might be shared according to the proportion of the business in each country. Analysis by the NIESR (Armstrong and Ebell 2014) suggests that the UK's liabilities exceed its assets by about £1.3 trillion. This is hardly surprising given the scale of pension liabilities. They estimate Scotland might gain a larger than per capita share of physical assets, but that it would emerge as a heavily indebted country. This emphasises the difficulty of the task: the negotiators will have to agree, overall, a division of all the physical and intangible assets and liabilities which they think is fair and defensible to the electorate of each country.

Defence and foreign relations

In the economic negotiations, Scotland will be very much the smaller partner seeking agreements from the UK to meet its own needs, and may not be in a very powerful negotiating position. The negotiations in relation to defence, however, might take a different tone. An independent Scotland could not possibly seek the same global role as the UK, and is unlikely to wish to have the type of Armed Forces, still less the size, that would enable it to do so. The UK, on the other hand, might well want to continue with the same defence posture and approach to international relations as at present. Since Scotland will represent the strategically important northern border and contain important UK defence assets, this may be an area where the UK will want Scottish agreement for its own purposes.

Scotland's own defence needs might be relatively modest, but would be unlikely to be met by a simple per capita share-out of the UK Armed Forces. Military bases in Scotland could readily become the responsibility of the new state (we discuss nuclear bases below) but rather than divide each type of military asset equally (it is not possible to have a bit of an aircraft carrier) a proportional allocation of equipment and material that formed a reasonably coherent defence force for Scotland might be agreed. A number of speculative attempts have been made to describe what would be needed, but it is ultimately a political decision for an independent Scotland to confirm.

Decisions as to the future careers of military personnel would also be necessary. Many regiments of the Army are traditionally Scottish, and recruit many of their personnel in Scotland, but the soldiers in those regiments are still members of the UK armed forces. It cannot be assumed that their members would wish to serve in a Scottish Army (though many might). Scots make up a disproportionately large number of those serving in the Army, and many will want the option as to which country to continue to serve. Royal Air Force and naval personnel do not have the same traditional geographical identities, and Scots are not overrepresented amongst them, but presumably all would have to be given the choice of which country to serve. However, the latest figures show that Scotland is home to less, not more, than its population allocation of HM Forces: 11,000 in Scotland out of about 180,000 in the whole UK (6% compared to a population share of 9%) (Scottish Government 2012c; ONS 2012b: p. 5). The difference is likely made up by Scots whose bases are outwith Scotland, for example, in Catterick or Colchester, though recent defence reviews will affect these numbers. The UK might, of course, in future choose to continue to recruit military personnel from Scotland, as it still does from the Republic of Ireland, and might choose to keep identifiably Scottish formations, some of which are currently based in England.

Whether an independent Scotland joins NATO will be an important consideration. As part of the UK, Scotland has played an important role in the NATO alliance. It seems likely that NATO would want an independent Scotland to remain a member, though the terms of membership would need negotiation. Until recently, the policy of the SNP was that an independent Scotland would withdraw from NATO, but this has changed. As a member of NATO, Scotland would participate in common defence as that is the key aspect of NATO membership. Air defence would be of particular importance, as Scottish airfields have been key NATO assets until now. Negotiations might agree that this could continue, using either suitable Scottish aircraft, or assets from a NATO ally, most likely the UK. All aspects of defence negotiations between Scotland and the rest of the UK would greatly be eased if Scotland remained a NATO member.

The most difficult defence issue, however, concerns the UK's nuclear deterrent. UK nuclear-powered and nuclear-armed Vanguard missile submarines operate out of Faslane on the Clyde, and there is a substantial facility nearby at Coulport where nuclear warheads are stored. They are maintained at the Atomic Weapons Research Establishment in Aldermaston. (The Trident missile system which delivers them is maintained by arrangement with the US government.) As we have seen, Scotland would not wish to be a nuclear power, and could not properly do so, because of the nuclear non-proliferation treaty. If the UK wishes to maintain a nuclear deterrent once Scotland is independent, it will have a strong incentive to negotiate the continuation of these arrangements on a basis which is consistent with international law. While it would in principle be possible for the missile submarines to operate out of an alternative port, and an alternative storage facility for the warheads to be built, in the short or long-term, this would be difficult and highly expensive.

The Scottish government White Paper says that Scotland will not host nuclear weapons, and indeed that this will be constitutionally forbidden. This is likely to be subject to intense negotiation linked to negotiations over NATO membership, and to the wider negotiating portfolio. A number of outcomes might be envisaged. First, the UK might agree to withdraw weapons. The process of withdrawal is likely to take a number of years. Experts at an autumn 2012 Commons hearing offered timescales of at least ten and possibly over twenty years to relocate them to operate from another UK site, though the Campaign for Nuclear Disarmament argued the weapons could be disarmed very quickly and removed from Scotland within two years (Scottish Affairs Committee 2012). Alternatively, the UK might succeed in negotiating an agreement to continue to use Faslane and Coulport either as leased bases (as was agreed with the Irish Free State in 1922 for naval vessels to operate from the so-called 'treaty ports' in Cork, Bantry Bay and Lough Swilly) or even as continued UK sovereign territory. An agreement might be reached for facilities to be available to the UK for a period of years, perhaps the lifespan of the present submarines or missile systems. Again agreement might be easier to reach if Scotland was a member of NATO and thus committed to Alliance policy of nuclear deterrence. The UK's nuclear weapons are under sovereign control, but are nevertheless also explicitly committed to the NATO strategic nuclear mission, with some coordination of operations with the United States.

An independent Scotland would also want some overseas representation. If it were to be a member of the EU and other international organisations, it would have to accredit representatives to them. This would be an early priority, especially Scottish representation in the EU, possibly in NATO, and in due course in the UN. Scotland would have to decide the extent to which it had representation in other foreign capitals or with other organisations, or whether it sought to negotiate a deal with the UK to have those services provided by sharing embassy or consular premises. This would not simply be a vanity project. Scottish citizens overseas will on occasion need consular help (if they get into trouble with the local authorities, or are the victims of crime) and they will expect arrangements to be made for this. International representation is also an important aspect of promoting trade and economic development.

Other UK public services

Although the Scottish government already has responsibility for devolved public services, the majority of expenditure on public services that benefit Scotland is in fact the responsibility of the UK government. These services will have to be disaggregated and provided separately in Scotland, although in many cases it is clear that to avoid disruption they could only be provided on a continuing UK basis for some time.

Two of the most significant such services are tax collection and benefit payment. The UK has a centralised tax collection system. Her Majesty's Revenue and Customs (HMRC) collects nearly all taxes, direct and indirect, apart from those collected by local councils. It collects direct taxes such as income tax, national insurance and corporation tax, and indirect taxes such as VAT and excise duties. In addition it is responsible for paying tax credits, which are distributed alongside the income tax collection system but are strictly speaking a social security benefit. Although HMRC has a number of local offices, the tax collection system is integrated across the UK, with processing and call centres in different parts of the country dealing with taxes for the whole UK. So, for example, the HMRC Enquiry Centre in East Kilbride ('Centre 1') deals with tax issues for Scottish residents but also for taxpayers elsewhere in the UK; national insurance contribution records are managed from Newcastle. Equally important, the computer systems which support the different taxes, notably for PAYE (which collects around 90% of UK income tax) and VAT, are the same for the whole UK.

An independent Scotland would have to create its own tax collection system. It is not clear how much this would cost to run, or what its compliance cost to business would be. One estimate (Scotland Office 2009) put the cost at £1bn a year. On the other hand, some small countries manage to have highly efficient tax collection systems, for example Finland (OECD 2009), but ultimately the cost of collection would depend on the tax policies of the independent country and the effectiveness of its tax collection, especially how well it uses IT systems. In the interim, however, Scotland would have to negotiate with the UK for a shared tax collection system for at least a transitional phase.

Similarly, social security benefits are paid out on a uniform basis across Britain by the Department of Work and Pensions (DWP). The DWP pays old age pensions, income support, job seekers' allowance, attendance allowance, disability living allowance and many other benefits. Apart from housing benefit and council tax benefits, which are administered by local authorities at present, all benefits are administered by UK-wide computer systems, and on uniform scales. In the same way as for tax, an independent Scotland would have to create its own social security system: but until it was able to do so it would have to negotiate with the UK to run common social security policies and administration. This is proposed in the Scottish government White Paper, which says that administration would be shared but that nevertheless Scotland would have the freedom to pay more generous pensions and benefits.

The UK is under no obligation to agree to shared administration, but in neither of these cases is it likely that the UK would completely refuse to assist an independent Scotland with the administration of tax and benefits for a period. As the Scotland Analysis paper on Welfare and Pensions points out, altering UK administrative and computer systems to pay different benefits in Scotland only would be difficult and expensive in practice.

How long the period of cooperation would have to last is unclear. Creating new administrative systems of this kind can take a notoriously long time and it would be in the UK's interest to set a deadline for Scotland to run its own independent systems.[2]

There are a number of other UK-wide public services that would have to be separated out in a similar way. Scotland would have to manage its own borders and immigration policy. Since the 1920s, the UK and Ireland (along with the Channel Islands and Isle of Man) have had a Common Travel Area, which means that passports are not needed to move from one country to another. Provided Scotland had not joined the EU Schengen area, it would be possible to negotiate the continuation of the Common Travel Area to include Scotland. This would make practical sense. Scotland would still have to police its own external borders, but not those with England or Ireland. In practice this would constrain Scotland's ability to operate a markedly different immigration policy from England and Ireland.

One significant issue is the future of the British Broadcasting Corporation. The BBC is a UK-wide service financed by the licence fee, which is in effect a hypothecated tax – set by the government but used to finance the BBC. As part of the BBC, BBC Scotland produces programmes for use in Scotland only, but these are a small minority of the total service provided. The White Paper says that Scotland would have the same licence fee and both a new Scottish Broadcasting Service and the same access to BBC services as today. If Scotland became independent, it could not reasonably expect to retain BBC services free, though no doubt many Scottish viewers would continue to watch British programmes if they could. So it seems likely that they would have to be paid for, possibly by individual viewers.

How much could be shared with the rest of the UK after independence?

One argument that is made is that even after it became independent Scotland could simply continue to share many of these public services with rUK, not merely on a transitional basis but permanently, so as to share costs and avoid disruption. Why not a tax collection agency, or a social security payment system? Or even a border agency or a public service broadcaster? Some transitional sharing is inevitable if disruption is to be avoided, and it might be that it continued for some years, but there are problems with doing so permanently. First of all, the administration of services is closely connected with the policy to be implemented: tax or benefit decisions, for example, are constrained by the ability of the relevant agencies to develop systems to administer them. So Scotland might find it had little real independence if tied into rUK administration. Secondly there is the problem of governance of shared arrangements: who would really be in charge of them? At present Scotland is represented at Westminster, which oversees these bodies. After independence the rUK would have to agree to some joint oversight. Therein lies the main problem: the government and Parliament of the rUK will have to put the interests of their citizens first and can only agree to share services with a separate state if those interests are not jeopardised. So they will hardly cede control and might want all the extra costs to fall on Scotland. Some such deals might well be possible, say for consular representation abroad, which countries do sometimes share; but agreements to keep the present UK-wide services are anything but guaranteed.

Immediate tasks for Scotland

As well as negotiating with the UK and the EU, Scotland would have to develop plans of its own. A new state has to be created. Some aspects of this will be significant but largely formal – drafting and agreeing a new independent Scottish constitution would be very important. This will include such important matters as citizenship – who was entitled to be a citizen of the newly independent country; how the country was to be governed – would there be one chamber of the Scottish Parliament or two, how would they be elected, and so on. A convention might be held to draft a constitution, which could be approved by a further referendum, though as long as there were interim arrangements this need not be before independence.

Other tasks would be immediate operational necessities, such as creating a new Scottish Treasury, ensuring that tax revenues flow into it and that it could fund and control Scotland's public spending, and borrow as need be to meet the country's deficit. An independent Scotland would have to establish its credibility with the markets very swiftly, particularly if its monetary and fiscal arrangements were unusual, as they might well be. Otherwise it would be forced to pay punitive rates of interest to borrow, imperiling its stability.

The path to independence

Putting independence into effect will be a very major task. It has already been suggested that it could take a period of two years from a referendum vote in favour to make the necessary arrangements. Given the scale of the task, even a period of that length would present challenges. Several processes of negotiation will have to proceed in parallel, across a range of subjects on which little preparatory work will have been done. The outcome of the negotiation is hard to predict. It will be in the UK's long-term interest to help Scotland become a stable and prosperous country, but in the negotiations the UK government will be obliged to look after the immediate interests of England, Wales and Northern Ireland, for whom it will continue to be responsible. As the smaller party, it is inevitable that Scotland will be looking for a significant deal of goodwill, particularly in the transitional phase. How much of that is available may depend in part on how the referendum campaign is conducted.

At the end of the period of negotiation, it would be expected that the UK Parliament would pass a law to declare Scotland independent, and to give up jurisdiction over it. That Act might, as has happened when the UK has given up colonies, provide Scotland with an interim constitution, but it would be up to the Scottish Parliament to adopt it or amend it in future. Implementation is likely to take even longer than the two-year period. Unless Scotland is willing to tolerate disruption to services, transitions to independent tax collection and social security systems are likely to take longer, and this may constrain Scotland's ability to operate distinctive policies.

If Scotland votes to remain within the UK

By contrast, if Scotland votes to remain within the UK, there will be change, but it is likely to be incremental rather than immediately radical: some further devolution will take place. The starting point will be the Scotland Act 2012. Those plans are already being put into practice. From 2015, the Scottish government will be able to decide on the level and type of stamp duty land tax, and landfill tax. From 2016, there will be a Scottish Income Tax, which may differ from the UK rate.

Additional borrowing powers to allow for investment in infrastructure began to be put into effect in 2012. Unless there is a vote for independence, these plans will proceed.

It is also possible however that other more wide ranging schemes will be put into practice. How that comes about will depend on how the proposals are taken forward. Chapter 4 discusses the full range of possible schemes which are being produced.

Plans for more devolution developed by political parties in Scotland are likely to be put to the electorate, not on the referendum ballot paper, but in the manifestoes for the next Scottish and UK general elections. If so, the outcome of the elections might give both a UK and Scottish mandate for the further development of devolution. All of the main UK parties supported the Scotland Act, and plans are likely to build on it, either using the powers in it to extend tax devolution step-by-step, or by legislating at Westminster, with the agreement of the Scottish Parliament, to extend its powers into other areas.

Conclusion

Whatever the decision of the electorate, it is clear that the referendum vote will be the start rather than the finish of constitutional change. A vote for independence would be the signal for a huge effort to separate Scotland from the UK and set it up as an independent country. Many important aspects of that would be the subject of intense and difficult negotiations, and not wholly in Scotland's hands. The process is likely to take a couple of years to negotiate, and then a much longer period to put fully into practice. A vote to remain in the UK will also be the start of a different process, of greater devolution, under existing plans or perhaps plans still to be agreed. When Mr Ron Davies, then First Minister of Wales, said that devolution was a process not an event, he was clearly speaking nothing less than the truth.

Coda: and what about the United Kingdom?

This book has concentrated on the choice facing Scotland, and how Scottish voters can make it. The choice of whether to stay in the UK or leave it is one for them to make. The UK will accept their decision, but it has profound implications for the rest of the country as well. A vote to remain within the UK would lead to more devolution, perhaps in time markedly more. This could gradually change the nature of the

Union, for Scotland but perhaps for England, Wales and Northern Ireland too. It might become looser, less centralised, but the price of greater devolved powers could be less influence at the centre, and a lesser claim on common resources. In time, we might hear more of a distinct English voice in the UK as well. Some further evolution of the relations between the nations of the Union is inevitable.

A vote to leave would have more dramatic effects. Scotland was never a conquered nation, nor a colonised one. Its leaving would not be Britain withdrawing from an overseas empire nor gradually separating from a Dominion, but splitting up the state itself, after 300 years of voluntary union. Its first effects would be immediate and practical, and both domestic and international. The border between Scotland and England might not have customs posts and passport controls, but travellers would still move to a country that was, properly speaking, foreign. British political institutions have been remarkably stable and flexible. They have operated continuously through profound periods of change – Irish independence, the end of empire, the growth of the EU: but losing nearly a tenth of the population and one third of the country's land mass would be a profound challenge to them. The UK's international status would be changed too, even if only through the formalities of EU representation. The most significant effects would be psychological and cultural, and might take years to become clear: who knows what they might be? We may find out, but only after we know Scotland's choice.

Notes

1. The Scottish government have recently indicated that they are open to this possibility (Scottish government 2013b).
2. In these and other public services there would have to be plans to allocate staff to one government or another; like members of the Armed Services, they too might hope to have some say in the matter.

Bibliography

Amior, M., R. Crawford and G. Tetlow (2013), Fiscal sustainability of an independent Scotland, IFS November 2013, <www.ifs.org.uk/publications/6952> (last accessed 30 March 2014).

Armstrong, Angus and Monique Ebell (2013), Scotland's Currency Options, NIESR, <niesr.ac.uk/publications/Scotland's-currency-options> (last accessed 30 March 2014).

Armstrong, Angus and Monique Ebell (2014), Assets and Liabilities and Scottish Independence, National Institute for Economic and Social Research, discussion paper no 426, February 2014.

Armstrong, Kenneth (2014), Scottish Membership of the European Union <www.cels.law.cam.ac.uk/Media/working_papers> (last accessed 30 March 2014).

Ashdown, Paddy (2001), *The Ashdown Diaries* Vol. II, Harmondsworth: Penguin Press.

Australian Electoral Commission (2011), *Referendum Dates and Results 1906– Present*, <http://www.aec.gov.au/Elections/referendums/Referendum_Dates _and_Results.htm> (last accessed 5 October 2012).

Barnes, Eddie (2012), 'Independent Scotland to Stick with Sterling', *Scotsman*, 2 February 2012, <http://www.scotsman.com/news/politics/top-stories/ independent-scotland-to-stick-with-sterling-1-2090953> (last accessed 5 October 2012).

BBC News (2012), 'Swiss Voters Reject Longer Holidays in Referendum', <www. bbc.co.uk/news/world-europe-17335444> (last accessed 20 June 2012).

BBC News (2014), 'Scottish independence: "No cross-party plan" on devolution' 14 February 2014, <www.bbc.co.uk/news/uk-scotland-scotland-politics-26189448> (last accessed 3 April 2014).

Beveridge, Sir William (1942), *Social Insurance and Allied Services*, CMND 6404, London: HMSO.

Black, Andrew (2013), Ruth Davidson supports more Holyrood financial powers 26 March 2013, <http://www.bbc.co.uk/news/uk-scotland-scotland-politics-21933791> (last accessed 3 April 2014).

Boadway, Robin and R. Watts (2000), 'Fiscal Federalism in Canada', Kingston, Ontario: Queen's University, <http://www.fiscalreform.net/library/pdfs/fiscal_federalism_in_canada.pdf.> (last accessed 28 March 2012).

Bogdanor, Vernon (1994), 'Western Europe' in D. Butler and A. Ranney (eds), *Referendums around the World*, Washington, DC: AEI Press, pp. 24–97.

Bogdanor, Vernon (1999), *Devolution in the United Kingdom.* Oxford: Oxford University Press.

Bogdanor, Vernon (2003), 'The elements of a codified constitution,' *Financial Times*, 8 December 2003.

Bogdanor, Vernon (2009), *The New British Constitution*, Oxford: Hart Publishing.

Bradley, A. W. and D. J. Christie (1979), *The Scotland Act 1978*, Edinburgh: W. Green.

Braithwaite, W. J. (1957), *Lloyd George's Ambulance Wagon* edited by Sir H. N. Bunbury, London: Methuen.

Brown, Gordon (1981), 'The Labour Party and Political Change in Scotland 1918–1929', Ph.D. thesis, University of Edinburgh.

Brown, Gordon (ed.) (1975), *The Red Paper on Scotland*, Edinburgh: EUSPB.

Bulpitt, Jim (1983), *Territory and Power in the United Kingdom*, Manchester: Manchester University Press.

Calman, Sir Kenneth [Commission on Scottish Devolution] (2009), *Serving Scotland Better: Scotland and the United Kingdom in the 21st Century*, Final Report 15 June 2009, Edinburgh: Commission on Scottish Devolution, <http://www.commissiononscottishdevolution.org.uk/papers.php> (last accessed 9 October 2012).

Calman, Sir Kenneth [Commission on Scottish Devolution] (2008), The Future of Scottish Devolution within the Union: A First Report, 2 December 2008, <http://www.commissiononscottishdevolution.org.uk/papers.php> (last accessed 9 October 2012).

Campbell, John (1987), *Nye Bevan and the Mirage of British Socialism*, London: Weidenfeld and Nicolson.

Campbell, Sir Menzies (2012), Federalism: The Best Future for Scotland, Edinburgh: Scottish Liberal Democrats, November 2012.

Campbell, Sir Menzies (2014), Campbell II: The second report of the Home Rule and Community Rule Commission Edinburgh: Scottish Liberal Democrats, March 2014.

Chalmers, Malcolm (2012), The End of an 'Auld Sang': Defence in an Independent Scotland, RUSI Briefing Paper, April, London: RUSI <http://www.rusi.org/downloads/assets/End_of_an_Auld_Sang.pdf.> (last accessed 1 October 2012).

Chalmers, Malcolm and Walker, William (2001), *Uncharted Waters: the UK, nuclear weapons and the Scottish Question*, East Linton: Tuckwell Press.

Clerk, Sir John of Penicuik, J. M. Gray (ed.) (1892), *Memoirs of the Life of Sir John Clerk of Penicuik . . . Extracted by Himself from his own Journals.* Edinburgh: Edinburgh University Press.

Commission on Scottish Devolution (2008), Financial accountability task group: Oral evidence session with Professor Francois Vaillancourt and Alan Morris, <http://www.commissiononscottishdevolution.org.uk/uploads/2008-11-30-note-of-evidence-with-vaillancourt-and-morris.pdf> (last accessed 28 March 2012).

Conservative Party (2010), *Invitation to Join the Government of Britain: the Conservative Manifesto 2010*, London: Conservative Party.

Crawford, Rowena and Gemma Tetlow (2014), Fiscal Challenges and Opportunities for an Independent Scotland, National Institute Economic Review, February 2014.

Crawford, Stuart and Richard Marsh (2012), *A' the Blue Bonnets; Defending an Independent Scotland*, Royal United Services Institute London, October 2012, <www.rusi.org/downloads/assets/Scottish_Defence_Forces_Oct_2012.pdf> (last accessed 12 February 2013).

Curtice, John and R. Ormston (2012), 'Scottish Independence' in A. Park, E. Clery, J. Curtice, M Philips and D. Utting, *British Social Attitudes 29th Report*, London: Sage.

Curtice, John and R. Ormston (2011), Is Scotland more Left-Wing than England? *British Social Attitudes*, 28 Special Edition No. 42 December, Edinburgh: Scottish Centre for Social Research, <http://www.scotcen.org.uk/media/788216/scotcen-ssa-report.pdf> (last accessed 8 October 2012).

Curtice, John, and B. Seyd (ed.) (2009), *Has Devolution Worked? The Verdict from Policy Makers and the Public*, Manchester: Manchester University Press.

Curtice, John (2014), 'How the SNP could win the referendum' Juncture Volume 20, Issue 4, pages 303–307, Spring 2014.

Cuthbert, J. and M. Cuthbert (2011). 'GERS: Where Now?' in Mackay (2011), 35–44.

Dalyell, Tam (1977), *Devolution: The End of Britain?*, London: Jonathan Cape.

Department of Finance Canada (2012), Federal Support to Provinces and Territories, <http://www.fin.gc.ca/fedprov/mtp-eng.asp> (last accessed 28 March 2012).

Devo Plus (2012a), 'A stronger Scotland within the UK: First report of the Devo Plus group', May 2012, <www.devoplus.com> (last accessed 8 October 2012).

Devo Plus (2012b), *Improving Social Outcomes in Scotland,* September 2012, <www.devoplus.com/storage/Improving%20Social%20Outcomes%20in%20Scotland.pdf> (last accessed February 2012).

Dicey, Albert Venn (1915), *Introduction to the Study of the Law of the Constitution* (8th edn), London: Macmillan.

Electoral Commission (2013a), *The Referendum on Independence for Scotland: Advice of the Electoral Commission on Proposed Referendum,* 30 January 2013, <www.electoralcommission.org.uk/__data/assets/pdf_file/0007/153691/Referendum-on-independence-for-Scotland-our-advice-on-referendum-question.pdf> (last accessed 12 February 2013).

Electoral Commission (2013b), *Electoral Commission advice on spending limits for the referendum on independence for Scotland,* 30 January 2013, <www.electoralcommission.org.uk/__data/assets/pdf_file/0004/153697/Report-on-spending> (last accessed 12 February 2013).

Ewing, Fergus MSP (2012), *Scottish Parliamentary Answer* (S4W-08289), 31 August 2012.

Fraser, Derek (2003), *The Evolution of the British Welfare State,* London: Palgrave Macmillan.

Gallagher, Jim (2012), *England and the Union – Why and How to Answer the West Lothian Question,* London: IPPR.

Garrett, Geoffrey (1998), *Partisan Politics in the Global Economy,* Cambridge: Cambridge University Press.

Gordon, Tom (2012), 'Salmond: Scots have a right to second question on devo max', *Glasgow Herald* 1 July 2012, <www.heraldscotland.com/mobile/politics/referendum-news/salmond-scots-have-a-right-to-second-question-on-devo-max.18013865> (last accessed 8 October 2012).

Grant, J. P. (ed.) (1976), *Independence and Devolution: the Legal Implications for Scotland,* Edinburgh: W. Green.

Greer, Scott L. (ed.) (2009), *Devolution and social citizenship in the UK,* Bristol: Policy Press.

Guthrie, Roger and I. McLean (1978), 'Another part of the Periphery: Reactions to Devolution in an English Development Area', *Parliamentary Affairs* 31: 190–200.

Hague, William (2004), *William Pitt the Younger,* London: HarperCollins.

Hallwood, C. Paul and Ronald MacDonald (2009), *The Political Economy of Financing Scottish Government,* Cheltenham: Edward Elgar.

Hansard (1977), 26 January 1977, c. 1608–19, <http://hansard.millbanksystems.com/commons/1977/jan/26/the-assemblies> (last accessed 20 June 2012).

Hansard (1998), 12 January 1998 c. 24, <http://hansard.millbanksystems.com/

commons/1998/jan/12/scotland-bill#S6CV0304P0_19980112_HOC_131>
(last accessed 20 June 2012).

Heald, David (1990), *Financing a Scottish Parliament: Options for Debate*, Glasgow: Scottish Foundation for Economic Research.

Henderson, A. and N. McEwen (2005), 'Do Shared Values Underpin National Identity? National identity and Value Consensus in Canada and the UK', *National Identities* 7(2):173–91.

HM Government (2010a), The Coalition: Our Programme for Government, May 2010, <www.direct.gov.uk/prod_consum_dg/groups/dg_digitalassets/@dg/@en/documents/digitalasset/dg_187876.pdf> (last accessed 9 October 2012).

HM Government (2010b), *Strengthening Scotland's Future*, Cm 7973, November 2010.

HM Treasury (2011a), European Union Finances 2011: Cm 8232 December 2011, <http://www.official-documents.gov.uk/document/cm82/8232/8232.pdf> (last accessed 1 October 2012).

HM Treasury (2011b), Measuring Tax Gaps 2011, Methodological Annex, <http://www.hmrc.gov.uk/stats/mtg-2011.pdf> (last accessed 7 November 2012).

HM Treasury (2011c), *Public Expenditure – Statistical Analysis 2011*, <http://www.hm-treasury.gov.uk/pespub_pesa11_natstats.htm> (last accessed 26 March 2012).

HM Treasury (2012a), 'Chapter 9: Public Expenditure by Country, Region and Function', Public Expenditure Statistical Analysis 2011, <http://www.hm-treasury.gov.uk/d/pesa2011_chapter9.pdf> (last accessed 1 October 2012).

HM Treasury (2012b), *Public Expenditure: Statistical Analyses 2012*. Cm 8376, <http://www.hm-treasury.gov.uk/d/pesa_complete_2012.pdf> (last accessed 4 October 2012).

HM Treasury (2013), Public Expenditure: Statistical Analyses 2013 < https://www.gov.uk/government/uploads/system/uploads/attachment_data/file/223600/public_expenditure_statistical_analyses_2013.pdf> (last accessed 27 March 2014).

HM Government (2013, 2014), Scotland Analysis series, <www.gov.uk/government/collections/scotland-analysis> (last accessed 30 March 2014).

Hogg, James (ed) (1819), *The Jacobite Relics of Scotland: being the songs, airs, and legends of the adherents of the house of Stuart*, 2 vols, Edinburgh: William Blackwood.

Holtham, G. (chair) (2009), Working Paper: Replacing Barnett with a Needs-Based formula, Cardiff: ICFFW, <http://wales.gov.uk/docs/icffw/news/091204needsworkingpaperen.pdf> (last accessed 11 September 2012).

Holtham, G. (chair) (2010), Fairness and accountability: a new funding settlement for Wales. Independent Commission on Funding & Finance for Wales: Final Report, Cardiff: Welsh Assembly Government, <http://wales.gov.uk/docs/icffw/report/100705fundingsettlementfullen.pdf> (last accessed 8 October 2010).

House of Commons Library (2011), Scotland, Independence and the EU – Commons Library Standard Note SN06110, London: House of Commons, <http://www.parliament.uk/briefing-papers/SN06110> (last accessed 4 October 2012).

House of Lords (2009), *Select Committee on the Barnett Formula – First Report*, 9 July 2009.

House of Lords Constitution Committee (2012), *Referendum on Scottish Independence: 24th Report of session 2010–12*, HL 263 17 February, <http://www.publications.parliament.uk/pa/ld201012/ldselect/ldconst/263/263.pdf> (last accessed 1 October 2012).

Hughes Hallett, A. and D. Scott (2010), *Scotland: a new Fiscal Settlement*, St Andrews: University of St Andrews Centre for Dynamic Macroeconomic Analysis, Working paper series CDMA10/09.

Independent Expert Group (2009), Natural Resource Taxation and Scottish Devolution, Edinburgh: Heriot-Watt University, <http://www.commissiononscottishdevolution.org.uk/uploads/2009-06-06-ieg-natural-resource-taxation-1.pdf> (last accessed 3 May 2012).

Institute for Fiscal Studies (IFS) 2012, An independent Scotland would face long term fiscal challenges, <http://www.ifs.org.uk/pr/Scotland_Fiscal.pdf> (last accessed 19 November 2012).

Jackson, Alvin (2003), *Home Rule: an Irish History 1800–2000*, London: Weidenfeld and Nicolson.

Jeffery, C., (2012), 'Dis-United Kingdom?', *Juncture* 19 (1): 14–16.

Jeffery, C., G. Lodge and K. Schmuecker (2010), 'The Devolution Paradox' in Guy Lodge and Katie Schmuecker, *Devolution in Practice 2010*, London: IPPR.

Jenkins, Roy (1968), *Mr Balfour's Poodle* (2nd edn), London: Collins.

Johnson, Simon (2012), 'David Cameron Backs Body to Divide Powers if Scots Reject Separation', *Daily Telegraph*, 4 October, <http://www.telegraph.co.uk/news/uknews/scotland/9588207/David-Cameron-backs-body-to-divide-powers-if-Scots-reject-separation.html> (last accessed 8 October 2012).

Johnson, Simon (2014), Daily Telegraph, 14 March 2014, 'David Cameron: Scotland to be allowed to set own taxes' <www.telegraph.co.uk/news/uknews/scotland/10698541/David-Cameron-Scotland-to-be-allowed-to-set-own-taxes.html> (last accessed 3 April 2014).

Johnston P. and D. Phillips (2012), Scottish Independence; the Fiscal Context, IFS November 2012, <www.ifs.org.uk/bns/bn135.pdf> (last accessed 3 April 2014).

Katzenstein, Peter, J. (1985), *Small States in World Markets: Industrial Policy in Europe,* Ithaca, NY: Cornell University Press.

Keating, Michael (2011), 'Meso-Level Policy Systems', Paper for ECPR Conference, Reykjavik, <http://www.ecprnet.eu/MyECPR/proposals/reyk javik/uploads/papers/491.pdf> (last accessed 15 October 2012).

Kemp, A. G. (2011), *The Official History of North Sea Oil and Gas,* 2 vols, Abingdon: Routledge.

Kemp, A. G. (2012), 'Memorandum submitted by Professor Alex Kemp, University of Aberdeen' in House of Commons, Energy and Climate Change Committee, The Impact of potential Scottish independence on energy and climate change, Written Evidence, March, <http://www.publicati ons.parliament.uk/pa/cm201012/cmselect/cmenergy/writev/1912/1912.pdf> (last accessed 10 September 2012).

Kemp, A. G. and L. Stephen (2011), *The Short and Long Term Prospects for Activity in the UK Continental Shelf the 2011 Perspective,* North Sea Oil Occasional Paper no. 121, Aberdeen: University of Aberdeen Department of Economics.

Kidd, Colin (2008), *Union and Unionisms: political thought in Scotland 1500–2000,* Cambridge: Cambridge University Press.

King, D., M. Pashley and R. Ball (2004), 'An English Assessment of Scotland's Educational Spending Needs', *Fiscal Studies* 25(4): 439–66.

Kobach, K. W. (1993), *The Referendum: Direct Democracy in Switzerland,* Aldershot: Dartmouth.

Lenihan, Brian (2009), 'Financial Statement by the Minister of Finance', <http://budget.gov.ie/budgets/2010/FinancialStatement.aspx#item24> (last accessed 8 October 2012).

Lodge, Guy and Rick Muir (2011), 'Localism under New Labour' in Patrick Diamond and Michael Kenny *Reassessing New Labour: Market, State and Society under Blair and Brown,* Chichester: Wiley-Blackwell.

Lodge, Guy and Katie Schmuecker (2010), *Devolution in Practice 2010: Public Policy Differences in the UK,* London: IPPR.

Lodge, Guy and Alan Trench (2014), Devo More and Welfare: Devolving benefits and policy for a stronger Union London: IPPR <www.ippr.org/images/ media/files/publication/2014/03/Devo-more-and-welfare_Mar2014_11993. pdf> (last accessed 3 April 2014).

Lord President of the Council (1975), *Our Changing Democracy: Devolution to Scotland and Wales,* Cmnd 6348, London: HMSO.

Bibliography

MacCormick, Neil (1999), *Questioning Sovereignty: Law, State, and Nation in the European Commonwealth*, Oxford: Oxford University Press.

Mackay, Sir D. (ed.) (2011), Scotland's Economic Future, Edinburgh: Reform Scotland, <http://reformscotland.com/public/publications/scotlandsecon omicfuture.pdf> (last accessed 10 September 2012).

Marshall, T. H. (1950), *Citizenship and Social Class, and Other Essays*, Cambridge: Cambridge University Press.

Matthew, Colin (1999), *Gladstone 1809–1898*, Oxford: Oxford University Press.

McHarg, Aileen (2011), 'Final Appeals in Scots Criminal Cases', <http://ukscblog.com/final-appeals-in-scots-criminal-cases> (last accessed 20 March 12).

McLean, Iain (1995), 'Are Scotland and Wales Over-represented in the House of Commons?', *Political Quarterly* 66 (4): 250–68

McLean, Iain (2005), *The Fiscal Crisis of the United Kingdom*, Basingstoke: Palgrave.

McLean, Iain (2006), *Adam Smith, Radical and Egalitarian*, Edinburgh: Edinburgh University Press.

McLean, Iain (2010), *What's wrong with the British Constitution?* Oxford: Oxford University Press.

McLean, Iain (2012), 'Challenging the Union' in T. M. Devine and J. Wormald (eds), *The Oxford Handbook of Modern Scottish History*, Oxford: Oxford University Press, 635–51.

McLean, Iain and Alistair McMillan (2003), 'The distribution of public expenditure across the UK regions', *Fiscal Studies* 24(1): 45–71.

McLean, Iain and Alistair McMillan (2005), *State of the Union: Unionism and the Alternatives in the United Kingdom since 1707*, Oxford: Oxford University Press.

McLean, Iain and Alistair McMillan (2009), 'How We Got Here' in J. Curtice and B. Seyd (eds), *Has Devolution Worked? The Verdict from Policy Makers and the Public*, Manchester: Manchester University Press, pp. 17–43.

McLean, Iain and Neil Shephard (2004), A Program to Implement the Condorcet and Borda Rules in a Small-n Election, Nuffield College Working Papers in Politics no. 2004–W11, <https://www.nuffield.ox.ac.uk/Politics/papers/2004/McLean%20and%20Shephard.pdf> (last accessed 16 November 2012).

McLean, Iain, G. Lodge and K. Schmuecker (2009), 'Social citizenship and Intergovernmental Finance' in S. L. Greer (ed.), *Devolution and Social Citizenship in the UK*, Bristol: Policy Press, pp. 137–60.

Microsoft (2011), 'Annual Report for Fiscal Year ending June 30, 2011' published under the *US Securities Exchange Act 1934*, Redmond, WA: Microsoft Corporation.

Mitchell, James (2003), *Governing Scotland: the Invention of Administrative Devolution*, Basingstoke: Palgrave.

Mitchell, James (2006a), 'Evolution and Devolution: Citizenship, Institutions, and Public Policy', *Publius* 36 (1): 153–68.

Mitchell, James (2006b), 'Undignified and Inefficient: Financial Relations between London and Stormont', *Contemporary British History* 20:1, 55–71.

Murkens, Jo E., Peter Jones and Michael Keating (2002), *Scottish Independence: a Practical Guide*, Edinburgh: Edinburgh University Press.

Murphy, James (2009), *Written Statement by the Secretary of State for Scotland*: HC Deb 15 June 2009 cc6–7WS.

NATO (2005), 'NATO and the Scourge of Terrorism', <http://www.nato.int/terrorism/five.htm> (last accessed 4 October 2012).

Northern Region Strategy Team (1976), *Public Expenditure in the Northern Region and other British regions*, Technical Report no. 12. Newcastle-upon-Tyne: NRST.

Oates, Wallace E. (1999), 'An Essay on Fiscal Federalism', Journal of Economic Literature 37: 1120–49.

Obinger, Herbert, Stephan Liebfried and Francis G. Castles (2005), Federalism and the Welfare State, Cambridge: Cambridge University Press.

Office for Budget Responsibility (2012), Fiscal Sustainability Report, July 2012, <http://cdn.budgetresponsibility.independent.gov.uk/FSR2012WEB.pdf> (last accessed 9 October 2012).

Office for Budget Responsibility (2014), Economic and Fiscal Outlook, March 2014, <www.cdn.budgetresponsibility.org.uk/37839-OBR-Cm-8820-accessible-web-v2.pdf> (last accessed 30 March 2014).

Office for National Statistics (ONS) (2011), Regional Gross Value Added (Income Approach), December 2011, <http://www.ons.gov.uk/ons/publications/re-reference-tables.html?edition=tcm%3A77-250308> (last accessed 26 March 2012).

ONS (2011a), Statistical Bulletin: Regional, Subregional and Local Gross Value Added 2010, published December 2011.

ONS (2011b), Statistical bulletin: Regional Gross Disposable Household Income [(GDHI) 2010].

ONS (2012a), Statistical Bulletin: Regional Labour Market Statistics September 2012, <http://www.ons.gov.uk/ons/dcp171778_278442.pdf> (last accessed 5 October 2012).

ONS (2012b), Statistical Bulletin: Public Sector Employment Q1 2012, <http://

www.ons.gov.uk/ons/dcp171778_268633.pdf> (last accessed 9 October 2012).

Oil and Gas UK (2011), 2011 Economic Report, <http://www.oilandgasuk. co.uk/cmsfiles/modules/publications/pdfs/EC026.pdf> (last accessed 8 May 2012).

Organisation for Economic Cooperation and Development (OECD) (2009a), Social Expenditure Database, <http://www.stats.oecd.org/els/social/ expenditure> (last accessed 16 October 2012).

OECD (2009b), Tax Administration in Selected OECD and non-OECD Countries: Comparative Information Series, <http://www.oecd.org/tax/ taxadministration/42012907.pdf> (last accessed 10 October 2012).

OECD (2012), Fiscal Decentralisation Database, <http://www.oecd.org/doc ument/32/0,3746,en_2649_35929024_47467040_1_1_1_1,00.html#section_ b> (last accessed 23 March 2012).

Quinault, Roland (2004), 'Churchill, Lord Randolph Henry Spencer (1849– 1895)' in *Oxford Dictionary of National Biography*, edited by H. C. G. Matthew and Brian Harrison, Oxford: Oxford University Press, 2004, online edn, edited by Lawrence Goldman, September 2010, <http://www. oxforddnb.com/view/article/5404> (last accessed 16 March 2012).

Registrar General for Scotland (2012), Population Projections for Scotland – 2010 based, Edinburgh 2010, <http://www.gro-scotland.gov.uk/statist ics/theme/population/projections/scotland/2010-based/figures.html> (last accessed 16 October 2012).

Rokkan, S. and D. Urwin (eds) (1982), *The Politics of Territorial Identity: Studies in European Regionalism*, London: Sage.

Rosie, George, and Magnus Linklater (2009), 'How the Treasury Redrew the Map of the North Sea to Keep Scottish Hands off Oil Reserves'; 'Thirty Years Ago, Whitehall Officials Succeeded in Diverting Oil and Gas Revenues to the UK' and 'Hands Got Dirty Keeping Hold of Revenue from North Sea Oil', *The Times*, 14 and 16 February 2009.

Royal Society of Edinburgh and British Academy (2012), *Scotland and the United Kingdom*, Edinburgh: RSE/London: BA.

Royal Society of Edinburgh and British Academy (2014), Enlightening the Constitutional Debate, <http://www.royalsoced.org.uk/1061_Enlightening theConstitutionalDebate.html> (last accessed 15 April 2014).

Schmuecker, Katie, Guy Lodge and Lewis Goodall (2012), *Borderland: Assessing the implications of a more autonomous Scotland for the north of England* London: IPPR, <www.ippr.org/images/media/files/publication/2012/11/ borderland_Nov2012_9885.pdf> (last accessed 3 April 2014).

Scotland Office (2009), Tax Administration and Constitutional Change in

Scotland, <http://www.scotlandoffice.gov.uk/scotlandoffice/files/Scotland %20Office%20Tax%20Paper%201711.pdf> (last accessed 12 October 2012).

Scotland Office (2012), *Scotland's Constitutional Future* Cm 8203, <http://www.scotlandoffice.gov.uk/scotlandoffice/files/17779-Cm-8203.pdf> (last accessed 1 October 2012).

Scott, Sir Walter (1826), *The Letters of Malachi Malagrowther* Edinburgh: Printed by James Ballantyne and Company, for William Blackwood, Edinburgh.

Scottish Affairs Committee (2012a), *The Referendum on Separation for Scotland: Do you Agree this is a Biased Question?*, House of Commons, May 2012.

Scottish Affairs Committee (2012b), House of Commons Oral Evidence taken before the Scottish Affairs Committee: The Referendum on Separation for Scotland: Defence 12 September 2012; Professor William Walker and Dr Phillips O'Brien, <http://www.publications.parliament.uk/pa/cm201213/cmselect/cmscotaf/uc139-ix/uc13901.htm> (last accessed 5 October 2012).

Scottish Affairs Committee (2012c), *The Referendum on Separation for Scotland: Terminating Trident – Days or Decades?*, House of Commons HC 676, October 2012.

Scottish Affairs Committee (House of Commons) (2012d), *The Referendum on Separation for Scotland, Session 2010–12: Oral and written evidence, HC 1608.*

Scottish Affairs Committee (2013), Seventh Report Separation Shuts Ship Yards, <www.publications.parliament.uk/pa/cm201213/cmselect/cmscotaf/892/892.pdf>.

Scottish Government (2007), *Your Scotland Your Voice*, <http://www.scotland.gov.uk/Resource/Doc/293639/0090721.pdf> (last accessed 5 October 2012).

Scottish Government (2009a), Choosing Scotland's Future: a National Conversation, <http://www.scotland.gov.uk/Topics/constitution/a-national-conversation> (last accessed 8 October 2012).

Scottish Government (2009b), Fiscal Autonomy in Scotland: Taking Forward our National Conversation, The Case for Change and Options for Reform, Edinburgh: Scottish Government, <http://www.scotland.gov.uk/Resource/Doc/261814/0078318.pdf> (last accessed 8 October 2012).

Scottish Government (2009c), *An Oil Fund for Scotland: Taking Forward our National Conversation*, Edinburgh: Scottish Government, <www.scotland.gov.uk/Publications/2009/07/28112701/0> (last accessed 7 November 2012).

Scottish Government (2009d), *Energy; Taking Forward our National Conversation*, Edinburgh: Scottish Government, <www.scotland.gov.uk/Publications/2009/11/25093815/6> (last accessed 7 November 2012).

Scottish Government (2011), *Government Expenditure and Revenue Scotland*

[GERS] 2010–2011, Edinburgh: The Scottish Government, <http://www.scotland.gov.uk/Publications/2012/03/9525> (Tables at <http://www.scotland.gov.uk/Topics/Statistics/Browse/Economy/GERS/Publications/GERS201011xls>), (last accessed 10 October 2012).

Scottish Government (2012a), *Your Scotland – Your Referendum – A Consultation Document*, <http://www.scotland.gov.uk/Publications/2012/01/1006> (last accessed 5 October 2012).

Scottish Government (2012b), Scotland's Global Connection Survey 2010, <http://www.scotland.gov.uk/Resource/0038/00385828.pdf> (last accessed 1 October 2012).

Scottish Government (2012c), Public Sector Employment in Scotland Statistics for 2nd Quarter 2012, September, <http://www.scotland.gov.uk/Publications/2012/09/8779> (last accessed 9 October 2012).

Scottish Government (2013a), *Fiscal Commission Working Group First Report –Macroeconomic Framework*, February 2013, <www.scotland.gov.uk/Publications/2013/02/3017> (last accessed 12 February 2012).

Scottish Government (2013b), *Scotland's Future: from the Referendum to Independence and a Written Constitution*, February 2013, <www.scotland.gov.uk/Publications/2013/02/8079> (last accessed 11 February 2013).

Scottish Government (2014), Government Expenditure and Revenue Scotland [GERS] 2012–13, Edinburgh: The Scottish Government, <www.scotland.gov.uk/Publications/2014/03/7888> (last accessed 30 March 2014).

Scottish Labour Party (2013), Powers for a purpose – strengthening devolution: Interim Report of the Scottish Labour Devolution Commission, April 2013, <news.bbc.co.uk/1/shared/bsp/hi/pdfs/18_04_13_scotdevoreport.pdf>.

Scottish Labour (2014), Powers for a purpose – strengthening accountability and empowering people: Final Report of the Scottish Labour Devolution Commission, March 2014, <http://s.bsd.net/scotlab/default/page/file/c07a7cdb97a522f4c5_h1m6vwh8l.pdf>.

Scottish Liberal Democrats (2006), The Steel Commission: Moving to Federalism – A New Settlement for Scotland, Edinburgh: Scottish Liberal Democrats, <www.scotlibdems.org.uk/files/steelcommission.pdf> (last accessed 8 October 2012).

Scottish Parliament (2009), Official Report, 25 June 2009 (cc18835–88).

Scottish Parliament (2011a), Official Report Debate Contributions: Scotland Bill Committee, 11 January 2011, <http://www.scottish.parliament.uk/parliamentarybusiness/28862.aspx?r=6054&mode=html> (last accessed 8 October 2012).

Scottish Parliament (2011b), *Report on Scotland Bill and Associated legislative Memoranda*, 3 March 2011.

Scottish Social Attitudes 2010 (2010), Edinburgh: Scottish Centre for Social Research, <http://www.natcen.ac.uk/study/scottish-social-attitudes-2010> (last accessed 8 October 2012).

Scottish Social Attitudes 2011 (2011), Edinburgh: Scottish Centre for Social Research, <http://www.natcen.ac.uk/study/scottish-social-attitudes-2011> (last accessed 8 October 2012).

Secretary of State for Scotland (2013), *Scotland Analysis: Devolution and the Implications of Scottish Independence*, Cm 8554, February 2012.

Sharma, C. K. (2012), 'Beyond Gaps and Imbalances: Re-structuring the Debate on Intergovernmental Fiscal Relations', *Public Administration* 90: 99–128. doi:10.1111/j.1467–9299.2011.01947.x.

Shetland Charitable Trust (2013), Trustees' Report and Consolidated Financial Statements 2013, Lerwick: Shetland Charitable Trust, <http://www.shetlandcharitabletrust.co.uk> (last accessed 30 March 2014).

Swinney, John (2012), *Scottish Parliamentary Answer from Mr John Swinney*, S4W–08278, 31 August 2012.

Tiebout, Charles M. (1956), 'A Pure theory of Local Expenditures', *Journal of Political Economy* 64(5): 416–24.

Townsend, P. and N. Davidson (eds) (1982), *Inequalities in Health: the Black Report*, Harmondsworth: Penguin.

Trench, Alan (2013), *Funding Devo more: Fiscal Options for Strengthening the Union*, IPPR London, January 2013, <www.ippr.org/publication/55/10210/funding-devo-more-fiscal-options-for-strengthening-the-union> (last accessed 12 February 2013).

United Nations (2012) 'Secretary-General Appoints Panel to Monitor Self-Determination in Sudan', *Press Release, 21 September 2010*, <www.un.org/News/Press/docs/2010/sgsm13123.doc.htm> (last accessed 20 June 2012).

Watts, Ronald L. (2008), *Comparing Federal Systems* (3rd edn), Montreal: McGill-Queen's University Press.

Whatley, C. A. and D. Patrick (2006), *The Scots and the Union*, Edinburgh: Edinburgh University Press.

Wincott, D. (2006), 'Social Policy and Social Citizenship: Britain's Welfare States', *Publius* 36 (1): 169–88.

Wolchik, Sharon L. (1995), 'The Politics of Transition and the Break-Up of Czechoslovakia' in Jiri Musil (ed.), *The End of Czechoslovakia*, Budapest: Central European University Press.

Wyn Jones, Richard, Guy Lodge, Ailsa Henderson and Daniel Wincott (2012), *The Dog that Finally Barked: England as an Emerging Political Community*, London: IPPR.

Index

Index

Goschen, George Joachim, 1st Viscount, 192, 194, 199
Government Expenditure and Revenue in Scotland (GERS), 24, 54–7, 92–4, 154–6, 170–7
Government of Ireland Bills and Acts 1886–1920, 185–90, 191–8
Greenshields case 1711, 189
Gretna, risk of hypermarkets in, 146, 159
GVA (Gross Value Added) *see* GDP

Hamilton by-election 1967, 166, 201
Harcourt, Sir William, 195–6, 199
head of state *see* monarchy
HFE *see* horizontal fiscal equalisation
Highland regiments, 189–90
HMRC *see* Revenue and Customs, HM
Hogg, James ('The Ettrick Shepherd'), 186, 191
Holtham Commission (Independent Commission on Funding and Finance for Wales), 80, 97, 105–6, 117, 148–9, 152, 157
Holyrood *see* Scottish Government
Home Rule *see* Government of Ireland Bills and Acts 1886–1920
horizontal fiscal equalisation, 144, 147–57; in Canada, 162–74
housing benefit, 65, 78, 107, 117, 135, 216
human rights
 Human Rights Act 1998, 130
 in Scottish criminal courts, 80
Hume, David, 158, 190

identifiable spending, 68
immigration *see* Schengen agreement
income tax, 70–4, 101–8
 higher rate of, 73, 82
 on savings, 73, 78
 see also Scottish Variable Rate
independence-lite *see* devolution-plus
Independent Expert Group *see* Calman Commission
inheritance tax, 69, 93, 194
Institute for Fiscal Studies (IFS), 55, 57
insurance principle, 118–19
Ireland
 Republic of, 97, 101, 160, 207, 213–14, 217
 union with Great Britain (1800–1921), 185, 191–8, 206
 see also Northern Ireland
Irish Free State *see* Ireland, Republic of
Irish Party, 191–5
Isle of Man, 40, 48, 88, 109
Italy, 32, 41, 135

Keating, Michael, 134
Kemp, Alex, 172–5, 183–4

Kidd, Colin, 191
Kipling, Rudyard, 190

labour market law, 90
Labour Party, in Scotland, 63, 76, 84, 89, 94–7, 107, 112, 116, 128, 129, 134, 166–7, 200–2, 204
Länder *see* Germany, Federal Republic of
Landfill Tax, 69, 77
Larne, 197
Liberal Democrats, Scottish, 23, 63, 76, 84, 94, 96, 104, 112–16, 128
Lloyd George, David, 178

Maastricht criteria (for EU member states' debts and deficits), 159
MacCormick, Iain, 171
MacCormick, Neil, 6
MacDonald, J. Ramsay, 200
Macpherson, Nicholas, xv–xvi, 28–9
macroeconomic policy, 27–8, 64, 74, 81, 108–10
Malawi, Scottish links with, 22, 30
Marshall, T. H., 123–30
massacre of Glencoe, 188
median line, 168–70
Mexico, 144
Microsoft Corporation, 96
Mitchell, James, 125–6, 199
monarchy, x, 15–17, 34–5, 111; *see also* individual monarchs listed by name
monetary policy, 26, 31, 46–8, 88, 100,110, 208; *see also* currency
monetary union *see* pound sterling
Montenegro, x, 3, 6, 32, 210
Morgan, Rhodri, 134
Morrison, Herbert, 124
Muscatelli, Anton, 50, 64

National Conversation (of Scottish government 2007–11), 63, 84, 86, 88–90, 96, 102, 109, 176
national debt, apportionment of, on independence, 58, 159, 208–11
National Health Service, 66, 126, 129, 133, 147–8; *see also* social union
National Institute for Economic and Social Research (NIESR), 211–12
National Insurance, 65, 68, 92, 95–6, 108, 117, 118, 119, 123, 132, 145, 159, 178, 180, 201, 216
 National Insurance Act 1946, 119, 123
 see also social union
National Statistics, as guarantee of protection from political interference, 54, 61, 154
nationalised industries, 23, 126

237

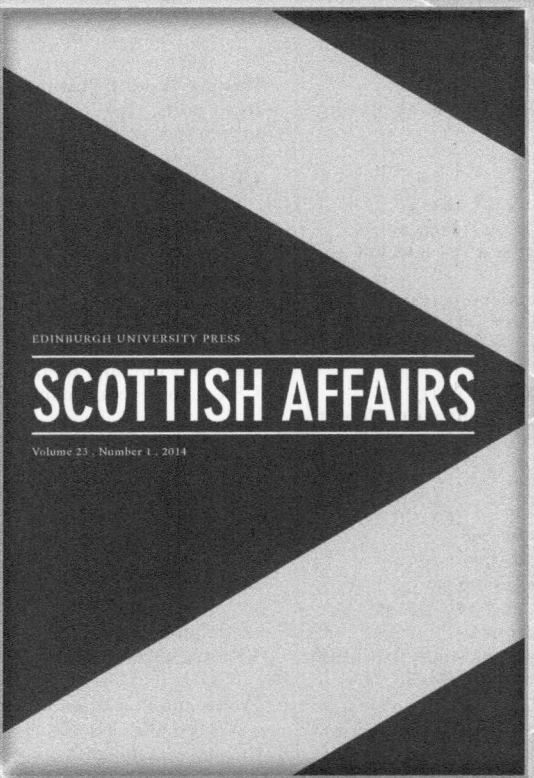